# THE LAST WHITE ROSE

# THE LAST WHITE ROSE

DESMOND SEWARD

Constable • London

Constable & Robinson Ltd
3 The Lanchesters
162 Fulham Palace Road
London W6 9ER
www.constablerobinson.com

First published in the UK by Constable,
an imprint of Constable & Robinson, 2010

A copy of the British Library Cataloguing in Publication
Data is available from the British Library

ISBN 978-1-84529-873-9

Printed and bound in the EU

1 3 5 7 9 10 8 6 4 2

# CONTENTS

**Part 1**
**Henry VII and the White Rose**

## Part 2
## Henry VIII and the White Rose

*For Tim and Marisa Orchard*

# 1. The Royal Descent of the de la Poles and the Courtenays

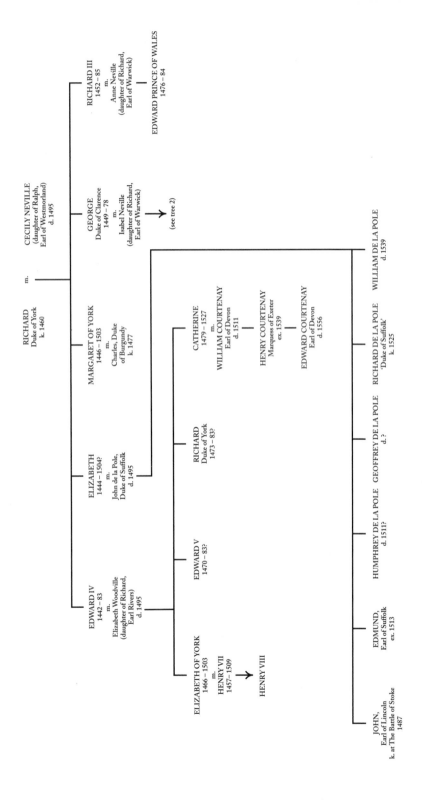

# 2. The Royal Descent of the Poles

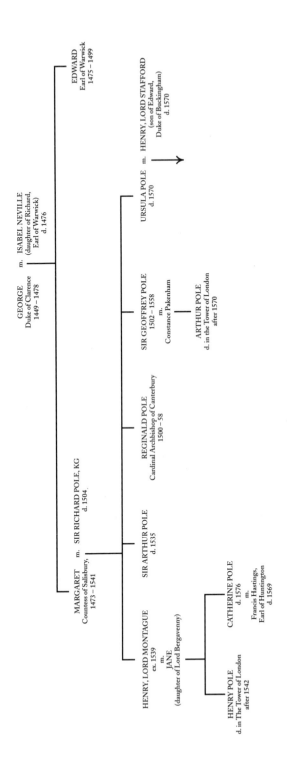

GEORGE
Duke of Clarence
1449 – 1478

m.

ISABEL NEVILLE
(daughter of Richard,
Earl of Warwick)
d. 1476

EDWARD
Earl of Warwick
1475 – 1499

MARGARET
Countess of Salisbury,
1473 – 1541

m.

SIR RICHARD POLE, KG
d. 1504

HENRY, LORD MONTAGUE
ex. 1539
m.
JANE
(daughter of Lord Bergavenny)

SIR ARTHUR POLE
d. 1535

REGINALD POLE
Cardinal Archbishop of Canterbury
1500 – 58

SIR GEOFFREY POLE
1502 – 1558
m.
Constance Pakenham

URSULA POLE
d. 1570

m.

HENRY, LORD STAFFORD
(son of Edward,
Duke of Buckingham)
d. 1570

HENRY POLE
d. in The Tower of London
after 1542

CATHERINE POLE
d. 1576
m.
Francis Hastings,
Earl of Huntington
d. 1569

ARTHUR POLE
d. in the Tower of London
after 1570

# ACKNOWLEDGEMENTS

Fifteen years ago I published a book called *The Wars of the Roses and the Lives of Five Men and Women in the Fifteenth Century* (Constable, 1995). This is the sequel, telling the story of what happened to the Yorkists in the decades after the battle of Bosworth and the death of Richard III – and why they so alarmed Henry VII and Henry VIII.

Once again, I owe much to the patient staffs of the British Library and the London Library. I am most grateful to my agent Andrew Lownie, to my editor Leo Hollis and copy-editor Elizabeth Stone, and to Sara Ayad for reading the proofs. I have to acknowledge two special debts – one to Sir John Hervey-Bathurst for reading my typescript and for helpful comments at every stage, the other to Richard Despard, who let me have access to his unpublished researches on the families of Foix-Candale and de la Pole. I must also thank Lucia Simpson for her sterling encouragement.

# Overview: The White Rose, 1485–1547

'"The White Rose is most true
This garden to rule by rightwise law."
The Lily White Rose methought I saw.'

*The Lily White Rose, c.*1500[1]

At Bosworth on 22 August 1485, at the head of his Knights and Squires of the Body, Richard III charged down on Henry Tudor's puny army in the field below. Killing Henry's standard-bearer, Richard hacked his way towards him – the two may even have exchanged blows. At the very last moment one of the king's followers, Sir William Stanley, changed sides in the battle. Galloping across the field with 3,000 troops, he annihilated Richard and the royal household. Henry owed his life and his throne to treachery.

As Shakespeare imagines the scene, after the battle Sir William's brother Lord Stanley offers the dead king's crown to Henry with the words, 'Wear it, enjoy it and make much of it'. Yet while it could be argued that nobody ever wore the English crown with greater skill or made more of it, Henry did not always enjoy the experience. 'From the start [Henry VII] was threatened with plots by fresh opponents,' says Polydore Vergil, a contemporary historian. 'He had to cope with armed uprisings by enemies who were also his subjects, surviving with difficulty.'[2] The future of the Tudor dynasty was uncertain, even in his son's time.[3]

Henry's campaign had been a desperate gamble. Most of his followers were ex-Yorkists, outraged by Richard's seizure of the throne, who supported him only because no other pretender was available. His claim to be king (through his mother, last member of a bastard branch of Lancaster) was far from convincing, even if he was crowned at Westminster Abbey by the same Archbishop of Canterbury who had crowned Richard III only two years earlier – and even if Parliament had passed an Act recognizing him as king. 'For all his high words about his just title, it was in fact as shaky as could be without being non-existent.' This is a good description of Henry's position in 1485. 'Thereafter, most revolts which he faced were similar pieces of high politicking about which family to put on the throne. His policy was to murder or neutralise as many likely rivals as possible, a policy which his son took up in mid life.'[4]

There was still a Plantagenet heir after Bosworth and many Englishmen were uneasy about replacing a dynasty that had ruled for over 300 years. 1486 saw a rising in support of Richard III's young nephew Edward, Earl of Warwick, while the following year Lord Lincoln led a revolt in the earl's name, using a boy called Lambert Simnel to impersonate him. During the 1490s the Tudors were threatened by Perkin Warbeck, who, encouraged by the Yorkist underground, posed as one of the Princes in the Tower and called himself the 'White Rose'. Indeed, there were so many plots against the Tudor king that a court poet compared the first twelve years of his reign to the Labours of Hercules.

Early in 1499 an astrologer's warning of yet more danger from the Yorkists caused Henry VII to suffer a complete nervous collapse, and a Spanish envoy reported that he had aged twenty years in a fortnight. Shortly afterwards, he decided to kill Warwick, the last male Plantagenet. Unluckily for the king, the earl's legal murder gave rise to the widespread rumour that his execution had brought a curse on the Tudors, dooming their male children to an early death. In any case Yorkism persisted – as a belief that there were men with a much better right to represent the Plantagenets than this new, self-invented royal family – and another White Rose soon emerged to claim the throne.

Another title for this book could have been 'The Shadow of Richard III'. As a boy Henry VIII must have known that if his father died, his line would probably disappear: as a king without a male heir, he became convinced that his own death would mean the end of the Tudors. When eventually he did father a son, he feared that if he died too soon the child might go the same way as Edward V. That is why anyone with Plantagenet blood lived under a death sentence, no English king having sent so many men – or women – to the scaffold. 'These, and many other such deaths, were a testimony to the profound disquiet that haunted Henry throughout his life,' comments Lucy Wooding. 'It was a direct inheritance from his father.'[5]

Henry VIII's disquiet first showed itself in 1513. When about to invade France he had Edmund de la Pole executed, to prevent him from being proclaimed king in his absence, while for the next decade Tudor agents tried to murder Richard de la Pole, Edmund's successor as the White Rose. Although Richard, the last man to challenge Henry VIII openly for the throne, was killed at Pavia in 1525 when fighting for the French, the king grew increasingly suspicious of any nobleman with Yorkist blood. Revealingly, the Treason Act of 1534 denounced as traitors those who wrote or said he was a 'usurper of the crown'.

During the early1530s England was rocked by Henry VIII's divorce from Katherine of Aragon and the Church's break from

Rome, and by new laws that increased the powers of the crown. No one disliked the changes more than Katherine's supporters, who included the White Rose party, by now centred around two families, the Courtenays and the Poles. The head of the Courtenays, the Marquess of Exeter, was a grandson of King Edward IV. The Poles, headed by Lord Montague, consisted of the four sons of Margaret Plantagenet, Countess of Salisbury (sister of the Earl of Warwick who had been Richard III's heir). They hoped to replace Henry with his daughter Mary, with Reginald Pole as a Yorkist king consort, and their ally Bishop Fisher implored the imperial ambassador to ask Charles V to come and overthrow Henry VIII, whom he claimed was even more unpopular than Richard. But the revolt never took place as the plotters lacked a leader.

In 1536 a rebellion known as the Pilgrimage of Grace broke out in Lincolnshire, and then in Yorkshire, Lancashire and Cumberland, with 30,000 men demanding an end to religious innovations and the dismissal of Cromwell and Archbishop Cranmer. The king tricked them into dispersing, before taking a savage revenge. This was the most dangerous moment of Henry VIII's reign and had it come to a fight he might easily have been toppled. But the White Rose families made the fatal mistake of sitting on the fence.

Next year Pope Paul IV appointed Reginald Pole to lead a 'mission' to force Henry VIII to bring England back to Rome or depose him. Pole hoped to revive the Pilgrimage of Grace, but was too late. In 1539 he led another unsuccessful mission, to persuade Charles V to invade England. Henry's reaction was to exterminate the White Rose families and their supporters, send assassins to kill Pole and execute his mother, the Countess of Salisbury – the last living Plantagenet. Even then, the king did not feel secure, destroying the Howards because he feared they would try and take the throne from his young son.

For over half a century after Bosworth the White Rose kept on producing pretenders, men who were either open or potential rivals for the throne. But while this is their story, the story of a forgotten lost cause, the underlying theme is the fear that the White Rose inspired in the first two Tudors. In Henry VII, suspicion turned into a disease, a sinister legacy he bequeathed to Henry VIII in whom it festered until it became mania.

# PART 1

# Henry VII and the White Rose

# 1

# Autumn 1485:
# 'this woeful season'

'The King was green in his estate; and contrary to his own opinion and desert both, was not without much hatred throughout the realm. The root of all was the discountenancing of the house of York, which the general body of the realm still affected.'

Sir Francis Bacon, *The History of the Reign of King Henry VII*[1]

On 23 August 1485, John Sponer, sergeant to the mace, galloped into York. A trusted official whom the city had sent to join the royal army and help the king put down a rebellion, he brought astounding news. Yesterday, 'King Richard, late mercifully reigning over us . . . with many other lords and nobles of these North parts was piteously slain and murdered, to the great heaviness of this city', the council recorded in their House Book. Horrified, the aldermen wrote a letter to the Earl of Northumberland, the greatest man in the North, asking his advice about what they should do 'at this woeful season'.[2]

The incident shows the entire country's bewilderment. Although Richard III's reign had been troubled by plots and rebellions, and he was disliked for deposing his little nephew, his head was on the coinage and he was accepted by most people as their king. A veteran commander, he had ridden out at the head of a large, well-equipped army that included the realm's leading magnates, against a small-scale rising by the unknown Henry Tudor that he should have crushed without any difficulty. News of his death must have come as a severe shock to the vast majority of his subjects.

Like anyone else in England of any standing, the aldermen of York had read Richard's recent proclamation against 'Henry Tydder', pretender to the throne, 'whereunto he hath [in] no manner interest, right title or colour, as every man well knoweth, for he is descended of bastard blood, both of father side and of mother side'. Among the rebels and traitors who supported Henry, adds the proclamation, 'many be known for open murderers, avouterers [adulterers] and extortioners . . . every true and natural Englishman born must lay to his hands for his own surety and weal'.[3] Yet the 'rebels and traitors' had won.

After King Richard's defeat, his surviving followers, save for a few key henchmen, simply rode off the battlefield unharmed and went home. Elsewhere, some of them refused to accept the change of regime, including 200 troops in the garrison at Calais who, along with one of their captains, Thomas David, marched up to 'Burgundy' – in those days a name for Flanders – and joined the Habsburg army (until the next century, there would be plenty of Yorkists at Calais). So did men from the tiny garrison on Jersey, under the governor Sir Richard Harleston, a former yeoman of the chamber to King Edward IV.

Even so, despite their astonishment, most Englishmen made a show of welcoming their hitherto unknown but now 'undoubted sovereign liege lord'. When Henry VII reached London on 3 September, he was met at Shoreditch by the lord mayor and the aldermen, with liverymen from seventy City companies – mercers, grocers, drapers, fishmongers, haberdashers, down to hatters and pouch-makers – 435 of them in gowns of scarlet and 'bright murrey' (mulberry), not to mention the fifty swordsmen of the mayor's bodyguard or the twenty armed servants guarding the sheriffs, each one in gowns of tawny, or the trumpeters who sounded a greeting.[4] Everybody kissed the new ruler's hand. Then he was escorted to St Paul's Cathedral to offer up the three standards under which he had fought (St George, the Red Dragon of Cadwallader and the Dun Cow). A great Mass of thanksgiving was celebrated, with ostentatiously joyful clerics at the high altar, and the singing of the *Te Deum*. There were pageants in the main thoroughfares, similar to those that had greeted Richard III's accession.

Unfortunately, the 'sweating sickness' – a lethal new disease brought over from France by Henry's troops – broke out, killing both the lord mayor and his successor. So deadly was this disease that a man healthy in the morning might be dead by evening. Polydore Vergil (who caught the sickness himself) believed it was an omen 'that Henry should only reign by the sweat of his brow, as turned out to be the case'.[5] An inauspicious start to the reign, it delayed the coronation. However, on 30 October 1485 Henry was crowned in Westminster Abbey by Cardinal Bourchier, Archbishop of Canterbury, who, just over two years before, had performed the same service for Richard. On 7 November Henry VII held his first Parliament.

Warmly supported by MPs and peers, the speaker of the House of Commons urged the new king to marry the lady Elizabeth, Edward IV's eldest daughter, whom his predecessor had contemplated marrying because of her dynastic significance even though she was his niece. Henry graciously assented, the wedding taking place on 23 January 1486. In theory it could be argued that his claim to the throne was twofold. Heir of Lancaster, he had married the heiress of York. Soon, court poets were writing songs about the union of the Red Rose and the White. Illuminators created the charming Tudor Rose of two colours as a decoration for their manuscripts, while chroniclers extolled the marriage for ensuring continuity with England's ancient monarchs.

Parliament passed an Act which declared that the crown should 'rest, remain and abide in the most Royal person of our now Sovereign Lord King Harry the VIIth and in the heirs of his body'.[6] Yet everybody knew that for years, Parliament had been legalizing new occupants after a previous incumbent's overthrow – Edward IV in 1461, Henry VI in 1470, Edward IV in 1471 and Richard III in 1483. How long would it be before another Parliament did so again? Nobody can have been more aware of this possibility than Henry Tudor.

The vast majority of Englishmen did not know what to make of the situation. King Richard had made a point of stressing that his rival was just an unknown Welshman whom he had never laid eyes on and whose father he had never even heard of – which was quite true. Henry's claim to be the heir of Lancaster was barely plausible. No doubt, through his mother, he was heir to the Beaufort Dukes of Somerset (descendants of John of Gaunt and his mistress Catherine Swynford), if not heir to their titles. But the Somersets' right to inherit the throne had been specifically denied by Parliament.

As for Henry's male line descent, it was unquestionably that of a parvenu. His great grandfather had been a bastard and the Bishop of Bangor's butler. The Tudors' membership of the ruling class was very recent indeed, having begun with the clandestine marriage of the new king's grandfather, Owain Tudor, to Henry V's widow, Catherine of France, by whom he had been employed as Clerk of the Wardrobe. If half Beaufort and a quarter Valois, Henry possessed precious little of the 'old blood royal of England'.

Elizabeth of York could add nothing to Henry's title: only their children would benefit from her Plantagenet blood. During the previous year she had been bastardized by an Act of Parliament, although this was hastily repealed in November 1485.

And while she might be King Edward's daughter, she was one of several – each an heiress who could also pass on the precious Plantagenet blood.

The new dynasty had one great asset, however, which was Henry himself. Few men could have persuaded such ill-assorted followers to join him in so desperate a gamble as the expedition of 1485, and held them together on the march to Bosworth. If he lacked the magnificent physical presence and overwhelming personality of Edward IV, Henry could summon up considerable charm. The chronicler Polydore Vergil, who met him in his forties, says 'he was good looking with a cheerful face, particularly when speaking'.[7] The most impressive image we have is Pietro Torrigiano's bust of 1508–9 in the Victoria and Albert Museum – although, admittedly, this is deliberately flattering – while the profile on his new shilling coin of 1489 hints at a genuinely regal appearance. Intelligent, decisive, iron-willed, he was a natural statesman and politician, who seldom made a mistake in choosing ministers – with one alarming exception. His foreign policy became as successful as his domestic policy, much admired by other European rulers.

Yet his task during his first years on the throne was a fearsome one. Since boyhood he had been a hunted exile, whom the Yorkists had sought to eliminate as the last possible Lancastrian claimant. At twenty-eight, he knew little about England and its people. A quarter Welsh (he was christened Owain but his mother insisted on the name being changed), he was brought up in Wales until he was fourteen, since when he had been a fugitive in Britanny without English friends or servants, so that his first language was, of necessity, French. Only in 1483 had English refugees begun to join him. From the start he distrusted the upper nobility because they were too powerful and, not having grown up among the great of the land, he was daunted by them. Instead, he relied on advisers who had supported him in exile, none of them born to a peerage apart from the Earl of Oxford. They included Cardinal Morton, Bishop Fox, Sir Reginald Bray,

Lord Daubeney and Lord Willoughby de Broke – the last two made peers by Henry. Henry never ceased to fear magnates, who might one day decide to support some Yorkist rival.

Secretly, no one can have felt more insecure. Henry knew he was on the throne because he had won at Bosworth, not by right of inheritance. Ousting the Plantagenets, who had governed England since 1154, he could not hope to avoid an aura of illegitimacy – of being a legalized usurper. In any case, he was unknown to all save a few of his subjects.

There were many people with a better claim to wear the crown. The most obvious was the ten-year-old Edward Plantagenet, Earl of Warwick – son of the Duke of Clarence, Edward IV's brother. After the death of his own son in 1484, Richard III briefly recognized him as his heir, but then set him aside in favour of another nephew. This was John de la Pole, Earl of Lincoln, who was about twenty-two in 1485, the son of Richard's sister, the Duchess of Suffolk. While there is no direct documentary evidence, it is almost certain that Lincoln had been publicly acknowledged as heir to the throne.

On the day after Bosworth Henry had sent a trusted follower to remove the young Earl of Warwick from Sheriff Hutton and bring him to London, to be confined in the Tower – as his cousin Edward V had been. As for the Earl of Lincoln, the king took a calculated risk in letting him stay at liberty, and (despite having fought for Richard at Bosworth) Lincoln appeared to accept Henry as his sovereign, riding in procession at his coronation. But the new king took no chances with Warwick: if he managed to reach his aunt in Flanders, a Yorkist restoration would be very much on the cards. So many men had served his father and then the boy himself on their vast estates in the west Midlands that they might be able to rally the whole country to his cause.[8] Despite being shut up in the Tower of London, closely guarded day and night, the boy was a magnet for Yorkists.

Undoubtedly, Henry possessed one or two excellent ministers in Sir Reginald Bray, Cardinal Morton and Bishop Richard

Fox – 'vigilant men, and secret, and such as kept watch with him almost upon all men'.[9] There was also his Lord Chamberlain, Sir William Stanley, who had won Bosworth and the crown for him by changing sides, and numerous less able, if dependable, figures such as the newly honoured Lord Daubeney.

But many of his apparent supporters could not be relied upon. Discontented Yorkists, they had only fought for him because they hated the late king. At the same time, his victory meant that a large group of Ricardian loyalists were deprived of lucrative posts or forced to hand back estates, such as all the Northerners whom Richard had rewarded with lands and offices in the South. Soon they began to show their hand in Yorkshire under assumed names – Robin of Redesdale, Jack Straw, Tom a' Linn, Master Amend-All – stirring up riots in collusion with Scots raiders. Even when the riots were put down, the disaffection remained. Throughout England, especially in the northern counties, there were people who, if not yet ready to revolt, felt much the same as the Yorkshiremen.

# 2

# Easter 1486:
# Lord Lovell and the
# Stafford Brothers

'[T]he old humour of those countries, where the memory of
King Richard was so strong, that it lay like lees at the bottom
of men's hearts; and if the vessel was but stirred, it would
come up.'

Sir Francis Bacon, *The History of the Reign of King Henry VII*[1]

Living, walking monuments to Henry VII's sense of insecurity
still exist, the Yeomen of the Guard. First raised in October
1485 as fifty archers to protect him at his coronation, these were
soon transformed into men-at-arms and their strength increased
to two hundred. Crack troops recruited from veterans who had
been with the King in France and fought for him at Bosworth,
their principal job was to mount guard every day and deter
assassins – the traditional Knights and Squires of the Body being
thought insufficient for the task – although in the absence of a

standing army the Yeomen also fought as an elite unit. It quickly became apparent that Henry needed them.

In a letter dated 18 December, just after Parliament had risen, Thomas Betanson informed Sir Robert Plumpton that there was an uneasy mood in London. A number of Yorkist lords and gentlemen, Richard's committed followers, had just been attainted by an Act that outlawed them, together with their families, confiscating their estates – men such as the Earl of Surrey, Lord Lovell and Lord Zouche. Although several MPs opposed the Act, the king insisted on it. There was talk in the city of war breaking out again: no one could say who was going to start it, but on the whole people thought it would be either the Northerners or the Welsh. Betanson adds, 'There is much running among the lords, but no man wot [knows] what it is: it is said it is not well among them.'[2]

Henry's most dangerous opponent was Francis, Viscount Lovell, who had been among his predecessor's staunchest supporters. At first believed to have fallen at Bosworth, according to a letter written by Henry soon after the battle, he had managed to escape and find sanctuary. A boyhood companion of the young Duke of Gloucester, during Richard's reign he had been chamberlain of the royal household and virtually the second most important man in the kingdom. Until now he had been a magnate not just of high standing and ancient blood – he was the seventh Lord Lovell as well as the second viscount – but one of enormous wealth, even before receiving lavish rewards from Richard. Some idea of how rich he was can be gained by walking around the ruins of his beautiful house at Minster Lovell in Oxfordshire, in woodland on the banks of the River Windrush, where he had been visited by his late master on at least one occasion.

After Bosworth, Lovell had made for East Anglia, hoping to go abroad. Failing to find a boat, he took sanctuary in the Benedictine abbey at Colchester. 'Sanctuary rights' gave a fugitive immunity from arrest for forty days, after which he must leave the kingdom. During the recent wars many had saved their lives in this way, although sometimes they were dragged out and executed, as happened to the Lancastrian leaders after their defeat at Tewkesbury in 1471. Remembering the widespread disgust caused by this vicious breach of legality, in which several of his cousins lost their lives, even when the forty days had elapsed King Henry made no attempt to remove Lovell from the abbey.

Also in sanctuary at the abbey were two more of the late king's supporters who had fought at Bosworth, Sir Humphrey Stafford and his younger brother Thomas. Well known in his county, Humphrey, who was to be attainted with Lord Lovell in December 1485[3], owned the valuable manor of Grafton in Worcestershire (near Tewkesbury and the River Severn), besides other big estates, including Blatherwycke in Northamptonshire. Fifty-nine but still hale and hearty, he had been MP for Worcestershire and high sheriff, as well as MP for Warwickshire. For most of his life he had shown himself not so much a Yorkist as an enemy of the Harcourts, a powerful Lancastrian family who were his neighbours in Northamptonshire. Sir Richard Harcourt had murdered Humphrey's father in 1448, to be murdered in turn, during an affray, by Humphrey's half-brother, the Bastard of Grafton. But in 1483, during the Duke of Buckingham's rebellion, Sir Humphrey had held the fords of the rain-swollen Severn against Buckingham's followers, earning King Richard's gratitude.

Locally, Humphrey had a name as a ruthless thug who was always ready to break the law. In a petition presented during the Parliament of November 1485 some Stafford cousins complained how, with 'great might and strength' (meaning a large body of armed men), he had seized their estates and kept possession of them because he was 'in such favour and conceit with Richard, late in deed and not of right, king of England'. Henry granted their petition, that the manors should not be included among those forfeited in Sir Humphrey's attainder.[4]

The three fugitives knew their one chance of rebuilding their fortunes was to replace Henry with the Earl of Warwick. They decided that in the spring of 1486, shortly before the king visited York, Lovell should break out of sanctuary, assemble a small force and kill Henry – helpers would be easy enough to find in a city where Richard had been so popular. Lovell would then proclaim Warwick king, and raise all Yorkshire in support. Meanwhile, the Stafford brothers were to rally the Yorkists of the West Midlands, where Warwick owned large estates, and then bring troops north to reinforce Lovell. While everything depended on liquidating Henry, the plan did at least have the advantage of surprise – no one expected a *coup d'état* from three men who were cooped up in sanctuary.[5]

Towards the middle of March Henry VII left London, riding north by way of Waltham, Cambridge, Huntingdon and Lincoln. He kept Holy Week at Lincoln – washing the feet of twenty-nine poor men in the cathedral, as he was twenty-nine years of age – where Sir Reginald Bray warned him that Lovell was going to leave sanctuary and was planning serious mischief. Henry immediately summoned Bray's informant, a Hugh Conway who had fought for him at Bosworth, but did not believe the story. 'I affirmed all to be true, as my said friend had showed, and the king said that it could not be so,' recalled Conway.[6] He grew angry when Conway refused to reveal the name of his friend, were he 'to be drawn with wild horses'. While they were still at Lincoln, news came that Lovell and the Staffords had escaped from Colchester and no one knew where they had gone. However, for the moment Henry remained unconcerned, riding on to Nottingham.

But when the king reached York he heard rumours of a revolt in the North Riding. Under the name of 'Robin of Redesdale', an unidentified Yorkist was raising support in an area around Ripon and Middleham that had been closely associated with Richard III. The rumours were confirmed, followed by a report that Lord Lovell was marching on York. Vergil says Henry was horrified – 'struck with great fear' – as he had neither an army nor weapons for his retinue, while it seemed unlikely he would be able to raise an adequate force in a city so well known for its devotion to King Richard.

Aware that he must act quickly, before Lovell's army grew any larger, Henry sent his ill-equipped retinue against the enemy, including the Knights of the Body and the Yeomen of the Guard, under his uncle Jasper Tudor, Duke of Bedford. According to Vergil, most of them 'armoured themselves in leather', meaning they bought padded deerskin jerkins (the poor man's armour) from the locals. He also sent heralds, promsing a pardon to any rebel, except for the leaders, who laid down his arms. The heralds won over so many men that Lovell lost his nerve and fled during the night.[7] However, still hoping for a chance to ambush the king, he took a band of reliable followers with him.

Meanwhile, reports that King Henry was in danger spread all over Yorkshire, with the result that local landowners came to York to offer their services. Somewhat improbably, in view of its former fervent loyalty to Richard, he is said to have been received in the northern capital with great enthusiasm and elaborate pageants, the crowds shouting, 'King Henry! King Henry! God preserve that sweet and well-savoured face'.

Even so, Lord Lovell regained his nerve. On 23 April, St George's Day, he very nearly succeeded in killing the king at York when he was celebrating the feast of St George. Although no proper account survives, the attack was made either at High Mass in the Minster, or afterwards when Henry was dining in state in the Archbishop's Great Hall with his court, including the earls of Lincoln, Rivers and Wiltshire. It looks as if he had a narrow escape. According to one source, the Earl of Northumberland personally saved Henry's life, which means that someone tried to assassinate him.[8] More than one man was involved, since the earl caught several people whom he hanged on the spot.[9] This had been the first attempt on Henry's life since Bosworth.

Yet the king was not too alarmed. In the words of Francis Bacon (echoing Vergil), Henry thought the rising was 'but a rag or remnant of Bosworth Field, and had nothing in it of the main party of the House of York'. Vergil and Bacon stress that Henry was not so much nervous about these particular rebels as worried he might not be able to raise a dependable force in northern England if a really serious rising broke out in the region, 'for that he was in a core of people, whose affections he suspected'.[10] It was impossible to estimate how much pro-Yorkist feeling had been stirred up.

Shrewdly judged promises of pardon caused the rebellion to disintegrate everywhere else in Yorkshire. Giving up hope, Lord Lovell fled across the Pennines by night, taking refuge on the coast of what was then northern Lancashire but is now Cumbria. There he found temporary shelter at the house of Sir Thomas Broughton of Broughton Tower – a peel tower built as a defence against Scottish raids – on Furness Fells in Broughton-Furness. Sir Thomas had been given confiscated estates in Devon and Cornwall by King Richard in 1484, but was forced by the new king to return them to their owners. He was another Yorkist diehard who remained loyal to Richard's memory, had been involved in the recent revolt and, with his Cumberland neighbour Sir John Huddleston, had held out for some time.

In the meantime, Sir Humphrey had set to work in Worcestershire. He overcame the problem of having been outlawed in the recent Parliament by claiming King Henry had pardoned him, producing forged 'letters patent' that rescinded his attainder. Clearly, he had plenty of friends in Worcestershire, such as Richard Oseney, to whom he sent a message, asking to meet him – presumably well armed – at Kidderminster in the north-west of the county. Another friend was Ralph Botery, who in his indictment was later to be accused, among other charges, of giving Stafford a brace of pheasants 'on account of the love that he then bore towards him'. Humphrey's bastard son, John Stafford, joined in the rising with enthusiasm, stealing horses from the king's close at Upton-on-Severn.

Humphrey assembled several hundred men, with whom he stormed into Worcester, raising the cry 'A Warwick! A Warwick!', and briefly took over the city. Later, the municipal authorities were charged with failing to post a proper guard at the gates, the implication being that they had been deliberately negligent. Stafford quickly put about inflammatory rumours – Henry Tudor had been captured by Lord Lovell in Yorkshire, while the Earl of Warwick had been freed from captivity on the isle of Guernsey and, having crossed to England, was riding north to join Lovell. The rising spread into neighbouring Warwickshire and Herefordshire – at the small towns of Warwick and Birmingham Stafford's supporters ran through the streets shouting 'A Warwick!' Obviously, there was plenty of grass-roots support for the Earl in the West Midlands.

Meanwhile, riots broke out in London, culminating with a rally at Westminster on 5 May. Most of the emblems on the mob's banners were ploughs, rooks, shoes and woolsacks, but one bore the Bear and Ragged Staff – Warwick's badge. Carrying weapons, they marched to Highbury in Islington where they clashed with the 'king's lieges' sent to disperse them.[11] Although they were demonstrating in support of the Plantagenet in the Tower, prompted by reports of the risings by Lord Lovell and the Staffords, no one was tried for treason because nobody of importance was involved and Henry's policy was one of leniency for the masses – his regime was too fragile for him to risk butchering ordinary folk.

News came of Lovell's failure, however, and the Worcestershire rising collapsed, forcing the Staffords to flee for their lives. Their first hiding place, an area of deep woodland near Bewdley, was soon surrounded by 400 men led by Thomas Cokesey, who had a commission from the king to arrest them. However, although he searched the woods thoroughly, he had to report that 'as yet we cannot get him nor hear where he is'. In fact, the brothers had been warned of Cokesey's approach by a neighbour, Sir

Richard Burdett, who was afterwards charged with aiding and abetting their escape.

Despite Henry's pretence of being unconcerned, the best informed chronicler of the period, Polydore Vergil, heard that he had been badly scared. He used carefully calculated leniency in dealing with the Midlands rebels, after twenty were tried and found guilty at Warwick and Birmingham, to the extent of intervening in the process of the law.

John Colard of Feckenham in Worcestershire had been indicted for treason, his lands, goods and chattels being granted to his accuser, Thomas Tolhoth. Petitioning the king for a pardon on 14 May, Colard said that while visiting Bromsgrove on market day, he had happened to meet 'Humphrey Stafford, now your rebel, which long before that time was no good master nor well-willer unto him', and because of rumours that Stafford had obtained a royal pardon, and because everybody else was doing so, 'more for dread than love' he had welcomed him, before going home. Although blameless, he had then been accused of treason 'by certain persons of malice and evil will'. Henry granted the petition, despite a protest by Tolhoth that 'sinister labour' had been used to persuade the authorities of Colard's innocence.[12]

After 'lurking for a time with Sir Thomas Broughton', as Bacon puts it, in May Lord Lovell made his way south. A hunted man, to avoid attention he must have ridden along lonely paths, often by night, avoiding towns. Once again, the former Lord Chamberlain hoped to find a boat across the sea. On 19 May 1486 the Countess of Oxford, the wife of one of Henry's right-hand men, wrote to John Paston, warning him that 'I am credibly informed that Francis, late Lord Lovell, is now of late resorted into the Isle of Ely, to the intent by all likelihood, to find the ways and means to get him shipping and passages in your coasts, or else to resort again to sanctuary.'[13]

Big rewards must have been offered for his capture and rigorous searches made, but the authorities were unable to lay hands on Lovell. They did not realize he had moved from

Cambridgeshire into Suffolk, almost certainly given shelter by the de la Poles. The head of the family, the Duke of Suffolk, was married to Richard III's sister Elizabeth Plantagenet, whose sympathies lay with the fugitive.

The Staffords were not so lucky. Avoiding capture, they had fled from Worcestershire to Culham in Berkshire, 'a certain obscure sanctuary betwixt Oxford and Abingdon'.[14] Here, the abbey of Abingdon, two miles to the north, possessed a church with long established sanctuary rights. Why the Staffords chose this particular place for a refuge only became apparent much later on, but they arrived there on 11 May. The king was taking no chances, however, and two days later they were forcibly removed at night by sixty armed men under Sir John Savage. No doubt there were protests from the monk in charge, and as soon as the abbot heard of it he sent a written complaint to the authorities about this outrageous infringement of his abbey's ancient privilege.

On 20 June Sir Humphrey appeared before the court of King's Bench, pleading that he had every right to be returned to sanctuary. Accordingly, he was assigned counsel and much to the king's displeasure the case was adjourned for eight days, so that the Abbot of Abingdon, Dan (as monks were styled then) John Sant, could be summoned to give evidence. Before the trial could resume, Henry tried to make the judges give him their opinion on whether or not Stafford had a good case. They refused. 'It is not good for us to argue the matter and give our opinions before it has come before us judicially,' was their answer. The king was so concerned that Chief Justice Hussey had to go before him and personally beseech his forgiveness. Even so, Henry had to wait.[15]

When the case came up again, Abbot Sant argued eloquently that the prisoners should be returned to Culham. He had a fairly good case in law, being able to cite charters in the abbey's possession by which an eighth-century king of Mercia had bestowed on fugitives from justice the inalienable right to seek refuge in the parish church. Although these charters were in fact thirteenth-century forgeries, they were accepted as genuine by the lawyers of the day.

Regardless of Sant's evidence, however, the judges decided that sanctuary could no longer be pleaded in cases of high treason, and on 5 July Sir Humphrey was condemned to the statutory death of a traitor. Three days later he was hanged but cut down before he was dead, then castrated and disembowelled while still alive, his guts being burned in front of him, after which he was beheaded and quartered. His head was tarred and set up on a spike over London Bridge, his body receiving similar treatment, although the tarred quarters were displayed at towns where he was well known – presumably in the West Midlands. Thomas Stafford was pardoned, on the grounds that he had been misled by his elder brother, but lost most of his property. It was still less than a year since Bosworth.

Yet even after Henry's countermeasures, Sir Thomas Broughton and Sir John Huddleston of Millom still held out in the North Country with other men who had fought for King Richard at Bosworth. Broughton was especially dangerous. Not only did he own very large estates, but he had unusually widespread influence all over Lancashire and Cumberland, and could rely on help from many important friends. He was hard to keep under surveillance as he was able to hide behind the separate legal jurisdiction of the Duchy of Lancaster, administered by neighbours who were well-disposed towards him.

The king cut his way through this legal jungle with a proclamation in July 1486 that accused Sir Thomas, with other northern gentlemen and yeomen, of 'great rebellions and grave offences . . . against the most royal person of our sovereign lord Henry VII', of hiding in secret places and ignoring numerous royal letters and commands. It ordered those named to present themselves in person to the king within forty days: otherwise they would be proclaimed 'great rebels, enemies and traitors, and so forfeit their lives, lands and goods at the pleasure of our sovereign lord'.[16] They came to heel, presenting themselves within the time stipulated and taking an oath of allegiance, after which they received letters of pardon. Yet neither their submission nor their oath meant that they were reconciled to the new regime.

The proclamation excluded five people from any hope of pardon: Geoffrey Franke, Edward (or Edmund) Franke, John Ward, Thomas Oter and Richard Middylton 'otherwise called Dyk Middylton'. All had fought for King Richard at Bosworth. Their exclusion meant they had been identified as irreconcilable diehards.

Another Lancashireman whose loyalty was very suspect was Sir James Harrington of Hornby Castle. For the moment, however, it was not quite clear whether his unruliness was due to Yorkist principles or a long-running feud with the Stanley family who coveted his estates. What made him especially dangerous was the sheer number of his kindred – there were well-endowed Harringtons all over the county.

As Thomas Betanson had predicted in his letter to Sir Robert Plumpton, some sort of Yorkist rebellion had also broken out in Wales, although no details survive. We do know, however, that Jasper Tudor, Duke of Bedford, had been sent there in February 1486, presumably to guard against a rising. The other evidence is that in October Thomas Acton was rewarded with a substantial property in Herefordshire, confiscated from a Thomas Hunteley because of 'his adherence to the rebels in Wales'.[17]

In January 1487, Lord Lovell at last found a boat whose skipper was ready to take him secretly across the North Sea, a vessel no doubt provided by the de la Poles. It was not the safest time of year for such a voyage, but he succeeded in reaching 'Burgundy'. Here, at Malines, as the late king's most loyal friend, he received a warm welcome from the Dowager Duchess of Burgundy, who was Richard III's sister. Henry Tudor's implacable enemy, Margaret of York was delighted to learn from Lovell that there was opposition to the new regime in many parts of England and Wales. No doubt he told her that all that was needed to overthrow the usurper was to unite the Yorkists.

In consequence, Henry VII found himself threatened by something much worse than the makeshift plot at Easter. On 29 November 1486 Thomas Betanson, who seems to have been good at picking up well-informed rumours in the capital, had written from London to Sir Robert Plumpton, that 'here is but little speech of the Earl of Warwick now, but after Christmas, they say, there will be more speech of [him]'.[18] This is infuriatingly discreet, but it seems that Betanson expected Sir Robert to read between the lines. Somehow, he must have heard that further trouble was coming, and on a more serious scale than anything Henry had faced since Bosworth.

# 3

# Early 1487:
# Margaret of York

'This Lady Margaret . . . invented and practised all mischiefs, displeasures and damages that she could devise against the King of England. And further in her fury and frantic mood . . . she wrought all the ways possible how to suck his blood and compass his destruction.'

Edward Hall, *The Union of the Two Noble and Illustre Famelies of Lancastre and Yorke* [1548][1]

Less than ten years earlier, there had been seven male members of the House of York. Now, only one was still alive – Warwick. Nobody resented this more than the Dowager Duchess of Burgundy. In the words of Polydore Vergil:

Margaret knew perfectly well the House of York had been destroyed by her brother Richard, yet . . . hating Henry [VII] with a truly insatiable hatred as she did, burning with unquenchable rage, she could never resist any scheme that might somehow do harm to the man who was the head of the rival family. Predictably, even if she thought their plan unlikely to gain much support (as turned out to be the case), when contacted by a group who had recently begun plotting against Henry she not only promised its agents she would help but took pains to put discontented English noblemen in touch with them.[2]

When Lord Lovell reached Burgundy, he made Margaret keener than ever to bring down Henry Tudor. The hopes of the duchess and Lovell rested on a young man whom Richard III had formally recognized as heir to the throne after the death of his only son. This was John de la Pole, Earl of Lincoln. A hundred and fifty years earlier, John's direct ancestor had been a Hull merchant known as 'atte Pool' (gentrified into 'de la Pole'), but his grandfather became Duke of Suffolk, while his father married Elizabeth Plantagenet, one of the Duke of York's daughters and a sister of King Richard.

Lincoln's father, John, Duke of Suffolk, was an ineffectual nonentity who took no part in politics but stayed on his estates, his only claims to distinction being his rank and his high-born wife, with whom he sired at least seven sons. Yet at least he had managed to survive the upheavals of the last thirty years. His funeral effigy, along with that of his duchess, may still be seen at the splendid church that stands next to their castle at Wingfield in Suffolk, a heavily fortified fourteenth-century manor house. Among the wealthiest magnates in the kingdom, the de la Poles owned land all over East Anglia and throughout the Thames valley, where their principal residence was a long since vanished mansion at Ewelme near Wallingford. They also had a family 'inn' or town house in London, in the parish of St Lawrence, Pulteney.

Ewelme had been acquired by the de la Poles in 1434, the duke's father having married its heiress who was Chaucer's granddaughter. Among many other powerful connections, through the marriage of a de la Pole girl they were related to the great French family of Foix, kings of Navarre and co-rulers of Andorra. In England the Foix were earls of Kendal – Gallicized as 'Candale'. (In the not too distant future this link with the Foix-Candale was going to save the life of a de la Pole on the run from the Tudors.)[3]

John de la Pole was born about 1462. We do not know very much about him but from his short career it is clear enough that he was tough, devious and self-controlled. He did not need to be reminded of his Plantagenet blood. In 1475 he had been created a Knight of the Bath with his cousins, the Prince of Wales and the Duke of York – the future 'Princes in the Tower', while in 1476 he attended the reburial of his grandfather the Duke of York at Fotheringay, an occasion of dazzling splendour, where the mourners included Edward IV with the Dukes of Clarence and Gloucester. In 1478 he was at the young Duke of York's wedding to the heiress of the Mowbray Dukes of Norfolk, and in 1480 he took a leading role at the christening of King Edward's youngest daughter Bridget at Eltham Palace. He was constantly at the Yorkist court, with his wife Margaret FitzAlan, a daughter of Lord Maltravers – heir to the Earl of Arundel.[4]

Lincoln and his father had each played prominent roles in Richard III's coronation at Westminster Abbey in 1483, Suffolk bearing the sceptre while Lincoln himself bore the orb. They could have made no more public demonstration of their support for the new king. John went on progress with Richard after the coronation, while later he was rewarded with a substantial number of confiscated estates for 'good service' in putting down the Duke of Buckingham's rebellion. After the death of Richard's only son in 1484, the late king had not only recognized John, Earl of Lincoln as heir presumptive to the throne, but appointed him Lord Lieutenant of Ireland and President of the Council of the North. Although Richard was a widower who hoped to remarry and beget another son and heir, in the meantime he saw Lincoln as one of the props of his regime. Obviously, he had complete trust in his young nephew, who spent a good deal of time with him.

At first it was thought that Lincoln had died with Richard III on Bosworth Field. However, he managed to survive, hastening to make peace with the man who had stolen his inheritance and despite being deprived of his great offices attended Henry VII's coronation, riding in the royal procession, and accompanied Henry on his northern progress, which left London on 9 March 1486. In consequence, he was in York at the end of April during Lord Lovell's abortive coup.

Despite this show of loyalty, the earl had secretly helped the Staffords and Lovell to escape from Colchester. While at York he was visited in his lodgings by rebels from Middleham and for a moment even considered joining them before deciding that Lovell's desperate attempt was bound to fail.[5] He continued to dissemble, riding south with the royal progress on the return to London. Because of Lincoln's claim to the throne Henry watched him closely but was inclined to believe in his loyalty because of his deferential manner. Lincoln was present at the baptism of Henry's eldest son, Prince Arthur, on 20 September 1486, then went to Greenwich at the start of November for the feast of All Hallows. After this, he left court to go back to his estates where he spent Advent and kept the twelve days of Christmas.[6]

It is more than likely that he was already in touch with Lord Lovell, whom he must have known for years. Lovell had been his father's ward after the Earl of Warwick's death in 1471, while he could scarcely have avoided seeing him at King Richard's court. Lincoln may also have been in contact with Margaret of Burgundy.

He returned to the capital for a Privy Council that Henry had summoned urgently at the royal palace of Sheen. When it met on 2 February 1487, it was told that a serious plot had been discovered, supported by people of high rank, and that a rising was imminent. The earl sat calmly through the discussions without betraying his involvement.

Someone who may perhaps have encouraged him to join
and recover his inheritance was his mother. Apart from the odd
reference in contemporary legal documents – and her aloof
marble effigy in Wingfield church – we know nothing about the
Duchess of Suffolk. Nevertheless, the third anonymous writer
who contributed to the continuation of the *Croyland Chronicle*
says specifically that 'King Edward's sister Elizabeth' longed for
Henry VII's overthrow and joined the conspiracy, but gives no
further details.[7] While it is plausible that a Plantagenet such as
the duchess should have resented the upstart Tudor, we have
no other information about her involvement.

The first solid evidence of insurrection appears in a writ of
8 February 1487 for the arrest of 'Henry Bodrugan, Knight,
and John Be[au]mont and others, who have withdrawn themselves into private places in those counties and stir up sedition
and rebellion'. The counties were Devon and Cornwall. In the
event, Sir Richard Edgecombe, the Sheriff of Devon to whom
the writ was sent, had little difficulty in preventing any local
disturbances. However, Bodrugan and Beaumont evaded all
attempts to capture them, and no one knew their whereabouts.

Alarming news arrived of trouble in Ireland, where the House
of York was remembered warmly. Towards the end of 1486 or
the start of 1487 a young priest from Oxford named Richard
Simonds had arrived in Dublin. He was accompanied by a young
boy, Lambert Simnel, the son of an Oxford joiner (or, possibly,
organ-builder), whom he had abducted from his parents and
was hoping to pass off as the Earl of Warwick.[8] 'This crafty
and subtle priest brought up his scholar with princely behaviour
and manners [and] literature, declaring to this child what lineage he was of and progeny,' says *The Book of Howth*.[9] The lords
of the Irish Pale were completely taken in, accepting that the
boy really was Warwick.

King Henry reacted swiftly. The day after the news arrived,
a Sunday, Lord Derby took the real Earl of Warwick out of the
Tower of London, parading him through the streets and then

bringing him into St Paul's where he was presented to a large assembly that included the entire convocation and the chancellor, Archbishop Morton, as well as the mayor and corporation. After spending a night with Morton at Lambeth Palace, he paid a visit to Sheen, under escort, where for a few days Lincoln spoke to him daily as someone who could vouch that he really was Warwick. Then his guards took him back to the Tower. This would turn out to be his last outing from prison. As a calculated piece of public relations it was not entirely effective, since Henry's opponents were able to pretend that the boy was merely someone impersonating the earl.

Despite the counter-propaganda campaign, the king's agents soon informed him that Lord Lovell, although still in Flanders, was in close touch with the Irish lords. This forced Henry to accept that a major conspiracy must be in the offing. It may also explain the savage way in which he turned against his mother-in-law. Edward IV's widow, Elizabeth Woodville, was a tragic figure who epitomized the dangerous life led by those of high rank during the Wars of the Roses, even by women. She was said to have ensnared the king into marrying her by refusing to sleep with him, even when he held a dagger at her throat, although Elizabeth and her mother were also accused of effecting the marriage by 'sorcery and witchcraft' in an Act passed by Richard III's Parliament. Her father, Earl Rivers, had been beheaded in 1469, her brother the second earl in 1483. Her son, Edward V, was deposed and bastardized, disappearing with his brother the Duke of York. She seemed to have embarked on a more serene life, however, when her daughter Elizabeth of York had married Henry, being lavishly provided for by the restoration of the valuable estates which formed her jointure.

Yet there was an unpleasantly opportunistic side to Elizabeth Woodville that made it reasonable to suspect her. She had made her peace with King Richard, the murderer of her sons, and in 1485 had tried to persuade the Marquess of Dorset, a son by an earlier marriage, to do the same and desert Henry Tudor.

King Henry must have thought that his mother-in-law was involved in the plot since he confiscated her entire jointure, giving the estates to her daughter Elizabeth. She was packed off to an undignified retirement on a paltry annuity at the convent at Bermondsey, where she died five years later.[10]

Someone definitely involved was the elderly Robert Stillington, Bishop of Bath and Wells, who had been in such favour with King Richard that he was imprisoned after Bosworth. Despite receiving a pardon on account of his 'great age, long infirmity and feebleness' and officiating at Henry's coronation, he never accepted the Tudor regime. Perhaps the real brains behind the conspirators, when he heard what had happened to the dowager queen he bolted, taking refuge at Oxford. On 7 March Henry wrote to the university, demanding Stillington be handed over. For a time the university refused, saying it was in breach of their privileges, but after some weeks they surrendered him. Because of 'benefit of clergy', he could not be tortured and revealed little about the plot. However, he was imprisoned at Windsor until shortly before his death in 1491.[11]

The council meeting and suspicions about his mother-in-law, let alone the flight of Bishop Stillington, cannot have enhanced Henry VII's sense of security. Lovell and the Staffords had been openly Yorkist, but secret enemies were now being identified. How many more did he have? He had no means of finding out the depths of his unpopularity, although the agents he employed must have sent in worrying reports. During the previous year he had refused to believe Hugh Conway's warning about Lovell, but he had learned his lesson. However, soon he received an even more unpleasant surprise.

Despite the danger of being denounced by an informer, John de la Pole kept his nerve, staying until the very end of the council. When he left Sheen on 9 March, he told the court he was returning to Suffolk, but when he got there, he immediately boarded a boat for Flanders. He sailed in the nick of time, lucky to have escaped detection.

Shortly after de la Pole's departure, Henry's secret agents learned that servants of the Earl of Lincoln, disguised as merchants, were on mysterious business in the North. One of the agents, James Tait, spotted them in Doncaster on 25 March, identifying the group as Lincoln's men because one rode a striking grey horse that he remembered seeing in the earl's household during the royal visit to York the previous year. Tait discovered their saddlebags were full of gold and silver coin, but could not find out why. All he was able to learn was that they were on their way to Hull and would visit Sir Thomas Mauleverer of Allerton Mauleverer (who had recently been made to hand back lands in Devon granted to him by Richard III), and then going to York where they would meet the Prior of Tynemouth at the Boar Inn. In fact, they were recruiting for the rising. On 31 March Tait sent a report on their suspicious behaviour to York, forwarded to the king the same day.[12]

The Act of Attainder later passed by Parliament refers to a lost document that describes a crucial meeting on 19 March between Lincoln and others in Flanders, just ten days after he left Sheen. The others can only have been Lord Lovell and Margaret of Burgundy, and a representative of Maximilian, King of the Romans, who was the husband of Margaret's stepdaughter. The meeting discussed ways of eliminating Henry Tudor. Those present resolved to exploit the Yorkist sympathies of the Irish Pale, of which they were kept informed by secret messengers from Dublin.

The Pale was the English-speaking area of Ireland, stretching 60 miles from Dundalk to Dublin and 40 miles inland, which possessed English institutions such as law courts and city corporations and its own fiercely independent parliament. The real ruler of the 'Lordship of Ireland' – not yet a kingdom – was the Lord Deputy, Garret Mór FitzGerald, Earl of Kildare, who owned vast tracts of land inside and outside the Pale. Like other Irishmen, he found it hard to accept the sovereignty of someone who was not a Plantagenet. By now Palesmen believed the boy in the Tower of London must be an impostor because Margaret of York had recognized Simnel as her nephew. He was accepted as genuine by Kildare and the Irish peers, as well as by the Lord Chancellor of Ireland (Sir Thomas FitzGerald of Lackagh, Kildare's brother), the Archbishop of Dublin, the Bishops of Meath and Kildare, the Lord Chief Justice, and the Prior of Kilmainham – head of the Irish Knights of St John.

On 5 May Lincoln and Lovell landed in Ireland, accompanied by a regiment of 2,000 Swabian and Swiss landsknechts in striped and slashed uniforms, hired with money lent by Margaret. They were commanded by a famous colonel, Martin Schwartz, originally a cobbler from Nuremburg, who had been ennobled by Maximilian for his distinguished services on many battlefields. Most of Schwartz's regiment were foot soldiers armed with an eighteen-foot long pike, although some carried a huge *zweihänder* (a two-handed sword for cutting down enemy cavalry or for hewing a way through pikes), while about one in eight were crossbowmen or arquebusiers.[13] The presence of such troops, the most professional in Western Europe, must have strengthened the Yorkist leaders' determination.

Among the Engilsh supporters who greeted Lincoln and Lovell at Dublin were Sir Henry Bodrugan and John and John Beaumont from Cornwall, by Sir Richard Harleston, once governor of Guernsey, and Thomas David, formerly captain of the Calais garrison. They too had valuable military experience.

Although the two English leaders knew that Simnel was an impostor, as did Duchess Margaret, they made a convincing pretence of believing he was the real Earl of Warwick. On 24 May, Whit Sunday, Simnel was proclaimed King Edward VI at Christchurch Cathedral by the Bishop of Meath in a sermon, after which he was crowned with a circlet taken from a statue of the Virgin in St Mary's church near Dame Gate. Lincoln and Lovell had been present at two coronations and no doubt gave advice on how to do it. The one notable who refused to take part in the ceremony or give it his blessing was the Italian Archbishop of Armagh, warned by a letter from Morton that Simnel was a fraud – the infuriated Lord Lincoln had to be restrained from knocking him down. Then, so that the crowds might all see the boy, he was carried through the streets from the cathedral to Dublin Castle on the shoulders of a giant of a man called Great Darcy of Platten.

Apparently, Lincoln and Lovell meant to keep up the pretence that Lambert Simnel was Warwick – 'Edward VI' – until they defeated Henry. No one knows what they planned to do afterwards. Had they won, the boy might have been replaced as king by the real Warwick, but it is more likely John de la Pole was going to claime the throne – the *Chronicle of Calais* comments that Margaret of York 'would have made him King of England'[14] – and become John II. This was also what Polydore Vergil heard from those who were well informed.[15]

What strategy should they use? One possibility was to lure Henry into crossing over to Ireland and attacking them. Yet if they stayed there too long, they would run out of money and be unable to pay their landsknechts. Their best chance was an immediate invasion of England. Encouragingly, the Irish raised four or five thousand troops for the expedition. Save for a handful of axe-wielding gallowglasses these were half-naked kern armed only with javelins and long knives, yet they were Kildare's men with a tribal loyalty to him and to his brother, Sir Thomas FitzGerald of Lackagh, who was their commander.

A further reason to invade was that having advanced funds to hire the landsknechts, Margaret of Burgundy wanted a return on her investment. She now gave Lincoln still more money to hire ships for the invasion. Judging from how much a later Yorkist expedition cost her, she must have lent him something like a million gold crowns. A notoriously hard woman where money was concerned, the duchess insisted on a bond being drawn up, to ensure the earl would pay her back in full – as soon as he had conquered England.

Lincoln and Lovell calculated that they would be joined by a host of northern Englishmen. All in all, they stood a better chance of overthrowing Henry VII than the Tudor had ever had of defeating King Richard.

# 4

# Summer 1487: 'Stoke Field'

'John, late Earl of Lincoln . . . continuing in his malicious and traitorous purpose, arrived with a great navy in Furness in Lancashire, the iiijth day of June last past, accompanied with a great multitude of strangers, with force and arms, that is to say, swords, spears, morris-pikes, bows, guns, harness, brigandines, hauberks and many other weapons.'

Act of Attainder, November 1487[1]

Henry VII's standing army consisted only of his new Yeomen of the Guard, with the Knights and Squires of the Body. The garrisons (600–700 troops at Calais and smaller forces at Berwick and on Jersey) were too far away to help. Awaiting an invasion, the king was forced to rely on the armed retainers of his magnates and leading gentry.

He had no means of knowing where or when his enemies intended to arrive. In early April he expected a landing in East Anglia, presumably at some place near de la Pole country, on the shore opposite Flanders. However, the news that Lincoln and Lovell had gone to Ireland made it more logical to suppose they would land somewhere along the west coast, and by 8 May the king had installed himself at Kenilworth Castle in Warwickshire, where he waited for news.

Henry could only guess how many secret sympathizers were going to join the Yorkist army. Would the Duke of Suffolk ride to the aid of his son, with his retainers and large 'affinity' from East Anglia and the Thames Valley? What about all those northern gentlemen who had been made to surrender estates in the South given to them by Richard III? Would the city of York rise? Was the Earl of Northumberland about to change sides with his vast following? The king was so nervous that when he heard that the notoriously unstable Marquess of Dorset was coming to join him, he had him arrested and put in the Tower, commenting that he would not mind a little discomfort if he were a true friend. Henry's fear that there were Yorkists everywhere came out in a proclamation he sent to the larger cities on 3 June 1487, ordering their councils to hunt down anyone who was found spreading rumours – 'feigned, contrived and forged tidings and tales'.[2] Offenders were to be put in the pillory.

On 4 June the invasion fleet made land at the desolate, treeless little island of Foulney in Morecambe Bay on the coast of what is now Cumbria, near the southern tip of the Furness Peninsula. It was an odd place to choose since it was guarded by a fortress, Peel Castle, a bastion against Scots raiders that luckily was undefended. Perhaps some of the invaders were seeking the first haven available after a stormy crossing. The fleet then sailed on, to disembark further troops and horses at Furness Fells, where they were welcomed by Sir Thomas Broughton, who brought his retainers and his Lancashire friends, including Sir Thomas Pilkington of Pilkington.

Lincoln wasted no time, marching towards York across the Pennines. This was country he knew well as a former President of the Council of the North. When his army reached Masham four days later, he sent a letter to the mayor and corporation of York, written in the name of 'King Edward VI'. It states that since his army is weary from 'travail of the sea and upon land', he will be grateful for 'relief and ease of lodging and victuals within our city', for which he will pay.[3] But although there was plenty of support inside York, the authorities were too frightened to admit him.

Several Yorkshire landowners joined the earl, such as Thomas Metcalfe of Nappa and Edward Franke of Knighton. The most important were Lord Scrope of Bolton and Lord Scrope of Masham, who later pleaded they had been forced into doing so by their tenants. Others included Sir Robert Percy of Scotton (whose father had died fighting for Richard at Bosworth), Sir Ralph Ashton of Fritton-in-Redesdale and Sir Edmund Hastings from Pickering. Abbot William Haslington of the great Cistercian abbey of Jervaulx was also implicated in some way – perhaps sending armed tenants – as he afterwards sued for a pardon. The Yorkist army had now grown to between 8,000 and 10,000 men but, as Lincoln and Lovell must have become sickeningly aware, it was not a big enough force for the job in hand. Even so, they did not lose heart.

On the night of 10 June, at Bramham Moor near Tadcaster, Lord Lovell and 2,000 followers overwhelmed a force of 400 Tudor supporters under Lord Clifford. Two days later, the two Lords Scrope made a sudden attack on one of York's gates, Bootham Bar, but with insufficient strength, before riding away northwards: they had probably expected the gate to be opened by other ex-henchmen of King Richard whom they knew were in York, each with a large following. The Earl of Northumberland thought the situation inside the city so threatening that he stayed nearby with his powerful forces, keeping an eye on the Scropes and York instead of hurrying south to reinforce Henry.

Unfortunately for Lincoln, too many of the gentlemanly sympathizers inside York were not ready to risk their necks by joining his army before he had won a battle. If he did so, they would support him with enthusiasm. Their caution proved fatal to his cause, although it is clear that both Lincoln and Lovell expected large areas of the North to rise in support. As Bacon comments, 'their snowball did not gather as it went'.[4] One reason why so many Yorkists did not join the rising may have been the outlandish appearance of the wild, bare-legged, Irish kern, who formed the bulk of the earl's army.

'Martin Schwartz was deceived, for when he took this voyage upon him, he was comforted and promised by th'Earl of Lincoln that great strength of this land after their landing would have resorted unto the said earl,' records *The Great Chronicle of London*.

> But when he was far entered and saw no such resort, then he knew well he was deceived, wherefore he said unto th'earl, 'Sir, I now see well that ye have deceived yourself and also me but, that notwithstanding, all such promise as I made unto my lady [Margaret] the duchess I shall perform', exhorting th'earl to do the same. And upon this sped them towards the field with as good courage as he had twenty-thousand men more.[5]

The earl decided that his only chance was to advance south as fast as possible, on the east side of the Pennines, and catch Henry before he could concentrate his full strength. He had only a few hundred mounted men-at-arms but Schwartz's *landsknechts* rode horses, while the kern could trot like ponies, so that he was able to cover 200 miles in five days. His route went through Rotheram, Mansfield and Southwell – taking him across the battlefield of Towton, which in 1461 had seen the Yorkists' greatest victory. Although small, this was a formidable army.

Outside Doncaster, Lincoln's troops ran into a troop of lances commanded by Lord Scales who, after three days of skirmishing in and around Sherwood Forest, retreated in confusion on 14 June, towards Nottingham. Encouraged, the earl and his men pushed on, fording the River Trent at Fiskerton, not far from Newark, to camp for the night on an escarpment near the little village of East Stoke. Yet Scales had seriously delayed him, gaining time for reinforcements to reach Henry.

As soon as the news of Lincoln's landing reached Henry at Kenilworth, he marched north with equal speed, hoping to intercept him, going by way of Coventry, Leicester and Loughborough, picking up levies as he went. Vergil attributes Henry's swift reaction to concern that any delay might allow Lincoln 'to assemble greater forces'.[6] But near Nottingham the king got hopelessly lost, with the result that he and his army were forced to spend the night of 12 June in a wood. Nor, according to his herald, did they manage to reach the city next day, wandering aimlessly – Henry was lucky to find a bed for himself in the isolated village of Radcliffe.

Lincoln's sympathizers spread defeatist rumours to deter others from joining Henry. According to *The Great Chronicle of London*,

> by subtle ways men were set atween the place of the field and many of the king's subjects which were coming towards his Grace, showing unto them that the king had lost the field and was fled. By such subtle means and report, many a true man to the king turned back again, and some men of name rode unto sanctuary, and tarried them there till to them was brought better tidings.[7]

A Burgundian source states that among those who deserted Henry was Lord Welles, who brought the stories to London where they were credited to such an extent that Yorkists emerged from hiding, attacking and robbing royal officials and known Tudor supporters, shouting, 'Long live Warwick! King Edward!'[8]

Matters improved for the king, however, when, on 14 June, he and the royal army at last reached Nottingham, camping outside. Here his army was doubled in size by the Earl of Derby's contingent of 6,000 well-equipped men who were commanded by Derby's son, Lord Strange. Henry's troops already included those brought by the Earls of Oxford, Shrewsbury and Devon, and by his uncle Jasper, Duke of Bedford.

Early on the morning of 15 June the Tudor army marched along the banks of the Trent, to engage the Yorkists at Stoke. Both sides sent out scouts to locate their enemy but, while Henry's spies were no doubt busy enough, one can scarcely accept the claim made by the chronicler Edward Hall in the following reign, that the king had been 'in his [the Earl of Lincoln's] bosom and knew every hour what the Earl did'.[9] We have no proper report of the ensuing battle. The only descriptions we possess are a sketchy casualty list drawn up by a Tudor herald, some details from an unreliable Burgundian chronicler and what Vergil was told twenty years later. There have been several reconstructions, however. What follows is a summary.[10]

The two forces went into action at about 9 a.m. on 16 June. Lincoln's Yorkists, less than 9,000, occupied an excellent defensive position on an escarpment, a low hill south-west of East Stoke, with their rear and one flank guarded by the Trent. The pikemen dismounted, forming their customary square. Then, despite its advantages, the earl suddenly abandoned the high ground, moving down to engage the royal troops as quickly as possible, as the bulk of Henry VII's 12,000 men had not yet formed up. Well over a mile away the king took no part in the fighting. After almost being killed at Bosworth, he had no intention of risking his life – his death would mean the speedy disappearance of his baby son and the immediate extinction of the Tudor dynasty.

Only Henry's advance guard, 6,000 picked men who were led by his most reliable commander, the Earl of Oxford, faced the Yorkists. Realizing that this force was isolated from the rest of the royal army, Lincoln hoped to annihilate it before the main body came up and joined in the engagement. As he lacked archers, he began the combat with a volley of quarrels from his Geman arbalestiers, after which he attacked with his entire force. Schwartz's gaudily uniformed pikemen loped downhill four deep to a deafening roll of drums while the wild kern ran beside them, yelling the FitzGerald war cry, '*Crom abu!*'. At the same time, his mounted men-at-arms launched their own charge.

Having never before encountered eighteen-foot German pikes and two-handed swords, or Irish javelins, the advance guard was understandably shaken. A sizeable number of men bolted, shouting that the battle was lost. Had the rest of the advance guard done so, too, it is more than likely that the Yorkist sympathizers in the remainder of the Tudor army would have turned on King Henry. For a moment, everthing was in the balance.

Despite substantial losses, most of the advance guard managed to survive the initial impact of the Yorksit charge, standing their ground, hacking and thusting at their opponents. At the same time, Oxford, a highly experienced solider with iron nerves, made full use of his archers' superior fire-power, which was a new experience for foreign troops. After two hours of murderous hand-to-hand combat, the odds started to turn in the advance guard's favour.

Unlike the *landsknechts*, who were equipped with steel helmets and breast-plates, the Irish had no protective covering other than frieze mantels, while those of their opponents not in armour wore 'jacks' made of thick layers of deerskin. In any case, the Irishmen's dirks and long-handed axes proved to be no match for the royal army's swords, bills and pole-axes, let alone for its bows. The kern began to drop like flies beneath the arrows, suffering horrific casualties that demoralized their German comrades.

After three hours, the Irish broke and finally the Germans ran, but there was no escape. Fleeing along a narrow ravine that led to the Trent, so many of them were killed before they reached the river, it became known by locals as 'Red Gutter'. (It has been suggested that the ravine was blocked by an upturned wagon or gun cart.[11]) Others drowned in the Trent. Lincoln, Sir Thomas FitzGerald of Lackagh, Martin Schwartz and Sir Robert Percy were all killed, with about 4,000 of their men – almost half their army. Even so, fighting with the utmost ferocity they had cut down at least half of Oxford's vanguard. The battle was over by midday. There is a tradition that the Yorkist leaders were buried with green willow staves driven through their hearts.

The only Yorkist leaders who escaped were Lord Lovell and Sir Thomas Broughton. Lovell was seen trying to swim his horse across the Trent: some said he drowned because the bank was too steep – the heavy armour worn by men of his rank cannot have helped him. Others suspected he got away safely, to hide in his great mansion by the Windrush. Bacon tells of a legend that he 'lived long after in a cave or vault',[12] and when part of Minster Lovell was demolished around the year 1700 (at least eighty years after Bacon was writing), a richly dressed skeleton was found in a cellar, seated at a table, giving rise to a gruesome story that, locked in for the sake of concealment, Lovell had starved to death.

In reality, both Lovell and Broughton succeeded in escaping to Scotland, where they were given refuge by James III, as his successor James IV gave them letters of safe conduct during the following year,[13] After this the pair disappear completely, neither being involved in later conspiracies.[14] It is not impossible that, sheltered by Yorkist supporters, Francis Lovell made his way back to die in hiding at his beautiful house. Because of his friendship with Richard III and mysterious end, he has left a sinister name, but no one can deny his courage or his loyalty. An enamelled brass plate bearing his arms (with the crest of a faithful dog) still hangs in St George's Chapel, Windsor. It has hung there ever since he was made a Knight of the Garter by King Richard in 1484.

Henry VII rode up with the rest of his army after the battle was over. There were no important prisoners to behead and he behaved with calculated moderation. Some of the Lancashire and Yorkist gentlemen who escaped, such as Thomas Metcalfe, Richard Middleton and Rowland Robinson, were attainted or fined. Sir Edmund Hastings received a pardon. The two Lords Scrope were imprisoned for a time and fined, but kept the bulk of their estates. When released, neither was allowed to travel north of the Trent, preventing them from returning home.

Although the king hanged a batch of less important prisoners at Lincoln, together with men found guilty of spreading rumours of his defeat, he stuck to a policy of mildness – he did not want to antagonize the North Country by overreacting as Richard III had done in the South after the Duke of Buckingham's revolt. When he went on progress through Yorkshire and Durham, an alarmingly large number of people came to him in search of letters of pardon, which they obtained without too much difficulty. If they had not ridden with Lincoln, clearly they had been involved in the rising in some way or other – some must have come from among the Scropes' followers or from those who had planned to take over York. Henry's clemency reveals his fundamental insecurity.

Richard Simons, the Oxford cleric who had trained Lambert Simnel to impersonate Warwick, could not be executed because he was a priest, but disappeared into perpetual imprisonment. Henry was more merciful towards the boy. 'Lambert is still alive today,' wrote Polydore Vergil twenty years later. 'He has been promoted to the post of falconer to the king, having previously been a turnspit and worked at various other menial jobs in the royal kitchens.'[15] This magnanimity was designed to demonstrate a self-confidence on Henry's part, which, in reality, he was far from feeling.

Although the king had won at Stoke, he might just as easily have lost. Only a small part of his army were involved in the fighting, which indicates that, as at Bosworth, their leaders were awaiting the outcome. According to Vergil, Henry regretted that Lincoln had not been captured because he wanted to discover from him the full extent of the conspiracy. Before the battle, noticing how confident the Yorkists appeared, he suspected they must have allies among the royal troops and had given orders for the earl to be taken alive. Vergil heard that these orders were disobeyed because some of Henry's men were terrified Lincoln might incriminate them.

The king knew the earl might well have found more supporters, and that there had been a growing groundswell of support for him all over the North Country. What was so alarming was the challenge coming within less than two years of Bosworth. Still more disturbing, when rumours circulated in London that Henry Tudor had been defeated, there was a breakout by the Yorkists in sanctuary at Westminster, while mobs rioted in the streets, shouting the name he dreaded most of all – 'Warwick! Warwick!'

Although the king could scarcely be expected to draft an Act of Parliament, the Attainder passed in November echoes the frenzied anger of Richard III on learning that the Duke of Buckingham had risen against him. It complains that:

> notwithstanding the great and sovereign kindness that our sovereign liege lord that now is, at divers sundry times, continually showed to the said late earl . . . but the contrary to kind and natural remembrance, his faith, truth and allegiance, [he] conspired and imagined the most dolorous and lamentable murder, death and destruction of the royal person[16]

Henry arranged for his wife, Elizabeth of York, to be crowned queen on 25 November, while Parliament was sitting. It was a gesture of insecurity – he wanted to remind England that his consort had Plantagenet blood. Unfortunately, there were other people with the same blood, and not just the Earl of Warwick. They included Elizabeth's sisters, together with Lincoln's brothers.

Most menacing of all was the Duchess Margaret in Burgundy. Bernard André, a French scholar in Henry's service, says the king was convinced that Lincoln had only acted as he did because of her encouragement. During the recent campaign, Henry described her to his courtiers as: 'That stupid, brazen woman, who despite knowing perfectly well her family was destroyed by her brother Richard, hates my own family with such bitterness that, deliberately ignoring the fact that her niece is my dear wife, she remains bent on destroying myself and my children.'[17] It was only a matter of time before this implacable enemy stirred up another dangerous plot.

Bacon believed Henry felt so unsafe that he distrusted even his wife, Elizabeth – 'he showed himself no very indulgent husband towards her, though she was beautiful, gentle and fruitful . . . his aversion towards the house of York was so predominant in him as it found place not only in his wars and councils, but in his chamber and bed'.[18]

# 5

# Winter 1489–90:
# The Conscience of Abbot Sant

'The Abbot of Abingdon, a most devout monk of the order
of St Benedict.'

Polydore Vergil, *Anglica Historia*[1]

If Henry VII did not expect any more trouble from pretenders,
he made a grave mistake. It was going to seem as though insurrection was a perennial disease for the new Tudor monarchy. In
Bacon's lapidary phrase, the king suffered from 'moles perpetually working and casting to undermine him'.[2]

Too weak to punish the Irish lords, in June 1488 Henry
sent Sir Richard Edgecombe over St George's Channel, to
make them swear allegiance. But when Edgecombe visited the
Lord Deputy, the Earl of Kildare, at Maynooth he was left in
no doubt as to who really ruled Ireland: the oath of allegiance
taken by Kildare and the other lords had to be modified since,
rather than give bonds for their behaviour, they threatened to
'become Irishmen' like those in the wild lands outside the Pale.

Still inclined to favour Yorkism, the earl bluntly declined a royal command to visit England.

At the end of 1488 the king declared war on France to preserve Breton independence and sent an army to Brittany. To pay for it, he was obliged to levy swingeing new taxes, voted by a very reluctant Parliament. The ensuing unpopularity encouraged the Yorkists and in March 1489 William Paston wrote to his brother Sir William of how Edward Heestowe [Hextall] of Dover had been accused of treason on 'many strange points'. At first neither the king nor his counsellors were inclined to believe the accusation, but then Hextall himself confessed his guilt 'and of many other things more'. As a result he was imprisoned in the Tower and facing death. There is no further information about his 'treason', which can only have been some sort of plot to release the Earl of Warwick.[3]

The previous year's harvest had been unusually poor, while the taxes were particularly resented in the North because the Border Counties were exempted (to pay for defences against the perennial threat from Scotland). In April a mob murdered the Earl of Northumberland at Topcliffe and the men of Yorkshire and Durham rose in rebellion, 'saying that they would pay no money'.[4] Sir John Egremont, a noted troublemaker, then led an attack on York. The rising was put down easily enough, the Earl of Surrey routing the rebels not far from the Northern capital. Mass executions followed, on a spectacular scaffold two storeys high that was erected specially in York, John a Chambre, Egremont's main accomplice, having the distinction of being hanged from the top tier.

The king linked the rising with the Hextall case, suspecting another Yorkist plot, and one of the motives for Northumberland's murder had undoubtedly been his betrayal of Richard III at Bosworth.[5] 'Divers affirm that the Northmen bare against the earl continual grudge sith the death of King Richard, whom they entirely loved and highly favoured,' was what Hall heard fifty years later.[6] Nor were the king's fears soothed when he learned that Egremont had taken refuge with Margaret of York. While Henry's eyes were fixed on Flanders, Northern England and Ireland, the next conspiracy emerged in the South, from a most unlikely personage.

A mitred abbot who had a seat in the House of Lords, 'Dan' John Sant, was as rich and powerful as many temporal peers. Abingdon Abbey was one of the oldest and wealthiest monasteries in England, dominating its beautiful little town amid the lush meadows of northern Berkshire. A fine bridge had recently been built over the Thames here, and during Lent the abbey's kitchener levied a toll of a hundred fish from every boat passing beneath. The monks' lands stretched in a block from Eynsham to Dorchester, with outlying properties as far south as Welford in the Lambourn valley.

The thirty or so 'black monks' of Abingdon (so called from the colour of their habits) lived a distinctly relaxed interpretation of the Benedictine rule. Instead of sleeping in a dormitory, each monk had his own cubicle, while wine was served at meals on not less than eighty feast days. As in other large monasteries, they employed a staff of at least a hundred servants (who were popularly known as 'abbey lubbers') to look after them. Resembling a combination of cathedral and Oxford college, the great abbey must have been an extraordinary sight in such a small town. Stuffed with treasures – jewelled reliquaries, gemencrusted vestments, gold and silver plate – it also had a fine library. Although the imposing church and most of the buildings were torn down during the Dissolution of the Monasteries, the gatehouse (built during Sant's abbacy) still stands to give us some idea of the grandeur of the place.

Abbot Sant mixed with Berkshire's leading gentry and merchants, entertaining them at his palatial lodging, in panelled rooms with stained-glass windows. It is likely that he had also been host to the Earl of Lincoln and Lord Lovell, who belonged to Abingdon's Fraternity of the Holy Cross. (Minsters Lovell and Ewelme were within a day's ride.) A member of the House of Lords, he was often in London, on excellent terms with the black monks of Westminster since he owned a large house nearby, The Mote in King Street. William Caxton had recently set up shop in Westminster Hall, not far from the abbey, and in 1476 Sant had commissioned the first English printed document from him – a papal indulgence that encouraged the faithful to go on crusade against the Turk.

The abbot of Abingdon must have been familiar with up-to-date political gossip. He had met Henry VII fairly often as the king had stayed at his monastery (twice in July 1488) on journeys to Kenilworth and back to Windsor,[7] and entrusted him with important diplomatic missions: during 1488 Sant was one of the ambassadors sent to France to negotiate with Charles VIII. He had also been the papal nuncio in England, Wales and Ireland. Vergil refers to him approvingly,[8] unaware of his later behaviour.

One has the impression, then, of a bland, smooth-talking, worldy cleric whose loyalty to the new regime seemed beyond question. Yet the king may have wondered why the Stafford brothers had taken refuge in a dependency of Abingdon, his suspicions perhaps further aroused by Sant's fury at the infringement of Culham's sanctuary rights: on 21 May 1486, eight days after the seizure of the Staffords, Sant was bound over for the huge sum of £800. Since then, however, it looks as if the abbot had completely exonerated himself – no doubt he held lengthy conversations with Henry when the king used Abingdon as a staging post and also when being briefed for his mission to France.

His brethren had elected Sant as abbot in 1468, presumably because he possessed the managerial skills needed to run the abbey's estates. In consequence, he had spent the best years of his life in a position of authority during Edward IV's second reign, the golden age of Yorkism: perhaps significantly, he was one of the two abbots who officiated at Edward's funeral. He remained unconvinced by Henry Tudor's tenuous claim to be the heir of Lancaster. Privately, he believed that the crown belonged to the Plantagenets and that the Earl of Warwick had been robbed of his inheritance and was ready to help anyone who was prepared to do something about it.

We only know of what is sometimes (wrongly) called 'Abbot Sant's conspiracy' from an indictment for treason dated January 1490. A certain John Mayne of Abingdon had been arrested, presumably after being betrayed by an informer and put to the 'question' – stretched on the rack or having his feet roasted. He admitted that three years earlier, he and Christopher Swanne, 'yeoman', of the same town, had met, 'falsely and traitorously [en]compassing, conspiring and imagining the destruction of the King'.

They had been collecting donations from Yorkist supporters to finance the Earl of Lincoln's expedition. (Interestingly, the indictment states that the abbot 'gave to the said John Mayne a certain sum of money', and as the date when Mayne and Swanne met was 1 January 1487, this means the earl had been planning a rebellion well before his flight.) A substantial amount of cash was no doubt collected, since he had so many friends in the area. The only study of Sant's conspiracy suggests that the Berkshire Yorkists were just a handful of monks in contact with one or two like-minded churchmen at Oxford, but its author does not appreciate that the De La Poles were such big local landowners, or that a large number of Abingdon townsmen may have met the earl.[9]

Undeterred by Lincoln's failure, on 1 December 1489 Mayne and a London priest called Thomas Rothwell (otherwise Thomas Even) met in the capital and plotted to release the Earl of Warwick, with the object of starting a 'war against the King, our said Sovereign Lord, to the intent to have destroyed his most royal person, and utterly to put this whole realm in confusion'. They then went to the house of Henry Davy where they found not only Davy but Edward Franke.

Franke, that veteran Yorkist irreconcilable, had been captured after the battle at Stoke and committed to the Tower, but had managed to escape. His unshakeable attachment to the former regime has already been demonstrated. Henry Davy, like Franke a gentleman, was another diehard Ricardian, faithful to the memory of a king who had made him his sergeant-tailor. With Franke, he had been ruined by Bosworth.

The plotters agreed on a plan, or at any rate on the outline of a plan. They decided to ask the Abbot of Abingdon for his advice. That they did so shows they were convinced he would give them a sympathetic hearing. It is likely that Franke had already met the abbot since he had been 'pricked' – chosen – as Sheriff of Oxfordshire and Berkshire in 1484, when he had farmed the manors of Bray and Cookham in the latter county. Clearly, the abbot was someone whom they were all convinced could be relied on not to betray their conspiracy to the authorities, and who might even consider joining them.

Mayne then travelled up to Abingdon and gave Sant an outline of what they had in mind, adding that Rothwell would come soon in order to explain the plan to him in more detail. The 'said Abbot was joyous and bade the said John Mayne choose what he would drink' (one has the impression of Sant gesturing towards a fifteenth-century drinks cupboard). At the same time, the abbot warned Mayne that the attempt was going to need extremely careful planning. He suggested that while Warwick was being rescued, a letter addressed to him should be dropped as if by accident so that it might be picked up by 'some good fellow': the letter would tell the earl to join the plotters at Colchester, presumably to put his pursuers off the scent after he had been released from the Tower.

But when Rothwell arrived Sant grew less enthusiastic, realizing that the man was half-crazy – 'light-witted'. Even so, he wanted the scheme to go ahead, promising he would talk about it with Edward Franke when he next visited London. Mayne, Rothwell and Christopher Swanne met in Abingdon on

20 December, for further discussions. (Swayne was more than a mere yeomen, being the town's bailiff – which was tantamount to mayor – and a person of some substance.) Franke remained in London, however. A monk of the abbey, Dan Myles Salley, brought the three a sum of money from Sant that would enable them to finance the conspiracy.[10] However, the plot never got off the ground. Within the next few days all the conspirators were arrested, together with the abbot, and charged with treason.

Little is known about Henry VII's 'secret service', but it had its successes and stamping out the Abingdon plot was one of them. Many of the agents seem to have been clerics. Understandably, no identifiable records were kept – although one or two reports have survived – but it is clear that informers were paid bounty money, sometimes on a regular basis: the regime had so many hidden enemies that it could not have survived without them. A number of otherwise inexplicable arrests can only be attributed to their activities. It was undercover spies of this sort who brought Mayne to the authorities' attention.[11]

He was swiftly tried and convicted. There was no need for a trial in the case of Edward Franke, who was soon hunted down: having been attainted after Stoke he was already a proscribed traitor whose life was forfeit. According to a contemporary herald's account, within a matter of days four men suffered on Tower Hill because of their involvement – Mayne, Franke, Davy and another, unnamed man.[12] The monk Myles Salley, who had brought the abbot's money to the conspirators, was also found guilty but eventually pardoned, as was Christopher Swanne, the Bailiff of Abingdon.

John Sant was found guilty, too, but being a cleric he escaped the death penalty. He appears to have been kept in prison until September 1490 when he was bound over and ordered to pay the enormous fine of £1,000 in instalments, besides forfeiting all his lands and goods, although these were restored to him in 1493. In any case, as they consisted of manors in Berkshire and Oxfordshire, they belonged to the abbey. In the same year he bequeathed all his movable goods – personal possessions – to King Henry, 'in token of all the grace shown to him . . . praying God for a good continuation of the king's royal estate'.[13] He remained Abbot of Abingdon until his death in 1496.

Yet it is plain that Abbot Sant was no fool. What is so interesting is that he and his friends among the Abingdon townsmen believed that a plot to release Warwick and make him king in Henry Tudor's place stood a fair chance of winning widespread support. They had been confident enough to risk their lives.

There is some evidence that Henry was seriously alarmed by the conspiracy. When riots broke out among the traders of Abingdon in spring 1492 and a large number were arrested, he stopped the proceedings and ordered their release – it seems that he was keeping an eye on the area, anxious to win support among the locals. It may not be a coincidence that in January 1494, when there was a distinct possibility of a rising in favour of Perkin Warbeck, the king went on progress through Berkshire.

# 6

# Winter 1491–Autumn 1494: One of the Princes in the Tower?

'At this time the King began again to be haunted with spirits, by the magic and curious arts of the lady Margaret, who raised up the ghost of Richard duke of York, second son to King Edward the fourth, to walk and vex the King.'

Sir Francis Bacon, *The History of the Reign of King Henry VII*[1]

Perkin Warbeck's arrival on the scene came as a profound shock to the king, who at first wondered whether this really was one of the Princes in the Tower, returned from the dead – Edward IV's son, the Duke of York. For at the start of his career Perkin seemed most convincing. Quoting people who had met him, the chronicler Hall says, 'he kept such a princely countenance and so counterfeit a majesty royal that all men did firmly believe that he was extracted of the noble house and family of the Dukes of York'.[2] Should this be true, he was infinitely more dangerous than the Earl of Warwick – and Henry was well aware that all too many of his subjects wanted it to be true.

In 1490 there had been yet another abortive plot to rescue Warwick, by Yorkists hoping to exploit the war with France. In February the king acknowledged a letter from the Bishop of Durham reporting the capture of Sir Robert Chamberlain (a former Knight of the Body to Richard III), his two sons and a group of friends at Hartlepool, who had been trying to leave the country for France. Henry asked for 'these rebels and traitors' to be sent to him urgently.[3]

An attainder of October 1491 explains why the king was so keen to lay hands on them. Chamberlain and Richard White, a Norfolk gentleman, had planned to kill him and start a civil war: they had been financed by Charles VIII of France, the 'ancient enemy to our said sovereign lord'. Their plot must have have hinged on a scheme to replace Henry with Warwick.[4] White was charged on 23 August 1490 with engaging in conspiracy and Chamberlain on 17 January 1491, which suggests that both had been under close surveillance for some time. Sir Robert was beheaded on Tower Hill within a month of his arrest but White received a pardon as he stood on the scaffold under the hangman's rope. (Dramatic reprieves were a feature of fifteenth-century justice, staged to show the king's merciful nature.)

The French then decided to send an expedition to Ireland in support of Warwick. The brains behind it were those of a Yorkist exile, John Taylor – 'the elder' as he signed himself – a middle-aged cloth merchant and former customs officer from Devon. On 15 September 1491 Taylor wrote from Rouen to John Hayes 'late of Tiverton, Devon', whom he appears to have met recently during a secret visit. A priest-bureaucrat who had also been in the Duke of Clarence's service, but was now a receiver of rents at Exeter and Dartmouth for many of the West Country's leading landowners, Hayes had confided in Taylor that he still felt a secret loyalty to Clarence's son Warwick.

Coloured by an exile's nostalgia, Taylor's letter reminded Hayes of 'words we spake together in St Peter's church of Exeter, and at the Black Friars when ye were at your breakfast'.

Telling him how to get in touch, Taylor recommends Thomas
Gale of Dartmouth:

> ye may speak with him by the same token that he and
> I communed together at matters touching your master's
> son in Stockingham Park when Sir John Halliwell hunted
> therin, and be you not afeared to show all your mind unto
> him for he is trusty . . . the token between you and me is
> that such as I shall send unto shall take you by the thumb.

(Gale was another staunch Yorkist. Once Clerk of the King's
Ships for Richard III, he had lost his job as a consequence of
the new regime. Living at Dartmouth, where he had been both
the MP and the mayor, he was the ideal man to help an invasion
force.)

The real message of Taylor's letter was that Charles VIII had
been advised by his council to help Warwick, 'your master's
son'. If the earl and his supporters could reach France, then
King Charles would provide troops, ships and money. Those
who arrived penniless would get financial assistance 'if they be
known for true men for the quarrel'. Taylor adds that help was
coming from two other places outside England, by which he
must mean Flanders and Ireland. It is likely he hoped to recruit
his old friend because he envisaged a Yorkist expedition landing
in the West Country and seizing Exeter.

After reading this exceptionally dangerous document, which
reached him on 26 November, Hayes threw it into the fire, but
it was saved and handed to the authorities, and he was arrested,
the letter being copied in his attainder as a traitor in 1492 – the
only reason for its survival.[5] When the king read it, he must
have smiled grimly at one sentence in particular. 'The [French]
king and his council say they will ask nothing in recompense,
but . . . do it for the wrong he did in making Henry King of
England.' John Taylor the Elder would bitterly regret that he
had ever put pen to paper.

Instead of landing in the West Country, the French went to Ireland, a mere 120 troops on board two small ships. Disguised as Englishmen, wearing surcoats with the Cross of St George and flying the English flag, they landed somewhere near Cork at the end of November 1491. Taylor, who accompanied them, quickly became aware that after the disastrous episode with Lambert Simnel there was little enthusiasm for taking up arms for Warwick – everyone knew he was locked up in the Tower of London.

Even so, Taylor's Yorkist agent at Cork did his best to find support, encouraged by the English-speaking Irishmen's dislike for the Tudor regime. The agent was John Atwater, a highly respected merchant who had twice been mayor of the city. He came to Taylor with a staggering proposal – to replace Warwick as pretender to the throne with the younger of the Princes of the Tower, the Duke of York. For, as if by a miracle, Atwater had discovered a doppelgänger.

In October or November 1491 the citizens of Cork had seen strolling along the front a handsome, fair-haired youth in his late teens, dressed in silken clothes, who had come ashore from a ship belonging to a Breton merchant, Pregent Meno, and was wearing his master's clothes. He looked so distinguished that they asked him if he was the Earl of Warwick, the Duke of Clarence's son. Seeming alarmed, in the presence of the Mayor of Cork and swearing on the Gospel and a crucifix, 'I took mine oath as truth that I was not the foresaid Duke's son, neither of none of his blood [no relation]', the youth recounted long afterwards. 'And after this came unto me an Englishman whose name was Steven Poytron, with one John Atwater, and said to me, in swearing great oaths, and said that I was King Richard's bastard son, to whom I answered with high oaths that I were not.'

Convinced he was a Plantagenet, Atwater and Poytron told him to forget his fears. If he would fight for his rights, they would do all they could to help him. They were certain that the earls of Desmond and Kildare would do the same if it meant being revenged on the English king. 'Against my will [they] made me to learn English and taught me what I should do and say. And after this they called me Duke of York, the second son of King Edward IV, because King Richard's bastard son was in the hands of the King of England.'[6]

All this comes from Perkin Warbeck's confession, made several years later. Although it sounds convincing enough, it should be remembered that he was desperately trying to exonerate himself from as much of the blame as possible. One cannot rule out the possibility that Atwater and Taylor had brought him to Ireland to impersonate the duke.

Taylor wrote to Maurice FitzGerald, Earl of Desmond, asking him to help the 'Duke' recover his throne and received an enthusiastic response. As a result, Perkin, Taylor and the French expedition – now his 'retinue' – stayed in Ireland for some months, almost certainly at one of the many castles of Desmond who was the great magnate in the area around Cork, ruling a huge swathe of south-western Ireland from which he took his title. Called '*an bacagh*' (the lame) by the kern, Desmond was a cripple who had to be carried everywhere in a cart or a litter, yet he possessed the power of life and death over his people, and used it. Perkin's stay with the earl may have been fairly nerve-racking. (At Strancally Castle on the Blackwater, the Desmonds had acquired a name for inviting enemies to dinner and then starving them to death in a dungeon before throwing their bodies into the river through a 'murdering hole' cut in the rock.)[7]

Taylor presumably spent the time with the Earl of Desmond in improving the young man's English and instilling the background of his 'royal' boyhood. Perkin was an apt pupil. Bacon, although relying more on imagination than documentary sources, recaptures his extraordinary charm: 'he had such a crafty and bewitching fashion, both to move pity and to induce belief, as was like a kind of fascination and enchantment to those that saw him or heard him.'[8]

It is likely that Kildare also encouraged him. Both FitzGerald earls welcomed a pretender, genuine or not, as long as he could make trouble for Henry VII. So did most Irishmen who came in contact with the boy, since nearly everyone in the Pale and the Irish seaports, and in much of the adjoining territory, remained Yorkist. The Scots were equally delighted: an entry in James IV's accounts for 2 March 1492 records a payment to a man who brought letters from 'King Edward's son and the Earl of Desmond'.[9] On the other hand, the Irish lords had no wish to invade England – they remembered what had happened to Sir Thomas FitzGerald and his kern at Stoke Field.

Henry's spies had reported the Duke of York's presence in Ireland fairly soon. Although at this stage unaware how dangerous the duke was, the king had reacted by sending a small force of troops to Dublin in December 1491 as a warning, besides releasing his Irish subjects from allegiance to Lord Deputy Kildare.[10] Perkin's principal Irish adviser John Atwater realized that the prospects of the 'Duke of York' in Ireland were not exactly promising.

Changing his plans, Taylor informed the French authorities that here was just the young man they needed and King Charles sent a flotilla over to Ireland to bring him back to France. Etienne Fryon, until recently Henry VII's French secretary, was on board. According to Henry's court poet Bernard André, Fryon, who had also been secretary to Edward IV, then spent several months in tutoring Perkin and furnishing him with details about the old Yorkist court and the Yorkist royal family, until he knew by heart the names of every member of King Edward's household 'as though he had known them from the days when he was a little boy'.[11]

In France, the 'duke' was received at court with full royal honours and given a retinue, together with a guard of honour commanded by an expatriate Scot, William Monypeny, Sieur de Concressault, who was an intimate friend of King Charles. He was also joined by about a hundred Yorkists. The most respectable of these were Sir George Neville, once an Esquire of the Body to Richard III who had been knighted at Stoke Field by Henry Tudor, and an outlawed Cumberland gentleman called Edward Skelton who had fought for Lincoln at Stoke. Members of the little court were told to hold themselves in readiness for an imminent invasion of England.

When the French acknowledged Warbeck, the cat was out of the bag. The fate of the young Princes in the Tower, the great mystery of the century, had stirred everybody's imagination and the report that one of them had survived aroused widespread excitement. Vergil tells us that the story was believed not merely by all the common people in England but by many of the ruling class. Old loyalties awoke among Englishmen who outwardly seemed to have accepted the new dynasty. In 1485 men with a lot to lose had risked everything to avenge Edward IV's children and, just as they had rebelled against King Richard, for the same reason they might rebel against King Henry.

In Hall's fanciful prose, then 'there began sedition to spring on every side, none otherwise than in the pleasant times of year trees are wont to bud or blossom'.[12] 'Widespread plotting started,' says Vergil, more prosaically. 'Many nobles got involved, some out of sheer foolhardiness.' He stresses that it happened only after people realized the implications – if the 'duke' was genuine, then the king's right to the crown was in question.[13]

Henry saw at once that he was in graver danger than at any time since Richard III had hacked his way towards him on Bosworth Field. In Vergil's words, the king's spies reported that 'rumours about Richard, the Duke of York come back to life, were dividing all England into factions, filling people's minds with either hope or fear, as nobody could fail to react deeply to such news. Depending on his particular temperament, everyone thought it was going to end in his own peril or profit.'[14] Henry knew that unless he defused the situation there would be an upheaval which might destroy him.

He possessed one great advantage, his subjects' dread of

attainder. They had seen, over and over again, that the new king knew just how to use such a terrible weapon. An attainder put a man outside the law, banishing him from the community – until the day he died he would be hunted for his life. A popular song of the time that apparently was sung all over London at this period, *The Ballad of the Nut Brown Maid*, gives us some idea of what it meant to be attainted.

> My destiny is for to die
> A shameful death, I trow,
> Or else to flee: the one must be,
> None other way I know
> But to withdraw as an outlaw,
> And take me to my bow . . .
> For I must to the greenwood go
> Alone a banished man . . .
>
> For an outlaw, this is the law,
> That men him take and bind,
> Without pity hanged to be,
> And waver with the wind.

Significantly, the ballad attributes high rank to the hero and heroine, the man being the heir to an earldom and the girl a baron's daughter. Even the most convinced Yorkist had reservations about joining a rising that might result in his attainder.[15]

Yet from the start, Henry VII suspected the 'Duke of York' might be a fraud. Obsessed with Margaret's implacable enmity, he thought she must have trained the boy before he arrived in Ireland, a mistake echoed by Vergil and Bacon. Even so, for months he had to face the devastating possibility that this might indeed be one of the Princes in the Tower.

Luckily for the king, French support for the Yorkists depended on France's foreign policy. Although Charles VIII had welcomed Perkin as a pawn in his war with England, his attitude changed when he decided he wanted a peace settlement that would leave him free to invade Italy without his kingdom being attacked by the English in his absence. As part of the Treaty of Étaples, signed on 3 November 1492, Charles gave his word not to help any rebellions against Henry. The invasion of England promised by John Taylor in his letter of the previous November was cancelled and the pretender forced to leave France.

Perkin moved to Flanders where Margaret of Burgundy welcomed the handsome, well-mannered young man and became convinced he was her nephew, although she had never met the real Duke of York. 'So wild was her joy that it seemed to unhinge her mind,' says Vergil. 'Eager for everyone to see how delighted she was, she made a point of constantly congratulating her nephew in public on his escape and never stopped making him repeat the story of how, having been saved from death by a ruse, he had wandered through different countries.'[16] In a letter from Margaret to Queen Isabella of Castile in August 1493, she wrote that she had recognized he was her brother's son by unmistakeable signs, his identity being confirmed by the way he answered questions about his childhood. 'Only too aware that he is now our family's sole survivor after all its disasters and misfortunes, I was deeply moved and . . . have accepted him as an only grandson, as an only son.'[17] Bacon claims that Margaret polished up Perkin's manners, and gave him 'the delicate title of the white rose of England', with a bodyguard of thirty halbardiers in striped liveries of murrey (mulberry) and blue.[18]

Believing that a restoration was merely a matter of time, the Yorkists sent an envoy to Margaret to find out when 'Duke Richard' was planning to arrive in England, so that they would be ready to rise in support. The envoy was Sir Robert Clifford who crossed over to Flanders in June 1493 with his father-in-law William Barley, a gentleman from Hertfordshire. When he reached Malines, Clifford explained to Margaret what the conspirators were planning at home. Ecstatic, the duchess presented

Clifford and Barley to Perkin, who impersonated Richard with his accustomed flair, after which Sir Robert reported to the Yorkist leaders in England that the young man really was the son of Edward IV.

The most important of the 'conspirators' mentioned by Vergil were William Stanley, the king's chamberlain, Lord FitzWalter, steward of the royal household, Sir Gilbert Debenham, a Knight of the King's Body, and Sir Humphrey Savage – Stanley's brother-in-law. Clifford had set the plot in motion, recruiting these four, who formed the core of a revitalized Yorkist faction, between mid-January and mid-March 1493. Their plan was to wait for an invasion and then rise: they also meant to assassinate Henry. Meanwhile, to encourage people to rally behind the cause they spread rumours all over England that the youth at Malines was indeed Richard, Duke of York, but so discreetly that no one hearing the rumours was able to learn of their origin.[19]

Although King Henry's agents alerted him that a rebellion was probably imminent, they could not discover the men who were behind it or what they had in mind, and while he himself sensed some sort of treachery among his courtiers he was unable to identify any of those involved. Expecting fresh trouble in Ireland, Henry again sent troops to Dublin. There are indications that during the summer of 1493 he also expected an invasion of England, on the same scale as Lincoln's, if not larger. He established his headquarters at Kenilworth and sent ships to patrol the North Sea.

Sir Robert Clifford, a younger son of Thomas, Lord Clifford (a Lancastrian killed at the second battle of St Albans in 1461), had once been a devoted follower of Edward IV. He had rebelled against Richard III and had fought for Henry's cause at Stoke where he was knighted on the field of battle. His presence at Malines, with that of Sir Gilbert Debenham from Norfolk who had arrived at the duchess's court before him, implied there was genuinely solid support for the 'duke' in England – although if Margaret and her 'nephew' had known how Clifford had received a pardon from King Richard in return for spying, they might have given him a less enthusiastic welcome.

As soon as he was established at the White Rose's court, Sir Robert contacted the key people behind the 'duke', working closely with them. One of these, of course, was John Taylor. Another was the treasurer for the 'duke', a humble Yorkshireman called Rowland Robinson, who had fought for Lincoln at Stoke and then escaped to Malines where he had been in Margaret's service ever since.

In England, Henry grew more increasingly nervous. Polydore Vergil tells us he sent chosen men to guard the coast and the ports – like King Richard before him. Besides being ordered to stop anyone who looked suspicious from either entering or leaving the country, they were given powers to prevent ships from sailing. As far as possible, all roads and paths near the sea were patrolled, while the local authorities were also told to watch for assemblies of armed men who might be planning a rising.

The royal network of agents stepped up surveillance, abroad as well as at home. 'During this time the king sent spies into Flanders, Some were instructed to pretend they had fled to the reborn Duke of York, and then find out the conspirators' plans as well as their names. Others were to persuade Robert Clifford and William Barley to come home by offering them a pardon,' we are told by Vergil. When the spies arrived they would have been helped by Flemish agents in Henry's pay, who were already working undercover at Malines – some recruited from among the duchess's courtiers.

Meanwhile, Henry's spies in Flanders had been trying to discover whether his rival was an impostor and, if so, to track down his real origins. By the late summer of 1493 they had learned the truth, but it was a long time before their story was generally accepted, despite the king circulating it as widely as possible. Recently, the story has been questioned by Anne Wroe.[20] On 20 July of that year, in a letter to Sir Gilbert Talbot, the king refers to a 'feigned lad called Perkin Warbeck, born at Tournay'.

For the agents had discovered that the duke's real name was Pierrequin Werbecque, a Walloon from Hainault in what is now south-eastern Belgium, who had been born at Tournai around 1474, the son of a well-to-do bargee on the River Scheldt. (This was a highly paid profession, the barges taking corn to the coast for export and bringing back the wines from Burgundy that were so popular at the ducal court.) In 1483 or 1484, 'from Christmas unto Easter' he had worked in the house of an English merchant at Middelburg called John Strewe, to learn his language. Later, he entered the service of Sir Edward Brampton, a Portugese Jew who had converted to Christianity and become Governor of Guernsey, but fled to Flanders after Bosworth. In 1487 Perkin accompanied Brampton's wife on a voyage from Middelburg to Portugal, picking up useful details about the Yorkist court.[21] Leaving the Bramptons, he spent a year at Lisbon, working for a one-eyed Portuguese knight called Pedro Vaez de Cogna. Then, because he wanted to see other countries, he took service with the Breton merchant Pregent Meno.

Many people wondered if this 'official version' of the young man's origins might be no more than a smear campaign. His supporters pointed out that he possessed an unmistakeably regal presence, while by the time the English authorities circulated their version he had developed an extremely plausible cover story that some historians think might possibly be true. The outlines of it are in a letter he sent to Queen Isabella of Spain on 8 September 1493, the gist of which is as follows:

His elder brother, the Prince of Wales, son of King Edward, had been assassinated, He himself had been delivered to a gentleman who had orders to kill him, but who, pitying such a little child, spared him and made him swear on the sacraments to conceal his name, birth and descent for several years. After this, he sent him away under the care of two persons who were both jailors and governors. He then led a wandering life of danger and misery for nearly eight years during which his governors kept him in concealment in different parts of the world, until at last one of them died and the other returned to his own country. In consequence, he was left alone while still almost a boy. Having spent some time in Portugal, he went to Ireland where he was recognised.[22]

A letter from King Henry to Talbot shows the strain was beginning to tell on him. While he spoke contemptuously of his rival as a mere 'boy', everyone knew that at the same age Edward IV had possessed sufficient leadership to win the terrible battle of Towton, the largest ever fought on English soil. Clearly agitated, Henry angrily referred to the 'great malice that the Lady Margaret of Burgundy continually beareth unto us'. He also mentioned an impending invasion of England by 'certain aliens, captains of strange nations', and asked Talbot to be prepared to bring as many troops as he can – 'ready to come upon a day's warning for to do us service of war'.[23]

During July Henry sent two of his ablest negotiators – Sir Edward Poynings and Dr William Warham, the latter Master of the Rolls and a future Archbishop of Canterbury – as ambassadors to Flanders. They lodged a formal protest with the council of Archduke Philip, the Duke of Burgundy, who was still only fifteen, at the help given to Warbeck, Dr Warham making a speech in which he went out of his way to insult Margaret of York. The council blandly insisted, however, that the Burgundian government was powerless to interfere in any way with the Duchess Margaret, who could act as she pleased in the lands of her dowry. It was all too plain that, under pressure from Philip's father, King Maximilian, and not just from Margaret, the government of Flanders had every intention of aiding Warbeck as much as they possibly could, without actually recognizing him as king of England.

Henry reacted furiously, transferring the Merchant Adventurers' Staple (the exclusive market for English goods, mainly cloth) from Antwerp to Calais in September 1493, forbidding Englishmen to do business with Flanders and banishing its citizens from England: Flemings were expelled and had their goods seized. It was as far as he could go without a full-scale war. Flanders retaliated with an embargo on English imports, but Henry strengthened his prohibition. This did serious damage to the Flemish economy, resulting in capitulation in 1496 and the signing of an agreement known as the *Intercursus Magnus*, which gave special advantages to Englishmen trading in Flanders.

Meanwhile, Warbeck was trying to find international support. In September 1493 he wrote the letter to Queen Isabella already mentioned. When it had no effect, he looked elsewhere. We know from a confidential report about the English Prior of St John,[24] that an unknown correspondent informed the prior in 1493 that, after finding it impossible to sell his wares in Flanders for the price he wanted, the 'Merchant of the Ruby' had decided to go to the court of the King of the Romans to see if he could obtain a higher price – which meant that Warbeck had been unable to obtain enough money from Margaret for an invasion. Although keen enough, she had already lost too much in financing the Earl of Lincoln.

He then obtained an introduction to Duke Albrecht of Meissen, Duke of Saxony, the King of the Romans' brother-in-law and principal lieutenant. In November 1493 Albrecht brought him to the Habsburg court at Vienna, where he attended the funeral of the Holy Roman Emperor Frederick III on 6 December and was presented to Frederick's son, the 'King of the Romans' and future Emperor Maximilian I. The king welcomed the young man warmly, giving him a place in his father's funeral cortège.

Maximilian had been angered by Henry making peace with France, breaking the long-standing alliance between the English and the Burgundians. He felt sure his guest was telling the truth when the young man told him he bore three birthmarks on his body that were recognizable by anyone who had known the Duke of York as a child – marks that would convince even Henry Tudor. The impecunious king tried to raise money in the Tyrol (the only part of his domains under his direct rule) so that Warbeck could equip an invasion fleet, but the canny Tyrolese refused, saying it seemed to be too risky a venture.

In mid-summer 1494, taking the young man with him, Maximilian went to Flanders where he announced that this was the real king of England. Henry responded by sending the Garter King of Arms to inform Maximilian and Margaret that their protégé was the son of a merchant of Tournai. When the king and the duchess ignored him, Garter marched through the streets of Malines, shouting that his master had proof that the 'Duke of York' was an impostor. However, he made little impression since his heralds believed it was just the sort of trick that someone as notoriously wily as Henry would use. Maximilian's good opinion of the 'duke' remained unshaken. With an invasion in mind, he ordered an enquiry into what people in England thought of the White Rose.

Maximilian might be showy, frivolous and unreliable, as well as virtually penniless, yet he was Holy Roman Emperor Elect. If he had little real power, he enjoyed enormous prestige throughout Western Europe as the theoretical Sword Temporal of Christendom. (Missals contained a bidding prayer for the Holy Roman Emperor that was said on Good Friday in all churches in every Christian country.) His recognition of the 'Duke of York' as king of England encouraged the Yorkists – and alarmed Henry VII.

Maximilian lost no opportunity of showing the world that he had complete faith in the 'duke'. At the end of August, he and his son made him ride with them to hear Mass in the cathedral at Malines. In October he was invited to attend when Archduke Philip, who had now come of age, took his oath as Duke of Brabant in Antwerp's cathedral church. Perkin was installed in the imposing Hôtel des Anglais at Antwerp (until recently the

Staple's headquarters), escorted everywhere he went by a body-guard of English gentlemen and twenty archers, who wore the badge of the White Rose of York. A shield bearing the royal arms hung over the door, with an inscription reading, 'The arms of Richard, Prince of Wales and Duke of York, son and heir of Edward IV, lately by the Grace of God King of England and France, Lord of Ireland.' This provoked an angry reaction from two Englishmen (possibly agents of Henry) who threw a chamber pot at the shield. They were chased away by a furious crowd, an innocent English bystander being killed during the uproar.

Ignoring the fact that officially he was supposed to be at peace with England, Charles VIII secretly offered to lend the Yorkists a flotilla of ships so that Perkin could invade England from Flanders. Diplomatically feigning ignorance of this offer, Henry sent Richmond King of Arms to Charles in August with a polite letter, in an attempt to dissuade him. After grumbling about the Dowager Duchess of Burgundy having hired Martin Schwartz to wage war on him, Henry wrote that it was notorious that 'the said boy [*garçon*] was no relation whatever to the late King Edward but a native of Tournai and the son of a boatman [*batellier*]', as the king had been reliably informed by those who knew the boy as a child, as well as by some of his old friends. The king complained bitterly of Maximilian's declared purpose of helping him to invade England.[25]

On All Saints' Day (1 November), in angry response to his rival's use of the title, the king created his younger son Duke of York. This was the future Henry VIII, still only three, who, with twenty other somewhat older aspirants, was dubbed a Knight of the Bath. During a fortnight of splendid celebrations at Westminster Palace, courtiers taking part in the jousts wore the old Yorkist colours of blue and murrey, while their chargers were caparisoned in black velvet sewn with white as well as red roses – it was a declaration to the world that the Tudors were the heirs of the House of York.[26]

During his negotiations with Charles VIII in August, King Henry had claimed that England was now in a better and more peaceful condition than at any time in living memory. He was about to learn that his claim was very wide of the mark indeed.

# 7

# January 1495:
# The Lord Chamberlain is
# a Traitor

'Though he were a dark prince, and infinitely suspicious, and his times full of secret conspiracies and troubles; yet in twenty-four years' reign, he never put down or discomposed counsellor or near servant save only Stanley the Lord Chamberlain.'

Sir Francis Bacon, *The History of the Reign of King Henry VII*[1]

A chronicler sets the scene for a confrontation that, he wrongly assumed, took Henry VII by surprise:

The king kept his Christmas at Greenwich and after he came to the Tower of London where was attached Sir William Stanley, called the Lord Chamberlain. And at the same season Sir Robert Clifford, which beforetime had fled the land

and was in Flanders with the king's enemies', came again
and was taken to grace.[2]

Embroidering on Vergil, Edward Hall recalls the impact on
public opinion made by the Duke of York's supposed survival.
It was 'received for an infallible verity and most sure truth, and
that not only of the common people, but also of divers noble
and worshipful men of no small estimation'.[3] Among these men
was Stanley who, by any reckoning, was among the most powerful figures in England. Brother of the king's stepfather, the Earl
of Derby, he had led the decisive charge at Bosworth that saved
Henry Tudor and won the battle. As Lord Chamberlain he ran
the royal household, besides arranging 'audiences' – deciding
who should or should not meet the king.

As has been seen, according to Polydore Vergil, at the end
of 1494 Henry had sent a new team of agents to Flanders, to
discover what the Yorkists were planning and persuade Robert
Clifford and William Barley to return by offering them a full
pardon. They were wholly successful in Clifford's case. By now
he knew that Perkin was not the Duke of York, while he had
learned the names of the Yorkist leaders in England. Following
the agents' advice, he waited for a few weeks before suddenly
fleeing to Calais, from where he was brought home. Barley
stayed on with the 'false duke' for another two years however,
possibly as a spy.

To avoid suspicion, after he had left the agents involved left
Flanders one at a time. What they had found out, presumably in
large part from Clifford, who possessed Warbeck's confidence,
must have shaken King Henry badly. An attempt on his life
was being planned, accompanied by a Yorkist invasion and an
armed rising. The amount of support for the scheme among
highly placed, influential Englishmen was especially alarming. The seventeen arrested and tried for treason at the end
of November included Lord FitzWalter, Sir Simon Mountford
of Coleshill, a big landowner in Warwickshire, Sir Thomas

Thwaites of Barnes in Surrey who, under Richard III, had been Treasurer of Calais, Robert Ratcliffe, a former gentleman-porter of Calais, and William Daubeney, once keeper of the jewel house to King Richard, together with other gentlemen of standing.

Four leading churchmen were also taken into custody: William Worsley, Dean of St Paul's, and Dr William Sutton, who was parson of St Steven's, Walbrook and a well known preacher, along with two Dominicans – Friar William Richford, his order's Provincial in England, and Friar Thomas Powys, Prior of Kings Langley in Hertfordshire. Later, it was discovered that other senior clergymen had also been implicated. As clerics, they would not have benefited all that much from a Yorkist restoration so their involvement stemmed from conscience rather than any hope of gain; they genuinely believed that Warbeck was the son of Edward IV.

On 27 January 1495 Mountford, Ratcliffe and Daubeney were beheaded on Tower Hill, while there were further executions on 29 and 30 January. Two of the conspirators, Thomas Cressyner (FitzWalter's steward) and Thomas Astwood (steward of Marton Abbey in Yorkshire), were reprieved on the scaffold at the last moment, 'which gladded much people for they were both young men'.[4] Lord FitzWalter was imprisoned at Calais, only to be beheaded after trying to bribe his gaolers into letting him escape. Thwaites was pardoned, while the clerics pleaded benefit of clergy.

What appeared to be the most dramatic revelation came after most of the plotters had been arrested and found guilty. On the day after Twelfth Night, 7 January, King Henry moved from Greenwich to the palace at the Tower of London. His reason for the move was that the Tower's smaller rooms enabled him to receive in secrecy Sir Robert Clifford who had returned to England a few days earlier. Only a few trusted counsellors were present at the audience. After falling at Henry's feet and begging for forgiveness, Clifford revealed that in March 1493 he had made a bond with Sir William Stanley to go to Malines and establish communications with Warbeck.

But the king already knew of Sir William's guilt. Long before, he had ordered the interrogation of Stanley's servants and Cheshire retainers, some of whom accepted bonds although none were later accused of treason, suggesting they had perhaps informed against their employer. The chamberlain's bastard son Thomas had been in the Tower for over a year and presumably he, too, had been closely questioned. Someone, either one of the Cheshire men or Thomas, reported that there were thousands of pounds in coin at Sir William's main residence, enough to finance a large-scale rising.

Despite having kept Sir William under surveillance, Henry made a show of being reluctant to believe the charge, ordering Sir Robert to repeat it over and over again. Finally, he gave orders for Stanley to be arrested and confined to his room, before questioning him – perhaps he hoped to trick Sir William into thinking every detail of his plans was known. But Stanley kept his nerve, pretending to make a full confession, while admitting no more than being in touch with Warbeck and disliking the prospect of fighting the House of York. Bacon comments that 'thinking to make his offence less by confession, he made it enough for condemnation'.[5] Yet the king must have known for some time that Stanley was planning his overthrow and death.

Stanley had been well rewarded by Henry. Besides being made a Knight of the Garter, he had become England's wealthiest commoner with estates all over the country, as well as a house in London, near Charing Cross. Manors and official posts brought him an income of £3,000 a year, while the money for the rising found at his castle of Holt in Denbighshire amounted to '40,000' marks (nearly £27,000), including £10,000 of gold coin in bags. Even so, according to Polydore Vergil, Stanley felt he had been insufficiently recompensed. Most of his lands were in Lancashire, Cheshire and the Welsh Marches, so he had asked for the earldom of Chester, an impossible request as it belonged to the Prince of Wales. The refusal rankled: as Hall puts it, Stanley's 'stomach began to canker and wax rusty'.[6] Aware of his dissatisfaction, the king had guessed he was planning mischief, but in his cold-blooded way allowed him to stay on as Lord Chamberlain, hoping to discover the names of his supporters. It was a calculated risk since Sir William possessed the resources to turn a Yorkist rising into a serious challenge to the monarchy.

He has gone down in history as a great traitor, but in a sense he acted out of loyalty – loyalty to York. Unlike his elder brother, he had always been faithful to Edward IV, possibly one of the reasons why he turned against King Richard at Bosworth. Besides asking Clifford to contact Warbeck, he had told Sir Robert that if he were sure the young man was Edward's son, he would never bear arms against him.[7]

It looks as if Sir William had refrained from telling Clifford about his own preparations for a rising and, unaware that he had been under surveillance, hoped to save his life. At his trial in the King's Bench in Westminster Hall on 30–31 January he denied the charges. Found guilty, none the less, by a jury of 'divers knights and worshipful gentlemen', he was condemned to be hanged, drawn and quartered.[8] But a chronicler tells us that, 'the xvj day of February, Monday, was Sir William Stanley, Lord Chamberlain, pardoned of the king of hanging and draw-ing, and the said day between xj and xij at noon was he led from the Tower of London to the Tower Hill, and there his head [was] smitten off and is buried at St Dunstan's'.[9] Henry gave the executioner £10 to behead him as painlessly as possible – he cannot have forgotten Sir William's charge at Bosworth Field.

It was widely rumoured that the Lord Chamberlain had been condemned solely for admitting that if he could be sure that Warbeck really was King Edward's son, then he could not fight against him; that he had been condemned for thinking a Yorkist claim to the throne better than the Tudor one. (This is what many other people thought, too, in private.) But Sir William went to the scaffold for planning a revolt. The rumour suited King Henry, however, since after Stanley's fall everyone was terrified of being denounced as a Yorkist, not daring to mention the 'duke'.

Although Robert Clifford did not destroy Stanley as many thought, his information averted an extremely dangerous conspiracy that might have ended the Tudor dynasty. On 20 January 1495 he was paid £500, which was an astronomical sum for the period – over five times the income of a modest squire for an entire year. Yet his services were worth every penny. Because of Clifford's report the Yorkists lost their leaders in England. For good measure, he claimed that the so-called 'duke' was a lovechild of Margaret of Burgundy by her confessor, the Bishop of Cambrai, a smear story the implications of which cannot have been wholly to the king's liking. They implied that not only did Clifford think that the young man bore a family resemblance to the House of York – and he had seen many of its members – but that he did not accept the official story of his real name being Perkin Warbeck.

Bacon says that after his return Clifford received no more favours from the king, which is not surprising. He had rebelled against Richard III and Henry VII, in each case turning his coat and betraying his fellow conspirators, and was scarcely a man who inspired trust. Even so, he was left unmolested, dying in 1508. The church at his village of Aspenden contains a contemporary stained-glass window which is clearly a portrait, if a rough one, and shows a proud, almost pompous face. A poor-quality brass below informs us he had been 'Knight for the Body to Henry VII and Master of his Ordnance'.

We shall never know what conclusions Henry VII drew from the revelations of the winter of 1494–5, but we can guess that they were uncomfortable ones. He could not rely on his most trusted courtiers, while devout priests opposed his reign. Although he had eliminated many leading Yorkists, Margaret of Burgundy and King Maximilian continued to encourage the

'Duke of York' who was still threatening to invade England. When his rival landed, would he find widespread support? The recent plot had shown that many influential Englishmen believed he was King Edward's son. It was a reminder, too, that most of those who fought for Henry Tudor at Bosworth had done so because they opposed Richard III, not because they had ceased to be Yorkists.

# 8

# Summer 1495:
# The Yorkist Invasion

'Yet [Perkin] determined not to leave the hope and trust he
had conceived in his mad head to obtain the crown and realm
of England: and so gathering a great army of valiant captains
of all nations, some bankrupts, some thieves, robbers and vagabonds, which leaving their bodily labour, desiring to live only
of robbery and rapine, came to be his soldier and servants.'

Edward Hall, *The Union of the Two Noble and Illustre*
*Famelies of Lancastre and Yorke* [1548][1]

Born in 1497, Edward Hall recalls not only the gossip but
the tone of voice of people who lived through these years.
Characteristically, he comments that Margaret of York, having
met Perkin, 'a certain young man of visage beautiful, of countenance demure, of wit subtle, crafty and pregnant', thought she
had 'gotten God by the foot when she had the Devil by the tail'.[2]
Yet while the dowager duchess may have been a poor judge of
pretenders, she knew the value of money.

Confident that her 'nephew' was going to be restored, on 10 December 1494 Margaret made him sign a document in which he promised to repay sums already owed to her in his future kingdom. Among these were the balance of her dowry, which was over 80,000 gold crowns, and a portfolio of lucrative customs concessions that she had been granted by her brother Edward IV. In addition, she was to be reimbursed for financing the Earl of Lincoln's expedition. She would also receive the manor of Hunsdon, together with the town and castle of Scarborough, which held special significance for the House of York. (Richard III had even made it a separate county in its own right.) The document was witnessed by Sir Robert Clifford, acting as chancellor for the 'duke', shortly before the upsetting news came that he had fled back to England.[3]

In a second document, signed and sealed on 23 December, Perkin acknowledged that he owed his 'aunt' the vast amount of 800,000 crowns, as well as other monies that had been spent on his future restoration. It is likely that the duchess had advanced these new sums to pay for the forthcoming invasion.[4] She saw him not just as her nephew but as a sound financial investment; however, in the light of Lincoln's failure, it appears she was something of a gambler.

Far from losing heart at Clifford's defection or at the betrayal of so many important Yorkists in what had once been her native land, Margaret sent an impassioned appeal to the pope, Alexander VI, in May 1495. Her fury at the throne of the Plantagenets having been stolen by an upstart is apparent in almost every line. She asks the pontiff to save England from the tyranny of 'Henry . . . called of Richmond, of the house of Sombreset [*sic*], reigning against the law by the use of force, claiming to be descended from the blood of Lancaster when we all know of the many adulteries committed on both sides of his parentage'. She begs Alexander to help 'The most illustrious Lord Richard, son of the late King Edward, legitimate son, successor and heir to his royal father the late King Edward'. We do not know whether she received any acknowledgement.[5]

For once, Maximilian made up his mind and decided to finance the Yorkist expedition. Perennially short of money, he was horrified by the cost, which forced him to delay an official visit to Augsburg and a Diet of the Empire. But he was as optimistic as Margaret.[6] What gave the King of the Romans and the duchess such confidence was the support the 'duke' was receiving from Yorkists who had made their way to Malines, and the fact that so many important men in England had supported his cause despite being betrayed by Tudor spies. They believed that as soon as the Plantagenet standard was raised on English soil, thousands more would join the son of Edward IV.

Although Clifford's defection and Stanley's elimination were a severe blow, the trust of Maximilian and Margaret in England's loyalty to the House of York finally nerved Perkin to embark on an invasion that he could not postpone for ever. At the end of June 1495 an expedition set sail from Flanders on board fourteen small vessels, several of which had been supplied by the Scots, such as the distinctively named *Keek-Out*. Despite Perkin's backers grumbling about the cost, the entire force amounted to a thousand troops at most: some eyewitnesses reckoned they numbered only 800.[7] The overall commander was Rodrigue de Lalaing, a Burgundian courtier and professional soldier.

The English government pretended that the Yorkist army was nothing but a motley collection of foreigners – Dutch, Flemish, German, Spanish, French – and that the only Englishmen among them were mercenaries or criminals on the run. In the next century the chronicler Edward Hall described them as 'a great army of valiant captains of all nations. Some bankrupts, some false English sanctuary men, some thieves, robbers, and vagabonds, which, leaving their bodily labour, desiring to live only of robbery and rapine, came to be his servants and soldiers . . . this rabblement of knaves'. Vergil contemptuously refers to them as 'these human dregs' [*hominum faece*].[8]

In reality, the expedition included a sizeable English contingent, most of the 'captains' (officers) being Englishmen – Corbet, Belt, White and Malyvery (Mauleverer?). There were even several gentlemen among them, such as Sir George Neville, who was probably second in command after Lalaing, together with Edward Skelton, who came from a well-known family of Cumberland squires, Thomas Mountford, son and heir of the recently executed Sir Simon Mountford, and William Barley. The most distinguished was a Knight of Rhodes (St John), Fra' James Keating, the former Prior of Ireland, who had been deposed by his Order for supporting the White Rose

The few ships of King Henry's small navy patrolled the North Sea coast opposite Flanders, keeping a sharp lookout. Theoretically, they were in the right place, since it is likely that the invasion's original destination was East Anglia where the Yorkists seem to have had many supporters, and where a reception committee may have been waiting for them. Later, a member of the expedition said they had hoped to take Yarmouth. But the Yorkist fleet was blown off course, into the Channel.

On 3 July it sailed into the tiny harbour of Deal, little more than a village, on the Kentish coast. An advance party of several hundred landed, apparently all Englishmen, who expected to be welcomed by local Yorkists. They intended to capture the nearby town of Sandwich, then an important port, which would make a useful beachhead. According to the Spanish envoy at the Tudor court, having heard the rumours about Perkin's real identity which the king had spread far and wide, the local Kentishmen joked that he ought to go home to his father and mother in France.[9] Vergil, however, says they were in two minds whether to join him or not when they saw his ships on the horizon, but – recalling that most of their previous uprisings had turned out badly – decided to stay loyal to Henry VII and ambush 'the feigned duke'.[10]

After making friendly overtures to the invaders and enticing them ashore by offering to bring barrels of beer down to the beach – although they failed to persuade the suspicious Perkin to accompany them – a band of armed countrymen led by the Mayor of Sandwich shot volley after volley of arrows into the Yorkists at close range. They killed 150 and wounded many more, before attacking at close quarters with bills.[11] The less badly wounded tried to run back to their ships, but most were cut to pieces, while others drowned. A further 150 were taken prisoner, including most of the English captains, although Neville, Barley and the Irishman Keating managed to get back on board. 'And after the said discomfiture the said rebels within the said ships drew up their sails and sailed westward,' says a contemporary chronicler, who was writing a little later.[12]

On 11 July a Norfolk man called Robert Albon returned to his home at Yarmouth and reported to the corporation how at Canterbury he had spoken with the captured 'English captains of the king's rebels'. One of them, Belt, had told him that while he knew himself to be 'a dead man', his friends would 'have Yarmouth or they shall die for it'. Albon warned the corporation to put the town on a state of defence without delay – the rebels' fleet might arrive that night or the next at the latest.[13]

The following day another Yarmouth correspondent informed Sir John Paston that the 'Admiral's Deputy' had intercepted a ship off Normandy, a hoy from Dordrecht, which was carrying eight horses with a consignment of saddles and bridles, intended for the rebels: the Dutch crew had been imprisoned, but eight or nine Englishmen on board had got ashore in the ship's boat and run off into the countryside. In the meantime, says the writer, Paston could depend on the authorities at Yarmouth sending word to him at once if they saw any suspicious vessels.[14]

Shortly after the expedition sailed, Maximilian received a report that it had landed in England and been joined by a great host of Yorkist supporters. Overjoyed, he told a Venetian embassy during an audience at Worms how confident he felt that, after regaining his kingdom, the Duke of York would attack the King of France. 'To this effect have we received every promise and certainty from the duke aforesaid.'[15] A week later, Maximilian was still optimistic, after another false report. The duke had arrived with his fleet near London but, because the population around the capital was unfriendly and prevented him from attacking the usurper's army, had decided to move his troops to a more welcoming area, explained Maximilian. He stressed that the duke was keen to attack the enemy, and from the way he was conducting the campaign there was every chance of his winning a decisive victory and putting an end to Henry Tudor.[16]

Meanwhile, the men who had been captured during the skirmish at Deal were brought to London by the Sheriff of Kent, tied up in carts or dragged along at the end of a rope. The Englishmen among them were put in the dungeons of the Tower, while foreigners went to Newgate. The trials lasted from 16 to 24 July.[17] 'The King thought that to punish a few for example was gentlemen's pay' and he wanted to reduce Perkin's forces to 'rabble and scum' explained Francis Bacon, about what then took place – 'he therefore hanged them all for the greater terror'.[18] They were executed along the coasts of Kent, Sussex, Essex and Norfolk, on tall gallows where their bodies could be easily seen from the sea. However, their captains' heads were stuck up on London Bridge. Henry had never previously reacted so savagely, but he had suffered a bad fright. If the Yorkist fleet had not been blown off course, it might have made land in a more welcoming spot and set off a very dangerous rising.

The invasion scare lasted for about three weeks, while the whereabouts of the Yorkist fleet continued to be unknown. In fact, it had sailed to Ireland, where its leader took refuge with his old mentor, the Earl of Desmond, whose household would have been a sobering experience after the decorous courts of Paris, Malines and Vienna. In Bacon's words, 'there was nothing left for Perkin but the blustering affection of wild and naked people'.[19] Yet the political scene had changed, isolating Desmond. There was a new, English deputy, Henry's able henchman Sir

Edward Poynings, who had arrived with 700 troops, arresting his predecessor, the supposedly all powerful Earl of Kildare, and sending him to London for imprisonment in the Tower. Even so, as yet Desmond took no notice of Poynings, as he had a grudge to settle with King Henry.

After Perkin's departure from Ireland in 1492, the Earl of Desmond had been reconciled with Henry VII, bribed by reinstatement as Constable of Limerick. Now, however, he was in a state of outrage at the arrest of his cousin and brother-in-law Kildare, which questioned the FitzGerald family's right to rule the Irish. In any case, as an evergreen Yorkist he was delighted by the return of a young man whom he insisted on treating as Duke of York – and no doubt as King of England and Lord of Ireland as well. To Desmond Perkin's arrival seemed heaven sent. Clearly, he expected that, as in Simnel's day, a reinforcement of crack troops would arrive from Burgundy and that he would be able to employ them in his unending struggle with the hated Butlers, his foremost rivals, who were staunch supporters of King Henry.[20]

The Duke of York did more than add legal justification for war against Poynings, he brought eleven ships. He swiftly added another, an English vessel, the *Christopher* of Plymouth, which his men had boarded and seized when it put in at the little port of Youghal, an area of miniature Cork that was controlled by Desmond. For his part, the earl had an army consisting of approximately 400 lightly armoured horsemen (riding bareback), 3,000 kern with knives and javelins, about 500 gallowglasses with long-handled battle axes and perhaps sixty to eighty men who had crossbows or primitive arquebuses.[21]

Together, the earl and the duke decided to capture the seaport of Waterford, always a thorn in Desmond's side. A bastion of loyalty to the English Lordship of Ireland, it had been the only place in the country that refused to recognize Lambert Simnel in 1487. On 23 July 1495 the earl and Warbeck invested the port by land and sea. But the Waterford men were accustomed to visitations of this sort, and possessed cannon they knew how to use. Aware that Sir Edward Poynings was on his way to relieve them, they fought with the utmost determination, launching sortie after sortie. Even so, at one point, when Desmond's wild kern were assaulting the walls and Warbeck's flotilla sailed into the harbour, it seemed that Waterford might fall. However, after one of the ships was sunk by gunfire from the bastion known as Reginald's Tower, the rest of the flotilla beat a hasty retreat out to sea. Then Poynings' fleet was sighted. On 3 August the besiegers were forced to raise the siege and flee, several of their vessels being captured.

The earl retired into a remote stronghold, protected by impassable bogs and forest, but Perkin could not abandon his fleet or his followers. For a short time, he anchored in the Haven of Cork, going ashore, and the mayor – his old ally John Atwater – smuggled him inside the city for suitable entertainment. However, a lookout sighted the fleets of Poynings and the Waterford men sailing towards the Haven, whereupon the 'Duke of York' and his ships hastily put to sea again. Despite the ingrained Yorkism of many Irish, it had become too risky to stay in Irish waters.

In retrospect, the Yorkist invasion of England in 1495 was of course an anticlimax. It failed to stir up the widespread rising of which the Tudor king had been afraid for the last three years, while further trouble in Ireland was prevented by the redoubtable Sir Edward Poynings. Yet the episode gave Henry VII some extremely anxious moments, even after learning of his enemy's flight from Waterford. Where, he must have wondered, was the duke now? For several days, the whereabouts of the Yorkist fleet remained a complete mystery.

# 9

# Autumn 1495–Summer 1497: The Scots and the Cornish

'When the news [of the Cornish rising] reached King Henry, he was completely taken by surprise and greatly alarmed, since he found himself being threatened by attack on two fronts at the same time – by a foreign war and by a civil war. The danger on either front seemed equally menacing. For some time he could not make up his mind about which of them to deal with first.'

Polydore Vergil, *Anglica Historia*[1]

Fifteenth-century English and Scots loathed each other. The Northerners' language, spoken or written, was largely incomprehensible to Englishmen, while the entire Border was in a state of undeclared, never-ending war, characterized on both sides by vicious raids and appalling atrocities. Although almost invariably defeated during major hostilities – as recently as 1482 the English had occupied Edinburgh – the Scots were brutally effective at hit-and-run frontier warfare. In addition there was a constant struggle at sea between the privateers who operated from Scarborough or Leith, with captured crews being thrown overboard. Intermarriage never took place between the two countries' royal families, while for over a hundred years Scottish troops had regularly fought for France.

Born in 1473, James IV, King of Scots, was the most personable monarch in Europe, very different from the mountebank at Vienna or the deformed dwarf at Paris. Handsome and charming, despite a nightmarish childhood during which he had been used as a pawn by the Scottish nobility against his inept father James III (murdered when his son was fifteen), he was an unusually effective ruler, popular not just with the lords but with the poor among whom he was said to wander disguised as a beggar. A portrait of him as a youth shows a cheerful, amused face of a sort that is rare in medieval portraiture.

According to the report of the Spanish envoy Don Pedro de Ayala, who met James in 1498, he had by then grown a beard and long hair he never cut, 'which suits him very well'. He spoke six languages besides Scots, including Spanish and 'the tongue of the savages who live in some parts of Scotland'. He adored war but was a poor soldier as he was insanely rash. 'When he is not waging war he hunts in the mountains.' Generous to a fault, humane and friendly, he was much loved by his people.[2] His great weakness was the sheer poverty of his kingdom, the poorest in Western Europe, with a population two-thirds less than that of England – the Scottish crown's annual revenues amounted to £30,000 at most.

In regular correspondence with Margaret of Burgundy and the Yorkists, King James was also in touch with the men who fitted out Warbeck's flotilla, as before the debacle at Deal, the Scots had taken steps to aid his invasion by supplying troops and money.[3] James now invited Perkin to Scotland. On 27 November 1496, surrounded by the Scottish nobility, James received him at Stirling Palace – probably in the new parliament hall. Escorted by a Scottish guard of honour, together with his more respectable followers, who presumably included Sir George Neville, his chaplain William Lounde and the bankrupt London merchant John Heron, the 'duke' was asked to justify his cause.

He struck just the right note, between pathos and drama, in a tearfully eloquent speech that was later reconstructed by Vergil, Hall and Bacon. 'You see before you the spectacle of a Plantagenet who has been carried from the nursery into the sanctuary, from the sanctuary into the direful prison, into the hand of the cruel tormentor,' he began. Then Warbeck described his escape from death, and the wanderings during which he had been made to do menial jobs. He said that the defamatory rumours about him were invented by Henry Tudor, 'calling himself King of England', who had spent large sums of money on turning friendly courts against him, besides bribing his servants to poison him and persuading advisers like Sir Robert Clifford to abandon him.

Yet 'the lady duchess dowager of Burgundy, my most dear aunt' had acknowledged the truth of his claim, and lovingly assisted him. Unfortunately, with no resources other than her dowry, she had been unable to finance a full-scale expedition against the usurper in London, which was why he had come to Stirling to ask for assistance. He reminded his listeners that once upon a time Scotland had given refuge to Henry VI, and ended by imploring the King of Scots to help him recover 'mine inheritance'. If James did so, he would be able to rely on his lasting gratitude and friendship.[4]

The bravura performance convinced King James that this really was the son of Edward IV. Although some of his more dour courtiers remained sceptical, James decided to do everything in his power to aid the charming, dignified young man, who was exactly his own age. From now on, he treated the adventurer not only as the Duke of York but as his brother, providing him with an expensive wardrobe suitable for his rank. The duke's new clothes included a 'great coat' for the Scottish winter, a tournament coat made of white and purple damask, and even a 'spousing gown' to wear at his wedding.[5]

In December King James gave 'Prince Richard of England' a bride. She was Lady Katharine Gordon, a daughter of the Earl of Huntley, by all accounts a beautiful, accomplished and courageous young lady, who as a great-granddaughter of James I belonged to the Scots blood royal. There could have been no stronger testimony to the king's belief in him.

If a letter supposedly written by the duke really was addressed to Katherine, it shows he had fallen deeply in love. It also conveys something of his charm. Her 'face, bright and serene, gives splendour to the cloudy sky, whose eyes brilliant as the stars, make all pain to be forgotten and turn despair into delight: whosoever sees her cannot choose but admire her, admiring cannot choose but love her, loving cannot choose but obey', he wrote. To him, she seemed, 'not born in our days but descended from heaven'.[6]

Through his spies, Henry VII soon heard of the speech at Stirling and of King James's reaction. No news could have been more disturbing. It meant that all his work in trying to maintain peaceful relations with the Scots had been wrecked. He had been to enormous pains in securing a seven-year truce between the two kingdoms, sealed in July 1493 – largely because he feared an alliance between James and the Yorkists. The implications of Warbeck's presence in Scotland were alarming: instead of the North Sea as a barrier against invasion, now there was only the Border. The Yorkist power base was no longer Malines but Edinburgh.

One of King Henry's principal agents north of the Border was Henry Wyatt, father of the poet. Among those who worked closely with Wyatt were two Scottish nobles, Sir James Ramsay, formerly Earl of Bothwell, and James Stewart, Earl of Buchan – both in Tudor pay for many years. Former favourites of James III, the pair were recruited when they took refuge at the English court after their master's death, but had since returned to

Scotland. A sinister, embittered figure, by any standards Ramsay was a traitor, who had already plotted to kidnap the king and his brother, the Duke of Ross, to sell them to the English, although nothing had come of his plan. Although initially driven by a desire to avenge his murdered patron, he was only too willing to be paid for his services by Henry.

Pretending to ignore the presence of the Duke of York at the Scottish court, and hoping to avert a Scottish invasion, King Henry did all he could to stay on peaceful terms. At the same time, with such a fine bargaining counter, James IV put off military action for some months, to see what he could get out of the English through diplomacy. Desperately, Henry offered him the hand of his six-year-old daughter Margaret.

No doubt Henry believed he could benefit from the international situation. The Italian states had formed a Holy League against France that included not only Spain but King Maximilian and his son Archduke Philip, and both sides were vying for English support. As a result, apart from Margaret, after the failure of Perkin's invasion Flanders had turned against the Yorkists despite Maximilian's wishes. Charles VIII sent a document to King Henry which helpfully testified that the 'Duke of York' was French and the son of a barber, and offered to send his parents over to England, undermining the widely circulated Tudor claim that his father was a Flemish bargee.

By the end of summer 1496 the King of Scots was preparing for war. Briefed by Wyatt, Ramsay and Buchan explored the possibility of kidnapping the duke. Ramsay wrote to Henry in September:

> Please your Grace, anent the matter that Master Wyot laid to me, I have been busy about it, and my lord of Buchan takes upon him the fulfilling of it, if it be possible: and thinks it best now in this lang nicht within his tent to enterprise the matter, for he has na watch but [what] the king appointed to be about him.[7]

In the same report Ramsay warns that potential English supporters had been in contact with the duke: a brother of Lord Dacre from Cumberland as well as men from Northumberland, including Edward Skelton's brother Michael.

At Berwick on 8 September Ramsay, who had just left the Scottish court, wrote a further report for King Henry, informing him that although he and his friends had done everything possible to persuade James not to give assistance to 'this fenyt [feigned] boy', a small Scottish army will assemble on 15 September at Ellam Kirk, ten miles from the Border, and that the invasion will take place two days later. Including the Yorkists, the army numbers about 1,400 men 'of all manner of nations', says Ramsay, commenting that he hoped James will be soundly defeated and punished for consenting to his father's murder. He adds that 'Perkyn' has signed a bond to pay the Scots 50,000 marks over two years after he has been restored, besides returning Berwick. Of the king, Ramsay states that 'he and the boy are every day in council'.

Ramsay also reports that Sir George Neville and others have lost heart and want to change sides. Neville says that if the King of Scots and Henry come to an agreement, he will 'quit him of Perkin'. Like Ramsay, Neville realized that James was on the brink of bankruptcy – in the spy's words, he has 'not a hundred pounds while now that he has coined his [gold] chains, his plate and his cupboards, and there was never people worse content of the king's government'.

Ramsay supplied two other important pieces of information in this lengthy report, a shameless piece of treachery. One was that reinforcements for the duke had arrived from Flanders, consisting of Rodrigue de Lalaing 'with twa little ships' that have brought 320 German landsknechts, besides 'sundry pleasant things for the war, both for man and horse'. He had had some difficulty in bringing them over because of Burgundy's new hostility towards the Yorkist cause. The other was a detailed description of the inadequate artillery at Edinburgh Castle, making the place vulnerable to assault. Ramsay ended by suggesting a well thought out strategy with which Henry could trap his fellow countrymen during the coming campaign.[8]

Henry may have feared the invasion would be accompanied by widespread rebellion. Messer Aldobrandini from Florence, who had been in London at Easter before going on to Bruges, told a Milanese acquaintance that Henry was hated because of his greed. 'No doubt the king is powerful enough where money is concerned, but if fortune allowed some lord of the blood royal to rise in revolt and he had to take the field, he would fare very badly owing to his avarice, as his people would desert him,' said the Florentine. 'They would treat him just as they did King Richard, whom they deserted, going over to the other side because he put to death his nephews to whom the kingdom belonged.'[9] Aldobrandini may perhaps have been repeating gossip he had heard in Flanders, from friends of the Duchess Margaret, yet there is other evidence of Henry's unpopularity. The king was well aware of it, since spies kept him informed of any signs of disaffection that they encountered. He had every reason to feel uneasy.

Significantly, Vergil says that the king was genuinely terrified when he heard that the Scots were about to invade. 'He was not only afraid of the enemy but of his own subjects, frightened that the gentry in the area, either from a mistaken belief [in the duke] or because they had been bought by him, would go over to Perkin.'[10]

As Ramsay had warned, the Scottish invasion crossed the Border on 17 September 1496, led by King James 'with banner displayed'. According to the 'reiver' custom, his troops ravaged the countryside 'with great boast and brag', although apart from the usual atrocities the only substantial damage they inflicted was to burn a couple of small peel towers. But the Scottish army was too small because the King of Scots did not have the funds for a larger force. As soon as James heard that an English army 4,000 strong was marching to intercept him, he hastily retreated back over the Tweed on 21 September, having penetrated a mere four miles south of the Border.[11] James IV might be as brave as a lion but (as he would prove at Flodden Field) he was hopelessly inadequate as a military commander. Nothing could have been more of an anticlimax.

During this brief campaign, Perkin was horrified by the way the Scots burned, killed and looted, so that in Northumberland 'nothing was heard but roaring, weeping and lamenting'. Instead of a crusade to restore him to his throne, this was merely a glorified frontier raid.[12] He complained to James at the way they were treating his 'subjects', receiving the tart reply that while he might call England his kingdom, there was no sign of Englishmen accepting his sovereignty. If some of the North Country people disliked the Tudors and remembered the Yorkist kings with nostalgia, all of them hated the Scots with a passionate intensity – together with anyone who was a friend of Scotsmen.

Although James remained convinced for some considerable time that his guest really was the Duke of York, his political position had deteriorated sharply. Scotland had been the last foreign power to support Warbeck, but after the Scottish invasion's abject failure and the strange reluctance of the Northumbrians to welcome their rightful sovereign, it was clear that the Yorkist rising which he had promised his hosts was never going to materialize. Henry VII was so angry with King James that he prepared to attack his northern neighbours in the spring of 1497.

Before the English army could march, the Cornish unexpectedly rose in rebellion against the taxes levied by Henry to pay for the war with Scotland and marched on London. Their leaders were Michael Joseph an Gof (in Cornish, 'the Blacksmith') and a lawyer from Bodmin, Thomas Flamank. Nobody describes what happened better than Bacon, who rephrases Vergil:

> The Cornish being a race of men stout of stomach, mighty of body and limb, and that lived hardly in a barren

land . . . muttered extremely that it was a thing not to be suffered that, for a little stir of the Scots soon blown over, they should be thus grinded to powder with payments, and said it was for them to pay that had too much and lived idly. But they would eat their bread that they got with the sweat of their brows and no man should take it from them.[13]

The rising was a desperate response to what they saw as unfair taxation – they wanted the dismissal of the members of the King's Council who were responsible for it. Armed with 'bows and arrows, and bills, and such other weapons of rude and country people',[14] they surged on towards the capital, much encouraged when Lord Audley joined them at Wells and took command, not realizing he had only done so to escape from his creditors.

Londoners were terrified by the news that the Cornishmen were coming. 'This was their outward colour,' comments a chronicler from the city, referring to their complaint about the new taxes, 'What their inward intent was, God knoweth.' The chronicler added that if they had succeeded, they would have behaved like Jack Straw, Jack Cade and others. The Peasants' Revolt and Cade's rebellion had not been forgotten.[15]

Yet hatred of the new dynasty undoubtedly played a part. One of the heroes in a miracle play written at about this time in the Cornish language, *Beunans Meriasek*, is a Duke of Cornwall who drives the self-styled Emperor '*Teudar*' out of the land. Beyond question the movement contained a strong Yorkist element. The sixteenth-century Spanish chronicler Zurita records (in his *Anales de la Corona de Aragón*) that the Cornish sent a message to the Duke of York in Scotland, offering to help him gain the throne, and an Act of attainder passed after their rising states that they wrote more than once. But he had left for Ireland and if the letter ever reached him, it would have been only after the rising had been defeated. It is also clear that the rebels had many secret supporters who wanted to see the downfall of Henry VII, as during their march through southern England they were

given food and shelter on a large scale. However, men of substance were reluctant to join the rebels because there were so
few gentry in their ranks.

Even so, when summoned to join the royal army, George
Neville, Lord Burgavenny, thought of joining the Cornish
instead. 'If a man will do ought, what will ye do now it is time?'
he asked the Earl of Suffolk. He was saying that if they were
going to topple Henry, this was their chance. The earl was of
a different frame of mind, however, and hid Neville's shoes to
keep him at home, before riding off himself to fight for the king.
There may have been other peers who thought like Burgavenny.[16]

King Henry was in a very ugly situation. About to embark
on a full-scale war with Scotland and threatened by the Yorkist
underground, he now found himself faced by a totally unex-
pected challenge from a large army determined to overthrow his
regime. Hastily he cancelled the invasion, patching up relations
with the Scots, and brought south as fast as possible the troops
he had assembled in the North.

Although disappointed that the notoriously unruly Kentish
men did not join them, the rebels marched on until confronted
by a royal army at Blackheath on 17 June. Here, Lord Daubeney
nearly lost the battle for the king by charging too rashly and
being captured, but was rescued by his troops. Badly led
and poorly armed, without cavalry or artillery, the Cornish
fought ferociously none the less and there was a moment when
they very nearly triumphed. Eventually, however, they were
forced to surrender after 2,000 of their number had been killed
and their leaders taken prisoner.

Had Perkin landed in Cornwall to lead them, they might have
attracted crucial support and defeated the royal army. The king
was lucky, too, in that James IV did not take advantage of the
situation and try to redeem his recent humiliation. Henry was
so alarmed by the revolt that he pardoned most of his Cornish
prisoners – only three were executed: Audley, Flamank and the
Blacksmith – and cancelled preparations for war with Scotland.

Warned that Cornwall 'was yet unquiet and boiling, he thought [it] better not to irritate the people farther'.[17]

Having dealt with the Cornish – as he supposed – King Henry sent ambassadors to negotiate a peace with James IV. His first demand was that the 'Duke of York' must be handed over to him, soothing the argument by adding that the King of Scots need feel no embarrassment at doing so because the young man was an impostor. However, a seven-year truce was agreed at Ayrton in September 1497, without the surrender of the duke.

During the negotiations Perkin left Scotland, sailing from the port of Ayr in July in a ship provided by James, with his wife and child on board. The vessel, ironically called the *Cuckoo*, was a merchant ship belonging to a Breton merchant named Guy Foulcart who had been hired by the king. It looks as though James had lost none of his liking for the young man, despite realizing at last that he was an impostor. He ignored his value as a bargaining counter and the high price, diplomatic and financial, that he might have got by handing him over. On the king's instructions, his boat was escorted out of port by Scotland's two most formidable privateers, Andrew and Robert Barton.[18]

Henry's spies soon informed him of the *Cuckoo*'s departure from Ayr. Yet it was impossible to intercept her as nobody knew where she was bound. Could her destination be Cornwall, whose inhabitants had such good reasons for disliking King Henry? Once again, the 'duke' had baffled his opponent.

# 10

# March 1496:
# The Grand Prior Plans to
# Poison the King

'the said Prior of St John and Sir John Tonge, and
Archdeacon Hussey, the three of them being at Rome . . .
sought ways and means of procuring the death of the King
of England.'

Deposition of Bernart de Vignolles, March 1496[1]

The Grand Prior of England of the Order of St John or 'Knights
of Rhodes' was a pillar of the realm. A monk-knight who had
taken vows of religion, he sat in the House of Lords where he
ranked as premier baron of England and was styled 'My Lord
of St John's'. His priory at Clerkenwell was one of the most
magnificent religious houses in London, with valuable estates
just outside the city (including St John's Wood and Hampton
Court) that brought in an annual income of over £2,300.

The Knights of Rhodes enjoyed huge prestige as Christendom's frontline troops, who confronted the never-ending Turkish threat in the eastern Mediterranean and the Aegean. Their magnificent defence of the island of Rhodes in 1480, when, despite being heavily outnumbered, they beat off an unusually determined and well-led besieging army, had earned them the admiration of all Europe. Several English brethren had taken part. Since the rents from the commanderies, as their houses were known, paid for such an excellent cause, few people begrudged them their large, meticulously run estates. Occupied by a commander and a chaplain, these houses also served as recruitment centres.

The current Grand Prior was Sir John Kendal, or Fra' John as he was known in his Order, who has been called 'the outstanding English knight of his generation'.[2] We know what he looked like from an Italian portrait medallion, which shows the profile of a tough if reflective-looking man in middle age with the long hair of the period, but little is known about his origins except that judging from heraldic evidence he belonged to a family of minor Westmorland gentry from near Kendal. Nor has much been discovered about his early career.[3] What can be deduced is that during the 1460s he joined the Knights at Rhodes as a very young man, taking vows and serving a specified number of 'caravans' on board the Order's galleys in the Mediterranean and Aegean, preying on Muslim shipping and raiding coastal villages in Greece or Anatolia. Once he had completed his sea caravans, he became eligible for a commandery.

He stayed on Rhodes for longer than most brethren, as Turcopolier (the officer who led the Turcopoles or native troops). He was not present at the siege of 1480, however, but instead travelled all over Europe seeking reinforcements. Four years later he was sent to Rome as a member of the Order's legation, acquiring a working knowledge of Italian, which he spoke and wrote fluently if ungrammatically. After becoming Grand Prior of England in 1489 and returning to his native land, he visited Flanders, France and Italy a good deal, on the business of both his Order and the king, serving on the royal council. He also went on diplomatic missions to the Scots, which made it necessary for him to spend a considerable amount of time at the Border city of Berwick.

The Grand Prior employed a servant called Bernart de Vignolles who, while Fra' John was away in Flanders, negotiating with Archduke Philip's government, obtained leave of absence, having said he wanted to go to Normandy, to see his brother. At Rouen, on 14 March 1496, he made a long and rambling deposition before French lawyers – who no doubt alerted their government – which he then sent to one of Henry's agents. The document contained a number of alarming allegations about his master.

The most serious allegation was that Kendal had been plotting to murder King Henry. Among those involved were his nephew Sir John Tonge, who was commander of Ribstone in Yorkshire, Dr John Hussey, Archdeacon of London, and the archdeacon's nephew, together with a man named Lilly and another called John Atwater, and also the Grand Prior's secretary, John Yolton. (Atwater is not to be confused with Perkin's ally.) All of these people were implicated in the conspiracy, alleged Bernart, their object being to procure the death of the king, his children and his mother Margaret Beaufort, and anyone close to him, in particular members of his council.

According to Bernart, when Kendal, Tonge and Hussey were at Rome together a few years previously, they had consulted a Spanish astrologer called '*mestre Jehan*' who told them he could arrange what they wanted, if they paid him: to demonstrate his power, he supposedly murdered a Turkish servant of Sultan Bayezid's brother Cem, who was a prisoner of the pope. The three conspirators then returned to England, leaving behind a Sardinian servant of the Grand Prior, Stefano Maranecho, who gave the astrologer a large sum of money on their behalf. However, the man kept on demanding further payments, while doing nothing to earn them.

Two years later, the three had sent Bernart de Vignolles to Rome with orders to kill the astrologer, as he was telling everyone in the city that they wanted to murder the King of England. But when Bernart reached Rome, instead of killing the man he went to another astrologer, who offered to come to England by way of Santiago, disguised as a friar, and arrange for Henry's death. Because Bernart did not have funds to pay for the journey, the astrologer made up a lethal poison. Contained in a little wooden box, this was an ointment which, so he said in a message for the Grand Prior, if smeared on the king's doorway was guaranteed to turn anyone passing through it into a murderer who would kill him.

Opening the box when he returned to his lodgings, Bernart found 'a vile and stinking thing' which he threw away in disgust, but on the way back to England he bought from an apothecary at Orleans a similar wooden box which he filled with a mixture of earth, quicksilver and soot from the chimney. In London, he gave the box to the Grand Prior, warning that if it remained in the house for more than twenty-two hours he would be in grave danger – he must keep it outside. Much alarmed, Fra' John told him to throw it as far away as possible, where no one could find it.

Three or four weeks later, when Bernart was very ill, Kendal had come to his bedside and offered him a horse and money if he would leave England. He replied that he was too weak to do so. The sickness lasted for six months but the Grand Prior kept on trying to persuade Bernart to go overseas, as though fearing that he might be arrested and, under interrogation, incriminate himself and his friends. He was delighted when Bernart asked for leave to return to France.

What should one make of this weird tale? At that date Rome was full of sinsister rumours of poisoning, used to explain the deaths of great personages that baffled physicians – although the vast majority of such deaths must have been due to natural causes. The only poisons available were belladonna and aconite, with a few other noxious herbs, none of them very effective, or arsenic which betrayed its presence by the excruciating agonies it inflicted. Yet even educated people believed that an expert poisoner was capable of killing anyone if he wanted to, and until 1491 Kendal had often been at Rome, where he was chamberlain of the hospice of St Thomas to which the Husseys also belonged.[4] It is of course just possible – but only just – that the Grand Prior was both murderous and credulous, and that Bernart was telling the truth.

The second half of Bernart's deposition was more plausible. He claimed Kendal had been in touch with the group around Warbeck, alleging that when Perkin first arrived in Flanders one of his followers had written several times to My Lord of St John's. Bernart had seen some, though not all, of the letters. These reported how 'the Merchant of the Ruby' (Perkin), having found that he was unable to sell his wares in Flanders for the right price, was going to try and sell them to the King of the Romans (Maximilian) – meaning, explained Bernart, that Perkin had been unable to find enough money or men in Flanders for his invasion of England. The writer of the letters was a sergeant of the Order of St John, Fra' Guillemin de Novion, who until recently had held a position in the Grand Prior's household.

Bernart also said that at a commandery belonging to Fra' John, Melchbourne in Bedfordshire, livery jackets bearing the Red Rose were stored, but that there were others in the commandery on which White Roses could be sewn. He added that a servant of Guillemin de Novion, called Pietres, had brought letters to the Grand Prior that were written in such a way as to mislead King Henry about where Perkin was going to land. My Lord of St John's was still receiving messages from Flanders, whose contents he always communicated to Thomas Langton, Bishop of Winchester, John Hussey, Sir Thomas Tyrell and Archdeacon Hussey, even if he did not send them the text.

Two or three times a year, sometimes just after Christmas, related Bernart, My Lord of St John's was accustomed to visit Sir Thomas Tyrell's manor house at Avon Tyrell in Hampshire. On one occasion, when the Grand Prior said he had heard that the late King Edward had been there several times in the old days, Sir Thomas replied that he was quite right and that the king had always 'made good cheer' – he hoped, please God, that one day King Edward's son was going to make no less good cheer. The present royal family had been set up with French money, he added, so there was some hope that another, just as good, might soon be put in its place. Both Bernart and Sir John Tonge were present when this conversation took place. He ended by repeating that all the men he named were implicated in the plot to murder King Henry.

The deposition denouncing the Grand Prior has only survived because it reached Henry. He endorsed it on the back, in his own hand, with the words, '*La confession de Bernart de Vignolles*'. Reading the document, he may well have thought that the plot to poison him was a malicious fabrication, but he took the second part seriously enough. Soon after Bernart sent in his deposition, the authorities raided Clerkenwell and seized Kendal's private correspondence. They kept five letters, all written by him in April 1496, no doubt because three were addressed to men mentioned in the deposition – two to Guillemin de Novion and one to Stefano Maranecho – and because their meaning is curiously unclear, as if by deliberate design. Yet there was nothing positive to incriminate the Grand Prior, and the king was always loath to take action unless he had convincing evidence in his hands. Nor did he arrest any of the men mentioned in the deposition. Even so, in the circumstances it seems significant that on 1 July Henry issued Kendal with a general pardon for all offences committed before 17 June.[5]

While it is improbable that the Grand Prior had ever been the centre of a Yorkist cell, there may be an element of truth in the accusation that he was in contact with Warbeck's circle at some stage during the young man's first days in Flanders.[6] If so, like William Stanley, he and his friends were hedging their bets, just in case Perkin really was the son of Edward IV and a Yorkist restoration took place, but had then changed their minds in the light of information about his true origins. None of their names seem to have been on the list given to Henry by Sir Robert Clifford.

The spiritual dimension can be overlooked in assessing the secret connections of Fra' John Kendal and his friends with Yorkism. He was very conscious of the vows he had taken. (In his letters he invariably addresses fellow members of his order as '*Spectabilis ac religiose in Christo frater praecarissime*' – 'Most beloved noble and religious brother in Christ'.) Like the clerics mentioned in the affair, such as Bishop Langton or Archdeacon Hussey, and many other clergymen, it is not impossible that Kendal's attitude towards the young man at Margaret's court was to some extent dictated by conscience, which made him anxious to find out whether he really was who he claimed to be. Had Kendal become convinced beyond all doubt that this was the Duke of York he might well have fought for him.

In the event, Henry VII took no action against Fra' John, who resumed his place on the royal council. Such a reliable administrator was too useful to lose. He never discovered that Bernart de Vignolles was a traitor, and the man remained in his service for some time to come, presumably spying on him for the king. Kendal stayed on at Clerkenwell as Grand Prior until his death nearly five years later. If Bernart had denounced him earlier, however, his career might have ended very differently.

Yet King Henry must have noted with considerable unease that at one point someone as respected as Fra' John had accepted that Perkin really might be the Duke of York. The seizure of the Grand Prior's correspondence in 1496 shows that despite the failure of the Yorkist invasion, the authorities suspected Warbeck was still being taken very seriously indeed. How many Englishmen remained loyal to the White Rose?

# 11

# September 1497: Cornwall Rises for Richard IV

'Eight thousand peasants immediately took up arms for him.'

Raimondo de Soncino to the Duke of Milan, *Calendar of State Papers and Manuscripts. . . at Milan 1385–1618*[1]

In September 1497 Andrea Trevisano, ambassador of Venice, sent a report in which he describes an audience with Henry VII at the royal palace of Woodstock. Leaning against a tall chair, the king wore a violet robe lined with cloth of gold and a jewelled collar, a large diamond and a beautiful pearl in his cap. Flanked by the young Prince Arthur and the Duke of Buckingham, he remained standing while the ambassador presented his credentials. Later, the king gave him a private audience lasting for two hours. In Trevisano's considered opininion, Henry was 'gracious, grave and distinguished'.[2] Yet despite his apparent serenity, the king must have been a very worried man. He knew that the Yorkists were about to start another rising, and he cannot have forgotten how his own slender chances had been crowned by success in 1485.

'Perkin Warbeck and his wife were lately set full poorly to sea by the King of Scots,' Henry informed Sir Gilbert Talbot shortly after this audience, in a letter of 12 September 1497.[3] The cause of the White Rose was fading fast when Perkin set sail from Ayr, yet he had not lost heart, convinced that Ireland remained staunchly Yorkist. He had been asked to return there by Sir James of Ormond, a bastard Butler who was currently up in arms against the head of his family, in the hope that the 'duke' might make him Earl of Ormond in his cousin's place.

But on 9 July 1497 Sir James was ambushed and killed near Kilkenny by a kinsman and old enemy, Sir Piers Ruadh Butler. Sir Piers wrote to the earl shortly after that this 'great and ancient rebel' had invited 'Perkin Warbeck to come lately unto this land for the destruction of the subjects and possessions here of our Sovereign Lord'.[4] The death of Sir James ended any hope of Irish support for the 'duke'. Unaware of this disastrous setback, after a voyage lasting a fortnight, round the north coast of Scotland and against contrary winds, Perkin landed in Ireland on 25 July, either in Kerry or in west Cork. In his letter to Sir Gilbert Talbot, King Henry reports him as landing among the 'wild Irishry'.

Still on board the *Cuckoo*, Perkin sailed on into the Haven of Cork. Here he learned that his ally Sir James had been killed, while he found a famine-stricken land with both of the FitzGerald earls in a far from welcoming frame of mind. Henry had reappointed Kildare Lord Deputy, as the only man who could rule the country and keep in check its dislike of the Tudor dynasty, while he bought Lord Desmond's loyalty with customs concessions throughout the south-western ports. In the letter to Talbot, the king says that Perkin 'would have been taken by our cousins, the Earls of Kildare and Desmond, if he and his said wife had not secretly stolen away'.[5]

When his 'two ships and a Breton pinnace' – in fact the *Cuckoo* – put into Cork harbour, John Atwater warned him of his danger whereupon he abandoned his little flotilla and fled.

Someone revealed that he was making for Cornwall and on 1 August the citizens of Waterford wrote to warn King Henry, their letter reaching him at Woodstock only four days later.

He replied at once, offering a large reward for the fugitive's capture, but the four big Waterford ships pursuing Perkin failed to catch him. From the Haven of Cork he had gone to an island near Kinsale, guided by the faithful Atwater, who hired a Basque merchant vessel from San Sebastian to take him to safety. Although the Waterford men boarded her shortly afterwards, Perkin managed to evade capture: he hid in a barrel, the crew insisting they had never heard of him, while his enemies did not recognize his wife and friends. What happened next is not entirely clear, but it seems that somehow the Basques brought Perkin back to one or two of his ships that had stolen out from Cork harbour while the Waterford men were busy elsewhere on a false scent.

In his letter to Gilbert Talbot, King Henry explained that Warbeck was still on course for Cornwall, so he had sent Lord Daubeney to organize a reception committee, while Lord Willoughby de Broke had been dispatched 'with our army on the sea . . . to take the said Perkin if he return again to the sea'. The king was taking the threat very seriously, adding that he would go there himself if it proved necessary and put down the rebellion, 'with Our Lord's mercy'. There is a definite hint of tension. Not only had the Cornish given him a bad fright, but his agents were reporting substantial pockets of Yorkist support all over the West Country.

The Yorkist ships had landed five days earlier, on 7 September, at Whitesand Bay, just a mile away from Land's End. Perkin went ashore with about 300 supporters. One report says they were of various nationalities, with eighty 'savage Irishmen', although it is likely that most were English. Writing to the Bishop of Bath and Wells on 20 September Henry admitted that 'our commons of Cornwall take his part', but claimed that two days earlier they had included 'not one gentleman'.[6] This was not strictly true, however. Humphrey Calwodely of Helland, John Nankevell of St Columb and Walter Tripcony of St Columb, later charged with having invited Perkin to Cornwall, were all gentlemen.

Within a week Warbeck had gathered an army of 3,000 men in an encampment at Castle Kynnock, not far from Bodmin. They were angry there had been no reduction of the tax that had provoked the recent revolt and eager to avenge the defeat at Blackheath where a large number of them must have fought. Few were well armed, however: Vergil says the majority only had swords, by which he presumably means the long Cornish knife.[8] They had had no military training and, save for the three gentlemen mentioned, were without local leaders. Communication must have been a problem, too, since a large number can only have spoken Cornish.

Had Perkin come to Cornwall in June, he might have had a chance of success. Now, he was too late. Afterwards, he admitted that when he landed he knew his cause was doomed, but had been unable to escape from his supporters. Foreign observers agreed. On 16 September the Milanese envoy in London reported:

> everyone is certain that this means the final annihilation of the Cornishmen and the end of the Duke . . . Everything is in the King's favour, especially his bottomless treasury, while the lords of the kingdom, well aware how shrewd he is, are either frightened or genuinely fond of him, so that it is unlikely that even a single nobleman will join the Duke.[9]

Even so, there was uneasiness in the city, where sinister rumours were circulating. The same letter reports, 'In London they say the Duke of York is coming nearer and nearer and is flying three standards, one with a little boy coming out of a womb, the second with a little boy coming out of a wolf's mouth and the third with a red lion on it.' These were all symbols of a rightful heir returned from the dead.

Moreover, Perkin recovered his nerve when the Cornishmen acclaimed him as king. The sheriff of the county attempted to attack the camp at Castle Kynnock, but his troops deserted and joined the rebels, who now numbered 8,000. When the Earl of Devon arrived with a small force of West Country gentlemen, he was horrified to find himself confronted by a large army and hastily withdrew to Exeter.

Perkin then issued a proclamation so eloquently phrased that it showed he must have possessed at least one extremely able adviser. 'Richard by the grace of God King of England' explained how 'We in our tender age escaped by God's great might out of the Tower of London and were secretly conveyed over the seas', and that in his absence Henry, grandson of 'Owen Tydder of low birth in the country of Wales' seized the throne. Henry had spread lies that Richard was an impostor, 'giving us nicknames', and tried to turn his supporters against him, 'some of them to murder our person' and others to desert, notably Robert Clifford. However, with the aid of our dearest cousin, the King of Scots, we have now 'entered into this our realm of England'.

The proclamation listed all the Yorkist leaders who had lost their lives or been hunted down, 'some of which nobles are now in the sanctuary'. It complained of the Earl of Warwick's imprisonment and of Plantagenet princesses being forced to marry Tudor kinsmen of 'low degree', of 'caitiffs and villains' being made ministers. Above all, 'our great enemy' had levied unbearably heavy taxes, impoverishing the entire realm with 'daily pillaging of the people . . . unlawful impositions and grievous exactions'. Those who fight for the cause of King Richard IV would be richly rewarded.[10]

Perkin's council – John Heron, Edward Skelton, Nicholas Astley, William Lounde – urged him to seize Exeter. Although he had no guns, he had a large army and the city's capture would attract recruits from all over the West Country. Leaving his wife at the little hamlet of St Buryan, he invaded England for the third time.

Arriving at Exeter at 1 p.m. on Sunday 17 September, the Cornishmen tried to storm the city at the north and east gates. However, the city was ready, reinforced by the Earl of Devonshire and local gentry, Courtenays, Edgecumbes, Carews and Fulfords, who knew that if they held out for only a few days, they could count on being relieved by a royal army. Undaunted, the besiegers attempted to climb the wall with scaling ladders, besides setting one of the gates on fire. Two hundred of them were killed by gunners and archers shooting from the wall, before the attack was called off for the night.

'And upon the Monday following he and his people made a new assault upon the said city, where again they were put off to their more damage. Albeit that they fired the gates: at which second assault the Earl of Devonshire was hurt in the arm with an arrow,' says a London chronicler.[11] What he does not tell us is that the Cornishmen succeeded in breaking down the east gate, apparently before dawn when the defenders were asleep, presumably with a battering ram, and then occupied the High Street. Beating back two savage attacks, Lord Devon eventually drove them out of the city, although there had been moments when he and his men came within an inch of being overwhelmed.

Both sides were exhausted and the earl negotiated a truce. The Cornishmen agreed to raise the siege and leave, while Devon promised not to pursue them.[12] They then began to panic. Perkin's council tried frantically to reassure them, saying it had a papal bull proving he was the Duke of York, that 'some lords of the realm' were about to join the rising and that money was being minted in the name of 'King Richard' which would shortly be handed out. Some of the Cornishmen were already drifting away when an advance party from Daubeney arrived, promising a pardon to anyone who laid down his arms.[13] Shortly after midnight on 21 September, Perkin himself fled with sixty mounted followers. When the remaining Cornishmen awoke, they found their leaders had deserted them and before dawn they too ran away. The Yorkist rebellion was over.

Guessing that the Earl of Devon had seized the vessels left behind in Cornwall, the fugitive horsemen rode towards the north Somerset coast, hoping to find a ship. Then they scattered. One group, led by the priest William Lounde, headed for London, to take sanctuary at Westminster Abbey or at the church of St Martin, which still provided immunity from arrest.

Perkin made for Beaulieu Abbey in the New Forest, which was near the Solent where a boat might be found to take them to France. His companions, Heron, Astley and Skelton, were friends of the abbot, who may have had Yorkist sympathies since the abbey owned manors in Berkshire – White Rose country. When they arrived, they were received in the lay brothers' refectory. Perkin concealed his identity, but the abbot guessed who he was and sent a message to the king at Woodstock. Within a short time the abbey was ringed by hundreds of armed men despatched by Daubeney, while a ballinger (an oared sailing barge) patrolled the Solent in case the fugitives tried to escape by sea. There was not much chance of this, however, as they had only 'ten crowns' left between them.

Unlike Culham, the abbey's sanctuary rights had a sound legal base and needed to be respected. Accordingly, Henry sent Roger Machado, Richmond Herald, to negotiate Perkin's surrender. John Heron, the former London merchant, was spokesman for the fugitives and it was agreed that he should go to the king and seek terms – if unsuccessful, he would be allowed to return to sanctuary in the abbey. Accordingly, Heron went to Taunton and, after informing Henry – untruthfully – that he had always believed Perkin to be the son of Edward IV, was sent back to Beaulieu to tell his leader he would be spared if he presented himself to the king.

Dressed in cloth of gold, Perkin emerged from sanctuary and was taken to Taunton by Richmond, escorted by a small guard. 'The young man is not too handsome, indeed his left eye lacks lustre, but he is intelligent and well spoken,' the herald told the Milanese ambassador. Kneeling before the king, Perkin begged for mercy. He was told to get up. 'We hear you call yourself Richard, King Edward's son,' said Henry. 'Several people in this room were the king's courtiers, so look round and see if you recognise any of them.' Perkin replied that he knew none of them and was not the Duke of York. He explained that he had been persuaded by some Englishmen and Irishmen to impersonate him, and had learned English for the purpose, adding that for the last two years he had wanted to give up playing the part, but had been unable to find an opportunity.[14]

Heron, Astley and Skelton were summarily packed off under guard. The last two were eventually pardoned, but John Heron remained in prison after it was discovered he had lied about believing Perkin to be the duke – he had always known that he was an impostor. The king then marched to Exeter, taking Perkin with him, where he was kept under strong guard, partly for his own protection. The Cornishmen wanted to murder the 'low born foreigner' who had tricked them into risking their lives.

King Henry stayed at Exeter for a month, in order to punish what he called, in a letter of 17 October to the citizens of Waterford, 'this great rebellion'. He says that captured rebels are appearing before him everyday, in their shirts and with halters round their necks, begging for mercy.[15] Many of those who had taken a leading part in the rising were hanged, drawn and quartered on scaffolds erected outside the city walls. Others filled the prisons and lock-ups of every town in the West Country.

The king was especially pleased when Perkin's wife Katherine was brought to him from St Buryan. She was dressed in black, perhaps in mourning for the death of their child of whom nothing more is known. Reassured to learn that she was not pregnant – he did not want Perkin to have an heir – he gave her rich clothes and a retinue of ladies, sending her with an escort to the queen at their palace of Sheen.

In his *Life and Deeds of Henry VII* Bernard André, the blind poet laureate, describes a meeting between his patron and the couple that took place in the West Country before her departure for London. After Henry had told Perkin he would spare his life, Katherine entered the room, looking particularly beautiful (*'egregia forma'*). Calling her 'illustrious lady', the king expressed his pity at her being placed in such a wretched situation by so worthless a creature (*'istius nebulonis'*), but promised that his queen would look after her. Weeping, Katherine reproached Perkin for dragging her down, declaring that her only hope lay in the king.[16] André adds that Henry complimented Katherine on her noble birth and dignity, telling her she was worthy of a man of high rank. He seems to have been smitten by her. Writing in the 1540s, Edward Hall says delightfully that the king 'began then a little to fantasy her person',[17] while nearer the time Polydore Vergil records how 'when the king saw the woman's beauty, he at once decided she was a captive worthy of a great general'.[18]

Despite having at last captured the 'White Rose' and routed the Cornishmen, Henry VII still did not feel safe. As Vergil tells us, the king knew that 'the population of all the neighbouring counties had been only too willing to feed and shelter the Cornishmen, not only when they were waging war on him, but when they had been beaten and become fugitives trying to get back to their homes.'[19] These non-Cornish neighbours can only have acted in such a way out of hatred for the Tudors or from Yorkist sentiment.

In September 1498 the king appointed a commission to levy fines on everyone in Devon and Cornwall involved in favouring or helping the Cornish rebels. A second commission was appointed for Hampshire, Wiltshire, Somerset and Dorset in March 1500, followed by another for these counties in August 1500. Over 4,500 people were fined which indicates the extent of the unrest. They included the abbots of Ford and Muchelney – two more cases of senior churchmen who remained loyal to the House of York. In Devon and Somerset the goods and possessions of whole districts were seized, reducing their populations to indigence, the fine rolls being endorsed by the king himself. His motive in establishing the commissions is often attributed purely to love of money.[20] Yet if greed played a part, insecurity is likely to have been the main reason: men ground down into poverty were less likely to buy weapons and revolt. Another factor was his obsession with identifying Yorkists.

Henry left Exeter only when he was sure there would be no more danger from the West Country, returning to London at the end of November. He brought Perkin with him. Writing in September 1497 of the king's reaction to the news that the 'White Rose' was besieging Exeter, Bacon comments that Henry had been overjoyed at the chance of laying hands on him. Now he would be 'cured of those privy stitches, which he had long had about his heart, and at some times broken his sleeps, in the midst of all his felicity'.[21] However, King Henry was wrong. Despite capturing Perkin, he would continue to suffer from sleepless nights.

# 12

# Autumn 1499:
# Bringing Down a Curse

'The tragic destiny of the House of York made it necessary
for Earl Edward to perish, so as to make absolutely sure that
no male representative of his family remained alive.'

Polydore Vergil, *Anglica Historia*[1]

In Westminster Hall on 21 October 1497 Henry VII was welcomed back to his capital by its mayor, aldermen and commoners.
Much to their surprise, Perkin was there too, instead of languish-
ing in a dungeon. During the next few weeks, well guarded, he
was regularly paraded on a horse through the main streets of the
city, some of the crowd yelling abuse as he passed.[2] According
to Soncino, the Milanese envoy, he was made 'a spectacle for
everybody and every day he is led through London'.[3]

On 28 November Warbeck was forced to accompany one of
his supporters when the man was taken to the Tower. This was
the former sergeant furrier to the king, who had been caught
disguised as a hermit. A few days later, the furrier and another

rebel, once a yeoman to the queen, were tried and condemned to death, the former being hanged, drawn and quartered at Tyburn although the other escaped with a mere hanging – it seems that betraying the queen was not so heinous an offence as betraying King Henry.

Soon after, the former White Rose signed a confession in which he admitted his real identity and described how he had been persuaded to impersonate the Duke of York. This was printed for circulation.[4] He also wrote to his mother at Tournai, declaring: 'The king of England is now holding me, to whom I have told the truth of the matter, most humbly beseeching him that he will please to pardon the harm I have done him.' This letter was given equally wide distribution, probably with the confession.[5]

Despite all the trouble he had given, for the moment his only punishment was mockery. The Venetian ambassador reported having seen Perkin and his wife in 'a chamber of the King's palace', adding that Henry was treating the couple well enough, but would not let them sleep together.[6] Perkin was never allowed into the royal presence, although occasionally the king took a surreptitious look at him from a window.

One theory for Henry's behaviour is that he wanted to make the White Rose an object of derision, as the best way of demolishing his claims. Another is that he really was Edward IV's son and Henry felt uneasy about executing him out of hand: some Yorkists remained convinced he was the White Rose, bullied into signing a false confession. There is a more subtle possibility, however. After his victory at Stoke, the king had regretted being unable to interrogate the late Earl of Suffolk and discover the full extent of his conspiracy. By keeping Perkin on display, he may have hoped to lure Yorkist supporters into plotting a rescue and revealing themselves.

Warbeck's nerve broke after eight months. About midnight on Saturday 9 June 1498, having persuaded the two yeomen warders who were his guards into giving him keys, he 'stole away out of the court, the king being then at Westminster', a London chronicler records.[7] He had only gone a short distance when he realized he was being pursued and that the roads were picketed. Instead of making for the coast as expected, he fled inland up the Thames – one source says he hid in the reeds – as far as Sheen (Richmond) where he threw himself on the mercy of the prior of the Carthusian monastery. The prior went to Henry and begged for the young man's life, which was granted. Brought back to London on Friday 15 June, he was placed in the stocks in Westminster Hall, on top of a pile of empty wine barrels. The following Monday he was again set in the stocks, on a scaffold in Cheapside opposite The King's Head tavern. Then he was taken to the Tower.

'The same hour he was arrested, the King of England sent one of his gentlemen of the bedchamber to bring me the news,' reported the Spanish ambassador to Ferdinand and Isabella.[8] Hoping to secure a bride from Spain for his eldest son, Prince Arthur, King Henry was anxious that the Spaniards should believe beyond any shadow of doubt that he was secure on his throne: they were not going to waste a daughter on a dynasty that might be toppled. The incident shows how much importance both Henry and international opinion still set on Perkin, however ridiculous he pretended to think him. During Perkin's brief escape, the king had sent letters to every port on the south coast, ordering them to search for the fugitive. He had been very worried indeed.

Once inside the Tower Perkin found himself in a cell, chained by his neck and ankles. De Puebla, the Spanish ambassador, saw him two months later, when he was brought to court to tell the Bishop of Cambrai (Archduke Philip's envoy) that he was not Edward IV's son and had tricked everybody, including most of Europe's rulers. 'He is kept with the greatest care in a tower where he sees neither sun nor moon,' wrote de Puebla. 'He is so much changed that I, and everybody else here, feel his hlife is going to be a very short one. He will have to pay for what he has done.'[9]

'After Perkin had been shut up in the Tower, for once the country seemed to be in a thoroughly peaceful condition,' Polydore Vergil informs us. 'Although there were plenty of people who wanted a change, nobody was prepared to do anything about it until a certain little friar called Patrick, a member of the Augustinian Order did so by persuading a young man to pretend he was the Earl of Warwick.'[10]

'A young fellow of the age of nineteen years, which was the son of a cordwainer [shoemaker] dwelling at the Bull in Bishopsgate street,' is how a London chronicler describes the wretched Ralph Wilford.[11] Early in 1499 Wilford, who was a Cambridge undergraduate and quite plainly crazy, deluded himself into believing he was Warwick and, abetted by his tutor Friar Patrick, wandered round the border of Norfolk and Suffolk, asking men to come to the aid of their rightful king. Caught by the Earl of Oxford, the pair were sent to London, Wilford being hanged on 12 February on a gallows by the Thames – where he hung in his shirt for several days – while the friar was condemned to life imprisonment. But the incident reminded the king that Warwick was still a threat.

It was not only Henry who thought so. 'Ferdinand, King of Spain, would never make full conclusion of the matrimony to be had between Prince Arthur and the lady Katherine his daughter nor send her into England as long as this earl lived', the chronicler Hall informs us. 'For he imagined that as long as any Earl of Warwick lived, that England should never be purged or cleansed of civil war and privy sedition, so much was the name of Warwick in other regions had in fear and jealousy.'[12]

According to a Spanish envoy, who wrote to Ferdinand and Isabella in March 1499, the constant strain took its toll on Henry VII. 'A few days ago the King asked for a priest who had foretold the death of King Edward and the end of King Richard, to tell him in what manner his latter end would come,' he reported. 'The priest, according to common report, told the King that his life would be in great danger during the whole year and informed him, besides many other unpleasant things, that there are two parties of very different creeds in his kingdom.'

This priest was the Italian astrologer Guglielmo Parron, at this period much trusted by Henry, who often asked him to look into the future.[13] The writer adds that the priest indiscreetly had told the secret to some friends, one of whom was immediately placed in confinement to prevent him from putting the rumour into circulation, although the other evaded arrest.

Coming after the Wilford affair, however ridiculous, the astrologer's prophecy and the fact that it might become widely known shocked the king to the depths of his being. 'Henry has aged so much during the last two weeks that he looks twenty years older,' reported the Spaniard, who was generally an objective observer. It is significant that Vergil says many Englishmen still wanted a change of ruler, even though there seemed to be no obvious pretender. Henry knew this. He suffered a complete nervous collapse.

Since 1498 France and England had been on better terms, the French agreeing to expel all Yorkist refugees. In July 1499 they handed over John Taylor. Commenting that here was the man 'who had thought up Perkin's expedition to Ireland when the latter first claimed to be King Edward's son', the Milanese ambassador said he suspected Henry of valuing his capture at more than '100,000 crowns' – a large sum for someone so notoriously avaricious.[14] Brought back to England under guard, Taylor went straight to the Tower of London, where he spent the rest of his life. (He was still there in 1509.) Surprisingly, this dangerous Yorkist escaped execution. It is not inconceivable, in view of what happened next, that Taylor saved his life by acting as an informer.

King Ferdinand's insistence on Warwick's elimination prevailed. According to the earl's nephew, Cardinal Pole, the Spanish king told Henry he did not believe the Tudor dynasty could survive if Warwick stayed alive, and would not let his daughter make a marriage that might endanger her life. Pole also mentions 'some disturbances which took place at this time, owing to the favour and good will borne by the people to my mother's brother the Earl of Warwick', but unfortunately he does not elaborate.[15] Other contemporary sources confirm the rumours of King Ferdinand's intervention.

Henry decided Warwick would have to die. Although there is no hard evidence, it really does look as if he used Perkin to destroy him. Realizing it was very likely that the former would try to escape, the king waited and watched until, as he had hoped, a plot emerged which involved the earl. In Bacon's words, 'it was ordained that this winding ivy of a Plantagenet should kill the true tree itself'.[16]

At first the conspiracy centred around Warwick. His education had been deliberately neglected and as a result, after years of close confinement, he was pathetically simple minded. He possessed so little knowledge of the world outside the Tower that according to the chronicler Hall he could not even tell a goose from a chicken. The prime movers were two impoverished gentlemen: John Cleymond, the earl's servant, and Thomas Astwode, who had been pardoned on the gallows in 1495 for supporting Perkin and was now in the service of the Constable of the Tower, Sir Simon Digby. The real brains behind the plot – if that is the right description – was Astwode, encouraged throughout by Cleymond who was almost certainly a double agent in the king's pay. Fairly soon, Astwode succeeded in recruiting over twenty conspirators.

Some of these were long-term Yorkist sympathizers, such as Thomas Warde, who had been in Richard III's service, and Thomas Masborough, who had been King Edward's master bowyer. Others were former followers of the 'Duke of York', like the priest William Lounde, who, from sanctuary, sent his old master a gold ducat with tooth marks – a recognized token between them. Half a dozen of the constable's servants were also recruited, presumably by Astwode, and included four of Perkin's warders. There was also John Fynche, haberdasher of Honey Lane in the parish of All Hallows, who had been in trouble before on account of Yorkist proclivities. An astrologer, he prophesied that the 'Bear' would soon be heard rattling his chains within the bounds of the city – the Bear being the badge of the earls of Warwick

The scheme Astwode decided on was to kill the constable and seize the Tower, and then smuggle Warwick and Perkin on board a merchant ship carrying a cargo of woollen cloth, which would take them over to the continent. Perkin's room was below the earl's so the two were able to talk to each other through a hole bored in the floor. Apparently Warwick agreed to help Perkin gain the throne if he really was the Duke of York. If he was not, then the earl would take the throne for himself.

It may well have been Perkin who suggested such imaginative additions as taking cash and jewels from the royal treasury and blowing up part of the building as a diversion to enable them to reach the boat which was anchored at a nearby wharf on the Thames. Once safely abroad, they could use the funds they had taken from the treasury to finance a rising. Won over by Perkin's no doubt lavish promises of reward, three of Digby's servants besides Astwode – Walter Bluet, Thomas Strangwysshe and 'Long Roger' – agreed to help Astwode murder him during the night and steal his keys.

It is surprising such a conspiracy could have found any support at all, with a half-baked plan that involved two pretenders to the same throne. Even so, the poor young Earl of Warwick, a prisoner since the age of ten, living in constant terror of being put to death at any moment, was overjoyed at the prospect. 'My lord, you are well-minded in what danger, sadness and duress you here remain, but you [must] help yourself,' the treacherous Cleymond told him soothingly. 'I will take you out of all danger.' Then as reassurance he gave him a hanger – a short sword – which was probably the first weapon Warwick had ever owned.

On 3 August the plot was betrayed to Sir Simon Digby, but by whom is unknown. The informant was rumoured to be Perkin after losing his nerve, but is more likely to have been Cleymond. Although Henry and his council were informed, no attempt to arrest the conspirators was made for three weeks – which indicates that the plot had been under close surveillance from an early stage. As usual, the king was obsessed with identifying every single one of his enemies, which would explain why he waited for so long before ordering their arrest – he was determined to catch as many as possible. He succeeded, judging from the mass of names in the indictments.[17]

Perkin was tried first, on 16 November in 'the White Hall at Westminster', along with John Taylor, John Atwater – the former mayor of Cork – and the latter's son Philip. Found guilty, all four were condemned to be 'drawn on hurdles from the Tower throughout London to the Tyburn, and there to be hanged and cut down quick [alive] and their bowels to be taken out and burned, their heads to be struck off and [their bodies] quartered'.[18] There was a certain logic in trying Warbeck with his first supporters.

The bulk of the remaining prisoners were tried at the Guildhall during the rest of November. Nearly all were found guilty of treason and condemned to death, yet only Astwode, Fynche and one or two others went to the scaffold. John Taylor's sentence was altered to imprisonment for life, while others were outlawed or given a spell in prison but eventually received pardons. The master bowyer Masborough escaped with being committed to the Tower, although usually the king was particularly severe with renegade servants of the crown. Most significantly, John Cleymond was not even sent for trial.

On 21 November the Earl of Oxford, Lord High Steward of England, presided over a grand jury of twenty-two peers that had assembled in the great hall at Westminster to try the Earl of Warwick, who stood indicted for treason. (Among the peers was John Kendal, Prior of St John's, who had once flirted with the idea of a Yorkist restoration.) Warwick was charged with having plotted with Perkin to raise a rebellion and overthrow the king. The bewildered young man, who was not even cross-examined, admitted he could not deny the charge and threw himself on the king's mercy, after which the last male representative of a dynasty that had ruled the country for three centuries was condemned to suffer a traitor's death. Although the first Plantagenet to suffer in this way, it was the fate he must always have expected since Bosworth.

On Saturday 23 November Perkin and John Atwater, with halters round their necks, were drawn through the muddy streets to Tyburn, where a small scaffold had been erected and a great multitude was assembled. The crowd seem to have felt sorry for Perkin, which may explain why he was spared castration and disembowelment.[19] From the scaffold he told them that he had been born a foreigner as he had already confessed, that he was not Edward IV's second son, and that John Atwater had forced him to take on the Duke of York's identity, and finally he asked God and the king for forgiveness. Then he was hanged. When Atwater took his turn on the scaffold, he told the crowd that what Perkin had said was true. Their bodies were buried at the Austin Friars' church, their heads stuck up on London Bridge.

A few went on believing that the young man really had been the duke, convinced that 'Perkin Warbeck' was a false identity foisted on him and that his 'confession' was untrue. Among them were the Earl of Suffolk and his steward Thomas Killingworth. In 1508 Thomas wrote to his master, referring to the 'abusion King H. hath made against the Duke of York, that he was a counterfeit' and insisting he had been 'right King of England'.[20] However, these sceptics were in a minority.

'This was the end of this little cockatrice of a king,' comments Bacon, adding that his conspiracy had been 'one of the longest plays of that kind that hath been in memory'. Yet he thought the play might have ended differently, if Perkin had not been faced with such a tough opponent as Henry VII.[21]

On the following Thursday, between two and three o'clock in the afternoon, the Earl of Warwick was led out from the Tower by two men, on to Tower Hill, where he was beheaded. Instead of being displayed on London Bridge as that of a traitor, his head was reunited with his corpse in a coffin and taken back into the Tower. 'And at the next tide following the body was conveyed by water unto Bisham, a place of religion, and there, by his ancestors, interred and buried,' records the London chronicler.[22] King Henry was trying to behave with as much decency as possible in the circumstances.

While the king had strengthened the Tudor dynasty's future by killing Warwick, he made himself deeply unpopular. There were rumours that he had used Perkin to trap the earl. 'The entire population mourned the handsome youth's death,' says Vergil. Normally a partisan of Henry, he adds, 'Why this unfortunate boy should have been sent to prison for no fault of his own but purely on account of his family, why he was kept there for so long, and what he could have possibly done in prison that made him deserve to die – these things people found hard to understand.'[23]

Knowing that the earl had been a simple soul, more than a little childish, every informed person in England was convinced that he was innocent of any plot against the king. Remembering Edward IV's sons, they were inclined to think of Warwick as the third Prince in the Tower. Many believed that by his murder – for that is what it was – King Henry had brought a curse upon his own family.

# 13

# Autumn 1499:
# Edmund de la Pole,
# Earl of Suffolk

'Edmund [de la] Pole, Earl of Suffolk, son to John, Duke of
Suffolk and Lady Elizabeth, sister to King Edward IV, being
stout and bold of courage, and of wit rash and heady, was
indicted of homicide and murder, for slaying of a mean person in his rage and fury . . . [and] fled to Flanders, without
any licence or safe conduct given to him by the king, to the
Lady Margaret, his aunt on his mother's side.'

Edward Hall, *The Union of the two Noble and Illustre
Famelies of Lancaste and Yorke* [1548][1]

If Warwick's killing brought a curse it wasted no time in striking
and Henry VII soon suffered a shattering series of bereave-
ments. In 1500 his third son, Edmund, Duke of Bedford died,
not yet a year old. In 1502 Arthur, Prince of Wales died at only
seventeen, so that the young Prince Henry was now the only

male Tudor other than the king. In 1503 Elizabeth of York died in childbirth.

Thomas More wrote 'A Rueful Lamentation on the Death of Queen Elizabeth'. For contemporaries, two of its lines had a hidden meaning.

> 'Was I not born of old worthy lineage
> Was not my mother queen, my father king?'[2]

There is nothing to suggest that More was a Yorkist – not yet, at any rate – but everyone knew that Henry Tudor had not been born of 'old worthy lineage'.

The story of a curse on the Tudors was not going to fade away. Years later, Bacon heard that when Henry VIII announced his intention to divorce her, Queen Katherine declared that it was God's judgement because her first marriage had been 'made in blood, meaning that of the Earl of Warwick'. During the reign of Henry VIII many people thought that the curse must be responsible for the eerie proneness of Tudor males to die in childhood.

Henry VII's own health was collapsing. He may already have contracted tuberculosis. (In 1508 he was rumoured to be in the last stages of consumption.) Whatever the reason, he had become an old man by his forties. There is no written evidence of his decline, but a portrait painted in 1505 by the Baltic artist Michael Sittow (now in the National Portrait Gallery, London) tells us a lot. This was commissioned by Emperor Maximilian's agent, for his master to send to his widowed daughter Margaret, whom he wanted the king to marry. It is hard to believe that the bleary-eyed, thin-lipped, exhausted old face leering out of the portrait is the same person as the young gallant sketched twenty years earlier. Torrigiano's portrait bust of about the same date shows a very different face, but it was designed to flatter. Some artists paint what they see, however, which is what Sittow seems to have done – perhaps he was given the commission because of the realism of his work. Other portraits by him are thoroughly convincing, such as that of the youthful Katherine of Aragon.

Although the calamities he experienced did not unbalance Henry's statecraft, they did little for his mental equilibrium. It is scarcely surprising that he grew ever more suspicious of the nobility, and continued to live in dread of the White Rose. There were strong hints that his mind was unbalanced in the way he dealt with the Earl of Suffolk.

'England has never been so tranquil and obedient as it is at present,' reported the Spanish ambassador in January 1500. 'There were pretenders to the English crown, but now Perkin and the Duke of Clarence's son are executed, not a drop of doubtful Royal blood can remain, the sole Royal blood being the true blood of the King.'[3] He believed there was no one left who could challenge Henry VII, and perhaps the king himself thought so, if only for a short time.

Yet Henry's astrologer had been justified in warning him that there were two parties in his kingdom, one of which questioned his right to the throne. The ballad 'The White Rose', dating from about 1500 – probably to be sung as a three-part 'carol' – shows that nostalgia for the House of York was still flourishing at this date. There were Englishmen who continued to regard the Tudor as a usurper, and were outraged at the Earl of Warwick's murder. He and Perkin might be dead, but the White Rose still bloomed, its new embodiment being Edmund de la Pole, Earl of Suffolk. Many must have recalled that less than twenty years earlier, John de la Pole, Earl of Lincoln – later killed at Stoke – had been named heir to the throne by Richard III. After the death of Warbeck and Warwick, Lincoln's younger brother, Suffolk, was the obvious Yorkist claimant as Richard's senior nephew.

Born about 1473, Edmund had showed no sign of disaffection, playing his role on ceremonial occasions and admired for his prowess at jousting – the great spectator sport of the age. A herald's account gives us a clourful glimpse of him at the tournament held at Westminster in 1494 to celebrate Prince Henry's investiture as Duke of York. He led the competitors as they rode out of Westminster Hall, his red silken banner bearing his motto, 'For to accumplisshe', while the crest on his tilting helm was a golden lion. During the tournament, he broke his sword on Sir Edward a Borough 'furiously and notably', and performed no less effectively in breaking his lance when charging his opponent. After supper, the five-year-old Princess Margaret, King Henry's eldest daughter, awarded the prize to 'the right noble lord, the Earl of Suffolk', a ring of gold with a diamond.

When the tournament was resumed a few days later, again he 'gave such a stroke to Sir Edward a Borough that his sword was almost out of his hand and bruised his gauntlet'. His opponent lost control of his horse so that many people thought that his aim had been damaged, but he recovered and managed to give Suffolk a light tap on the helmet with his own sword. This time it was Sir Edward who was given the tourney prize, another diamond ring. The earl was still only twenty-one, while the other competitors were all seasoned veterans.[4]

After campaigning against the French in 1492, when he took part in the siege of Boulogne, Suffolk was made a Knight of the Garter. In September 1495 the king paid him the supreme royal compliment of visiting his Oxfordshire house, Ewelme.

But Suffolk was his own worst enemy. He was haughty, not terribly intelligent, a nobleman 'of an hasty and choleric disposition' who had an uncontrollable temper, and Vergil calls him. 'bold, impetuous, readily roused to anger'.[5] Despite having been at Oxford, he was more or less illiterate, to judge from his few surviving letters. It has been suggested he felt close to his first cousin, Queen Elizabeth, which was why he stayed loyal to her husband for some years.[6] Yet there is no evidence for such affection other than his frequent attendance at court. In reality, he nursed a grievance. When his father, the Duke of Suffolk, had died in 1491 the de la Pole lands became forfeit to the crown under Lincoln's attainder as a traitor. The king allowed Edmund to inherit them, but only on payment (in instalments) of £5,000, which forced him to mortgage a large proportion of his heritage. He was then reduced to the rank of earl on the pretext that his estates were so diminished and impoverished that he could not afford to be a duke.

In consequence, Edmund had been plunged into debt, besides feeling insulted by his 'degradation'. At the same time he was very conscious of his royal blood, having been treated as a close kinsman by Edward IV and Richard III. There is no reason to think he had designs on the throne while Warbeck and Warwick were alive but, given his royal background and his brother Lincoln's rebellion, it was understandable that Henry should wish to keep a close eye on him.

The earl's loyalty was pushed to breaking point during the autumn of 1499. After dining in London with his kinsman Lord William Courtenay and other friends, near the Tower, in a fit of rage he killed a 'mean person' named Thomas Crue. Indicted for murder, he had to 'plead' in the law courts before being pardoned by Henry VII, and, as 'a prince of blood royal', he felt resentful that he had been tried at all. The fact that his victim was a plaintiff in a case under investigation by the King's Council made him fear he might be charged again. On 1 July 1499 he fled the country. The date suggests he was implicated in the plot to rescue Warbeck and Warwick from the Tower – we know he believed that Warbeck really was Edward IV's son.

On hearing that Edmund had left England secretly – like his brother Lincoln before him – the king assumed he was on his way to Margaret of Burgundy. The previous year she had sent Henry an apology for any wrong she might have done him, but he was convinced that as soon as the earl reached Malines she would make her nephew claim the throne – if he had not done so already. This new threat emerged just as the Warbeck–Warwick business was reaching a crisis.

On 20 August Henry sent writs to the sheriffs of Kent, Norfolk, Suffolk and Essex, and to the wardens of the Cinque Ports, ordering them to prevent anyone from leaving the kingdom without royal permission, in case they planned to join the earl. The principal Tudor henchman in East Anglia, Lord Oxford, was clearly following royal orders when, on the same day, he asked Sir John Paston to find out who had left the area with Suffolk: Paston was also told to arrest those who had escorted him to the coast but stayed behind, as well as anybody else who had known of his flight. The letter's clumsy prose obscures the sophistication of the security machine it set in motion – information gathering and close surveillance of the region by a wide network of experienced agents, accompanied by systematic interrogation of suspects.

Edmund had not gone to his aunt Margaret as the king supposed, but to Guisnes, one of the two castles guarding Calais, as a guest of its captain, Sir James Tyrell, once a loyal henchman of the House of York. He soon left English territory for St Omer, across the border in Burgundian Artois, where he begged its governor to give him refuge. Henry reacted by sending the comptroller of his household, Sir Richard Guildford, and an experienced diplomat, Richard Hatton, to Brussels to see Archduke Philip, who was the Duke of Burgundy. Having made it plain to Archduke Philip that there would be another full-scale trade war if he did not help, they then went to see Suffolk at St Omer.

They told Suffolk that every European sovereign was bound by treaty to repatriate English rebels, and that if he became a mercenary fighting for another country he would commit treason, and never see England again. Should he return, however, his escapade would be forgiven. He gave in and went home,[7] and was able to produce such a convincing excuse for his behaviour that the king pardoned him.[8]

Even so, Edmund was fined £1,000. Still more damaging from his point of view, King Henry rehabilitated the Howard family – out of favour since 1485 – and helped them to build up their power in East Anglia at the expense of the de la Poles. Distrusted by the king, growing poorer every day and losing local influence, he was being driven further and further down the social scale.

# 14

# Summer 1501: White Rose and White King

'Solicited, allured and provoked by that old, venomous serpent the Duchess of Burgoyne, ever being the sower of sedition and beginner of rebellion against the King of England, or else stimulate[d] and pricked with envy . . . with his brother Richard [he] fled again.'

Edward Hall, *The Union of the two Noble and Illustre Famelies of Lancaste and Yorke*[1]

In 1501 an English courtier in the service of Emperor Maximilian told him England was tired of the 'murders and tyrannies' of Henry VII – a reference to Warbeck and Warwick – and argued Edmund's claim to the throne. Maximilian replied that he would be only too willing to help 'one of King Edward's blood' regain the crown of England and was ready to spend an entire year's revenue on doing so. The courtier, a friend of Suffolk, immediately sent word to him.[2]

The courtier was Sir Robert Curzon, a figure who could only
have existed in the late Middle Ages, a professional soldier,
jousting hero and self-proclaimed knight errant. When Captain
of Hammes, one of the fortresses guarding Calais, despite his
duties, Curzon had often been at court and with Suffolk had
taken part in the tournament held to celebrate Prince Henry's
investiture as Duke of York. Vergil says he was of humble
origin and owed his career to being knighted by the king, but in
fact he was of impeccable gentry stock, a Curzon of Kedleston.
After repeated requests, Henry had allowed him to resign his
captaincy and go on crusade, which he performed by fighting
for Maximilian against the Turks in the Balkans, so gallantly that
he was created a *Reichsfreiherr* (Baron of the Empire) and in
England was often referred to as 'My Lord Curzon'.

Suffolk received Curzon's message shortly before the marriage of Prince Arthur and Katherine of Aragon. No doubt he
had learned that he was expected to play a major role in the customary tournaments, which would involve expenses and further
financial troubles. By now he had grown to hate Henry. While
Vergil says that a need to escape from heavy debts played a part
in Edmund's decision, he makes it clear that 'party feeling' was
the key factor. This means the earl was in touch with diehard
Yorkists – and that there were more than a few of them.[3] In July
or August 1501, shortly before the royal wedding, Suffolk again
took ship secretly, with his younger brother Richard de la Pole.
This time, he made up his mind to claim the throne of England.
Once more, the Yorkist cause had a leader with a better right to
the throne than Henry Tudor and who possessed at least some
experience of soldiering.

It was learned that a week earlier Edmund had 'banqueted'
in London with the Marquess of Dorset, the Earl of Essex and
Lord William Courtenay, who all fell under suspicion. (A ban-
quet was not a dinner but a selection of exotic sweetmeats eaten
in a luxurious setting – a celebration rather than a meal.) It was
also learned that before he sailed Edmund had dined with

Courtenay – son and heir of the Earl of Devon, the saviour of Exeter from the 'Duke of York'. Courtenay was even suspected of advising Edmund to land in the West Country when he launched his invasion.[4]

Whatever the chronicler Hall may say, Margaret of Burgundy had nothing to do with Edmund's defection. Although at the beginning King Henry was convinced she was behind it, because of her long record of support for the White Rose and hatred of the Tudors, there is not the slightest hint that Edmund ever tried to contact her. While she may have welcomed the news of his flight, she made no effort to help him. By now she was a disillusioned old woman, who had given up all hope of seeing any of her nephews on the English throne.

Instead of making for Malines, the earl – calling himself 'The White Rose, Duke of Suffolk' – made his way to Maximilian's court at Imst in the Tyrol. The emperor, an impressive-looking man with an eagle's nose and a lanthorn jaw, not only disliked Henry for more than once outwitting him in diplomatic matters, but also regarded the Tudor as an upstart: like many others in Europe, he had been shocked at the news of the execution of the Earl of Warwick and of Warbeck whom he was still inclined to see as the younger Prince in the Tower. Edmund's adoption of the title 'The White Rose', once used by Warbeck, may have appealed to a man who, as King of the Romans, sometimes called himself 'The White King'. Edmund denounced Henry VII as a murderer, adding that the king wanted to kill both him and his brother. He then declared he was the rightful King of England, asking Maximilian to help him overthrow the Tudor usurper. He was supported by Sir Robert Curzon, who either fled with him or met him at Imst.

Welcoming Suffolk as a 'kinsman' (which meant he recognized him as a fellow sovereign), the emperor explained that for the moment he was unable to help because of his son's treaty with England. Even so, he gave him a safe conduct to travel anywhere in the empire, while promising to find a way of assisting him. He invited the earl to stay at Imst and after six weeks wrote a letter to Edmund in which he offered to supply him with up to 5,000 troops under a German captain and to find ships for them.

The earl found himself a player on the international stage, recognized as a king in exile. Maximilian sent him to Aix-la-Chapelle with letters of introduction to the city fathers, promising that the ships he needed would be hired in Denmark. It seemed there was every chance of a full-scale Yorkist invasion, especially when Suffolk found another supporter in John, King of Denmark, Norway and Sweden.

His steward, Thomas Killingworth, went to Brunecken in the Tyrol to inform the emperor that Heinrich, Count of Ardek, had offered to find the troops, with his son as their commander, together with the necessary funds which would be made available on St George's Day (23 April) 1502, when the force would go to Denmark to embark on ships provided by King John.[5] But then the emperor – one of the most inept soldiers in Europe – decided he must take a hand. His meddling was so infuriating that Ardek withdrew his offer, thus putting an end to the latest Yorkist invasion.

Ironically, Maximilian was the House of York's obvious ally. Superficially, he seemed no less formidable than Margaret of Burgundy, although he had no family motive for hating Henry. But the earl had not got the measure of his new friend. Impulsive, fond of theatrical gestures, Maximilian could never accept that his resources were too small for his ambitions: ruling over no more than Austria, the Low Countries, Franche Comté and a few isolated fragments of Germany, he nonetheless dreamed of being a Holy Roman Emperor who governed all Christendom. Yet if the prospect of securing a Yorkist restoration appealed to his vanity, he was, however, known throughout Europe as 'the man of few pence' and simply did not have enough money to subsidize an invasion force.

Henry's frenzied reaction to yet another Yorkist challenge shows that, like Suffolk, he failed to appreciate the emptiness of Maximilian's promises. 'And the second Sunday of Lent [22 February 1502] was Sir Edmund de la Pole pronounced accursed at Paul's Cross, at the sermon before noon,' records the *Chronicle of the Grey Friars.*[6] This ceremony of excommunication by the Church, which was repeated at Paul's Cross every February for several years to come, reveals the extent of the king's fury and fear.

Carefully briefed, a highly effective commission under the Earl of Oxford and Lord Willoughby de Broke had purged East Anglia of Yorkism, using more than just the usual machinery of arrests or surveillance and flooding the area with agents. Another commission had purged the adjoining counties of Berkshire and Oxfordshire. Suffolk's retainers and tenants, his friends and neighbours – including a knight, 24 gentlemen, 15 esquires and scores of yeomen – were hauled before the local courts and placed under bonds to keep the peace, preventing them from taking any action in support of the earl. The fact that none of these people were attainted in the months that followed shows the bonds' effectiveness – infringing them meant ruin.

In addition to small landowners, others of higher rank were rounded up in the eastern counties and the Thames Valley. 'And soon after [the end of February 1502] was the Lord William of Devonshire, Sir James Tyrell and his eldest son, and one Wellesbourne, a servant of the said James Tyrell, taken and committed to safe keeping for favouring of the party of the Earl of Suffolk,', a London chronicler tells us.[7] William de la Pole, Edmund's youngest brother, was also sent to the Tower, where he remained a prisoner until his death in the late 1530s. At the same time, according to Vergil, many 'of the common people' [*de plebe hominibus*] were arrested throughout the country.[8]

Having married a younger daughter of Edward IV, it was understandable that William Courtenay should support a Yorkist restoration. As for Sir James, in the old days one of Richard III's most trusted henchmen, he had probably remained a staunch Yorkist (which explains why Edmund took refuge with him during his first flight) although until now he had enjoyed the king's complete confidence. His defection came as another shock for Henry. It needed a siege by the entire Calais garrison to prize the Tyrells out of Guisnes, and James only emerged in order to negotiate terms for a safe conduct – promptly broken by Henry's officers, who arrested him.

A mass trial took place at the Guildhall during the first week of May 1502, conducted by a commission that included the mayor, the Duke of Buckingham and the Earl of Oxford and other peers, together with several judges and a number of distinguished knights. Sir James Tyrell and Sir John Wyndham were sentenced to death, as also were a former yeoman of the crown, a herald, a London barber, a sailor and various others. Tyrell and Wyndham were beheaded on Tower Hill, but the rest suffered all the ghastly penalties reserved for treason.[9] Another Yorkist supporter, Charles Ryppon, keeper of Portchester Castle, was beheaded at Winchester.

Tyrell was widely believed to have confessed before he died (perhaps to ensure a merciful death under the axe) that he had killed the Princes in the Tower. The confession, the details of which are given by Polydore Vergil and Thomas More, has been questioned by modern historians who suggest it was an invention of Henry VII, to dispel any doubts that the boys were dead and discourage the emergence of another 'Duke of York'. Yet, in view of his own murder of the Earl of Warwick in 1499, it seems unlikely that the king should have wanted to remind his subjects of the Princes.

Always methodical, King Henry used not only spies but a species of filing system to identify potential enemies. His carefully updated lists included the names of men implicated in previous rebellions – fined, reprieved or pardoned – and those of everyone executed, since their kinsmen were likely to be hostile. It appears he made a clean sweep of Edmund's leading supporters, which according to Vergil plunged the earl into despair, and made him abandon his plans for an invasion.[10] Even so, the extent of King Henry's fear that Suffolk might revive the Yorkist challenge was apparent from the vast sums of money he spent on ensuring Maximilian's neutrality during the years when the earl was in imperial territory. The money was disguised as subsidies to help the emperor's crusade against the Turks.

Suffolk stayed on at Aix-la-Chapelle until 1503, waiting for the emperor to provide him with troops, and heartened by letters from Maximilian addressed reassuringly to his 'Very Dear and Most Beloved Cousin'. In June 1502 the emperor told 'My Lord Curzon' that despite having a treaty with Henry VII, secretly he would aid him as much as possible. But he then admitted his complete inability to do so by advising Curzon to ask the King of France for help. When Curzon asked, 'how are we going to live in the meantime?', Maximilian said he felt sure that Margaret of Burgundy would pay for their keep.

Understandably, the earl was encouraged when Arthur, Prince of Wales died in April 1502. It seemed to be divine intervention and in May Edmund told his steward Thomas Killingworth that, were the king's second son to die, his claim to the throne would be beyond any possible doubt.[11] Other people besides diehard Yorkists began to take Suffolk seriously, while Henry VII saw him as an even bigger threat. On the same day that the earl wrote to Killingworth, he informed the emperor: 'I have been warned for certain that King H. [*sic*] is looking into every means of destroying me, bribing anyone he can with gold and silver.'[12] He meant assassination by English agents. As Alison Hanham stresses, Edmund had ceased to believe Maximilian's promises and abandoned any idea of invading England. But he was convinced that he merely needed to wait for the ailing king to die, before returning home for his coronation. An eleven-year-old Tudor could in no way be a threat, he assured Killingworth.[13] Presumably he intended to arrange for young Henry's disappearance.

Increasingly dependent on Henry VII's subsidies, Maximilian replaced his promise to help Edmund become king by an assurance that he would do his best to see he recovered his duchy and his estates.[14] In February 1503 he told an English embassy led by Sir Thomas Brandon that he wanted King Henry to pardon Suffolk. When they asked him to expel the earl from imperial territory he made a joke they did not catch but which sent his courtiers into roars of laughter – 'a great laughing'. Even so, the envoys doggedly complained of the 'aid, comfort and relief' given by the emperor to the English 'rebels' at Aix.[15] The Spanish ambassador, too, was demanding that Suffolk should be banished from the empire.

In 1504 Henry ensured the passing of an Act of Parliament giving the towns of the Hansa League exceptional trading advantages very much to the disadvantage of English merchants. The only condition was that the Earl of Suffolk must not be allowed to take up residence in them, or be given help in any way whatsoever. This extraordinary gesture, detrimental to England's commercial interests, was prompted by Maximilian's lack of cooperation. Once again, it shows how frightened the king was of Suffolk.[16]

As has been seen, when Edmund was cursed at St Paul's Cross Sir Robert Curzon was cursed with him. But the knight errant turned traitor. Hall infers that for some time Curzon had been working for King Henry who, 'like a wily fox', included his name in the cursing to convince the earl of his loyalty.[17] Vergil, too, suggests that while remaining at Edmund's side, Curzon sent Henry the names of the leading Yorkists: Edmund's brother William, Courtenay, Tyrell and Sir John Wyndham.[18] He may also have implicated Lord Bergavenny and Sir Thomas Green who were arrested, although nothing could be proved and so they were released. 'Soon after, Curzon, when he saw time, returned into England and withal into wonted favour with the king, but worse favour with the people,' is Francis Bacon's reconstruction. 'Upon whose return the earl was much dismayed and seeing himself destitute of hopes, the lady Margaret [of Burgundy] also by tract of time and bad success being now become cool in these attempts.'[19]

Vergil, Hall and Bacon were convinced that Sir Robert had been a double agent all the time, yet the public anathema at Paul's Cross makes this unlikely – unless Hall's theory is correct. So, too, does the fact that those who had pledged large sums for his good behaviour forfeited their money. It is more likely that Henry's spies contacted Curzon, offering him a huge bribe to change sides. The date when Curzon left Suffolk is unknown – certainly not before 1504 – but in 1506 the king settled an enormous annuity on him and he was frequently at court until well into the next reign.

There was at least one other informer among the little group of Yorkists around the earl at Aix, who by now were almost starving. A report by one of Henry's spies has survived from about 1503. Possibly an agent of Sir Richard Guildford, ordered by the king to keep close watch on them, he seems to have been singularly inept. Although claiming to be expert at consulting astrologers, he could not find anyone to cast Suffolk's horoscope as he did not know the date of his birth. Nor was he able to learn what sort of help the earl expected or where it was going to come from, or any details about ships or who would rally to him when he landed in England. The agent claimed, however, that he had done his best to dissuade Edmund from launching an invasion, telling him not to do so until he was sure of really solid support. 'Trust not the commons for in them without their heads [leaders] never was nor shall be steadfastness.'[20]

During the summer of 1503 Maximilian asked the Master of the Hunt at Guelders to inform the authorities at Aix that he had ceased to encourage the Earl of Suffolk in his struggle against the King of England. He was also to add that the emperor could not in any way be responsible for Suffolk's debts but, as he pitied the earl's miserable state and because he had sent him to Aix with letters of recommendation, he would pay 3,000 Rhenish florins towards settling them.[21] Unfortunately, the imperial treasury did not forward even this inadequate sum.

Instructions signed – and probably to some extent dictated – by the king in 1503 to an agent who was to contact a 'Messire Charles' reveal his continuing obsession with the earl. The agent, Sir John Wiltshire, was the Controller of Calais. His instructions are in French, so he can show them to 'Messire Charles' who is in Henry's pay. His first job was to learn the plans of the 'rebels' through Charles's spies. He was to find out the name of every rebel so that Maximilian could be asked to banish them from his territories: if he heard that George Neville had not yet been expelled from Maastricht, he should see it was done as soon as possible. He was also to bribe Edmund de la Pole's household to inform on their master. 'If any other of the gentlemen and servants of the said Edmund de la Pole desire to have pardon and absolution, the King will be pleased to give them their lives so long as they tell everything they know.'[22] Wiltshire was almost certainly ordered to arrange for the earl's assassination.

Meanwhile, the last Yorkists who remained active in England were being methodically hunted down. In May four of them, including two sailors, were tried at the Guildhall and executed at Tyburn. Yet Henry VII still did not feel safe, although by now he had very little to fear from the White Rose.

Pursued by German creditors and English assassins, Suffolk had fled from Aix-la-Chapelle, leaving his brother Richard as security for the monies he owed. Towards Easter 1504, crossing the imperial frontier he set out for the coast, seeking shelter with George, Duke of Saxony. While travelling through Guelderland, he was arrested and imprisoned at Hattem Isel by Duke Charles of Guelders, who tried to sell him to King Henry but asked for such an exorbitant sum that the negotiations ended in failure

Edmund's dream of toppling the Tudors had turned into a squalid, hand-to-mouth existence of beggary or imprisonment. Throughout, he knew Henry was in unrelenting pursuit, and that two great powers, Spain and France were doing their best to help the king to catch him. For the moment, however, he seemed safe so long as he could remain in Guelderland or the

Low Countries, even when in July 1505 Hattem was captured by the troops of Archduke Philip and he became the archduke's prisoner. A Venetian envoy, writing from Antwerp the following month, informed the Signoria that the Flemish believed Philip would use Suffolk to 'keep the bit in Henry's mouth'.[23]

Apart from a few servants, Edmund's household had dwindled to his chaplain 'Sir Walter Blasset', his steward Thomas Killingworth and another retainer named Thomas Griffiths. The only gentleman left was that irrepressible Yorkist Sir George Neville (pardoned three times by King Henry), who was now calling himself 'Lord Neville.' They must all have been very shaken by Curzon's defection. They were also in financial peril, facing arrest for debt. Living in an inn at Zwolle, they could not pay the bill. 'None of my friends will help me with a penny,' the earl wrote to his steward.[24] By now he had been forced to pawn even his signet ring, while both he and 'Lord Neville' were in rags.

There was a ray of hope during the summer of 1505, however. In July we find him writing to Paul Zachtlevant as 'My most faithful friend' Zachtlevant was a wealthy Baltic merchant at Amsterdam with commercial interests in Denmark, who had been one of the main backers behind Warbeck's abortive invasion in 1495. Determined to recover his money, he planned to present King Henry with documents signed by Warbeck or else persuade the Duke of Pomerania and the King of Denmark to impound English shipping: he wanted Suffolk to authenticate the documents. He also threatened that if Henry would not pay, then he would help to finance the earl's cause.

Despite his abject poverty, Suffolk was too proud to beg Zachtlevant for ready cash. Instead, his steward Killingworth suggested to 'Mr Paul' that the first step was to restore his master's credibility by paying his bills. He also asked for money to buy him new clothes. Probably during the second half of 1505 – no date is specified – the steward wrote a letter to the earl, describing what he had extracted from Mr Paul, which included

satin for doublets and cloth for two pairs of hose – velvet for a
gown was also promised. There was also a bonnet for Neville.
So far nothing had been said, however, about settling the inn-
keeper's bill at Zwolle – 'an ye had therin spoken plainly to him
it had been otherwise, for he is a kind and a friendly man'.

Unfortunately, nothing came of the high hopes aroused
by 'Mr Paul'. As for Archduke Philip, 'He was my good lord
and would do for me many things, but I cannot perceive it,'
Edmund wrote at the end of November 1505. 'I lie here in pain
and shame, and also spend [only] what I can get of my friends,
and I have nothing but fair words.'[25]

Yet for all Suffolk's miserable circumstances the Venetian
envoy at Amsterdam, Vincenzo Quirini, was still taking him
seriously as a pretender. The next month he reported having
heard (presumably from Venetian merchants in London) that
'the people of England love and long for him'. Quirini thought
that even now Edmund might deal a blow against King Henry
who, he claimed, saw him as 'a great thorn in his eye' and
remained desperate to lay hands on him.[26]

# 15

# September 1504:
# A Conversation about
# the Future

'But none of them, he said, spake of my lord prince.'

John Flamank's report to Henry VII[1]

Some experts on the Tudor period regard Edmund de la Pole as a mere footnote to the history of the reign, a figure without any real political significance – which is precisely how Henry VII wanted his subjects to see the earl. Yet however wretched Edmund's adventures in Germany and the Low Countries may have been, they showed that more than a few foreign rulers accepted him as a serious claimant to the English throne. And Henry knew that a fair number of Englishmen recognized Suffolk's claims, judging from a spy's report from Calais that reached him during the autumn of 1504. It showed that some of his most trusted subjects thought the White Rose might become their next ruler.

Although taking just a few hours if the English Channel's uncertain weather was kind and the tides had been properly reckoned, a crossing from Dover to Calais in the early sixteenth century, on the whole, was a thing to be dreaded. All too often it could turn into a long and frightening voyage. The clumsy little ships – tubby, clinker-built 'cogs' – might easily be driven off course for days on end, tacking to and fro against a contrary wind, their skippers fearful of hoisting too much sail in case a squall blew up. In a high sea, vessels like this rolled and pitched horribly, shipping an alarming amount of water, the waves drenching everybody on board and swamping the rudimentary cabins under the 'castles' fore and aft. Passengers and crew were profoundly thankful to make land.

Going ashore at Calais, they found themselves on English soil in a thriving English town that housed the English merchants of the Staple, a tightly knit, and to some extent intermarried, community, who controlled the export of their country's wool, selling the bulk of it in Flanders where textile production was booming. In consequence, Calais – 'Calis' as it was pronounced at the time – was the entry point through which most of the foreign gold and silver earned by trade went back to England, so that its streets were full of luxury shops and expensive taverns selling best quality wine. Its merchants lived in fine, richly furnished mansions with glass windows and tall chimneys. The town was a jewel in the English Crown and Henry VII found time to visit it twice – the second occasion being in 1500 when he was paid a state visit here by Archduke Philip, who was also Duke of Burgundy.

Yet there was something claustrophobic about life at Calais. Its inhabitants felt dangerously isolated, cut off from home by rough seas and in constant fear of a siege as, understandably, the town's occupation by the English was resented by the French. But its massive fortifications looked impregnable (even though outdated), while the land around it, known as the Marches of Calais, was defended by two particularly strong castles – Hammes and Guisnes. A widespread network of secret agents, reaching as far away as Paris, was always on the look out for any sign of hostile preparations by the French government so as to give the garrison good warning of an attack.

For Henry VII, however, 'Calais and the Marches of Calais' were more than just a strategic and commercial bridgehead across the Channel. The garrison was the nearest thing he possessed to a standing army. In England he merely had a bodyguard of 200 'yeomen', but over in Calais he maintained a regular force of 700–800 regularly paid men-at-arms, archers and gunners. If necessary, Guisnes and Hammes could be used as maximum security gaols for state prisoners.

However, for many years Yorkist support was embedded in Calais. Although many hardliners had been hunted down and eliminated or chased away, devotion to the old royal family remained entrenched among some of the merchant families and even among the troops. The king took exceptional care when choosing the garrison's officers. These consisted of lieutenant and deputy lieutenant, governor and deputy governor, treasurer, captain and gentleman porter, posts that were only given to trusted courtiers whom he knew well. If he could not depend on them, then he could depend on no one. Needless to say, Henry relied on spies to make absolutely certain of his officers' loyalty. One of these agents was a certain John Flamank, the deputy governor's son-in-law. (He was also the brother of Thomas Flamank, the lawyer who had been executed for his part in the Cornish rebellion of 1497.)

A secret report by Flamank, written in 1504, must have made uncomfortable reading for the king. It provides a rare insight into just how worried many Englishmen of standing were about the succession to the throne, even those who were most loyal to the king. It also reveals that a substantial proportion of Henry VII's subjects heartily disliked their ruler. Even now the Tudor dynasty had not yet been securely established and some important people were taking Edmund de la Pole very seriously indeed.

The report concerns a meeting held at Calais. In attendance was the treasurer, Sir Hugh Conway, who had fought on Henry's side at Bosworth and later been treasurer of Ireland. Another of those present was the deputy governor, Sir Richard Nanfan of Trethewell in Cornwall, Flamank's father-in-law. 'A very grave and ancient knight'[2], Nanfan was born in 1445, had also fought for Henry at Bosworth and led several important diplomatic missions to Spain. (He employed a chaplain, a clever young man called Thomas Wolsey.) Also present at the meeting were Sir Sampson Norton, the master porter, who had been Master of the Ordinance, William Nanfan, who was probably Richard's brother, and Flamank himself. Conway made them swear not to reveal what they were going to discuss to anybody else, except 'to the king's grace if need shall require'.

Conway began by warning Sir Richard that he was in grave danger and should thank God he had so far escaped, adding that he knew the identity of the men sent to murder the deputy governor and who was behind them. Naturally, Nanfan wanted to know at once who they were, but Conway said he would tell him later. Everybody present had enemies at Calais, he explained, especially among those who had secured their posts through the influence of the Lord Chamberlain, Lord Daubeney. 'I and master porter [are] as far into the dance as ye be.' The only possible reason for their enmity that he could think of – he suggested with a perhaps assumed naïveté – was that 'we follow the king's pleasure'.

Conway then hinted that Lord Daubeney's loyalty to the dynasty might be suspect – 'hard it is to know men's minds if God should send a sudden change'. Sir Richard broke in at this point, to say that he would swear on the sacrament that the chamberlain (who had also fought for Henry at Bosworth) was as loyal to the king as any man living. Sir Sampson Norton agreed with him. Nanfan conceded, however, that Giles Daubeney had been very 'shlake' (slack) on at least one occasion, when he had failed to disperse the Cornish rebels of 1499 before they reached Kent, a failure that angered Henry.

After further discussion, Sir Hugh was forced to retract and to admit that 'my lord chamberlain . . . loveth the king as well as any man living'. He added, however, that 'it hath been seen that change of worlds hath caused change of mind'. Perhaps he was afraid that he might be replaced by one of Daubeney's numerous protégés.

What he really wanted to talk about was something more serious still. He went on to remind the meeting that 'the king's grace is but a weak man and sickly, not likely to be long lived', and only recently had fallen dangerously ill at his manor of Wanstead in Surrey. At the time, Sir Hugh had found himself 'among many great personages', who were discussing what would happen should Henry die. He did not give the meeting their names, but he recalled how 'some of them spoke of my lord of Buckingham, saying that he was a noble man and would be a royal ruler', reported Flamank. 'Others there were that spoke, he said, likewise of your traitor, Edmund de la Pole, but none of them, he said, spoke of my lord prince' – by this Sir Hugh meant the late Prince Arthur.

Clearly, the 'great personages' who were cited by the treasurer remembered all too well how Edward V had been turned off the throne and murdered when he was twelve. (After twenty years the late Richard of Gloucester's coup still cast a very long shadow.) In 1504, the new heir to the throne, the Duke of York – the future Henry VIII – at thirteen was only a little younger. His younger brother Edmund had died only recently so that, apart from his widowed father, he was the sole surviving member of a dynasty which might easily be supposed to be on the edge of extinction.

When Sir Sampson asked him if he had told the king, Conway asked to be allowed to finish. Since his arrival at Calais, he continued, he had repeated what he had just said to Sir Nicholas Vaux, lieutenant of Guisnes and to Sir Anthony Browne, lieutenant of the castle at Calais. Both had given him the same answer: they felt safe enough in their fortresses 'and should be sure to make their peace how so ever the world turn'. The entire meeting then vehemently insisted that Conway should tell the king.

'If you knew King Harry, our master, as I do, you would beware how . . . you broke to him . . . any such matters, for he would take it to be said but of envy, ill will and malice,' replied Sir Hugh. He then explained how this sort of thing had got him into trouble before. In 1486, hearing in confidence from a friend that Richard III's former henchman Lord Lovell, in sanctuary at Colchester, was plotting mischief, he had immediately told Sir Reginald Bray, who had brought him to the king. When Henry asked him to name his source, Conway had refused because he had been sworn to secrecy by his informant, so that his warning only served to irritate the king.

Sir Richard Nanfan reluctantly agreed that Henry was a little too prone to question warnings. He recalled that when he and Sir Sampson reported their suspicions about Sir James Tyrell – the murderer of the Princes in the Tower, who had recently been executed as a de la Pole supporter – the council refused to believe them, saying they were motivated by malice. When Nanfan had written to the king that Sir Robert Clifford was going round Calais insisting that Perkin Warbeck was Edward IV's son – 'Never words went colder to my heart than they did' – Henry had demanded proof from Sir Richard, who made Clifford repeat it in front of the town marshal, 'Else I had like to be put to a great plunge' – by which he means he would probably have been hanged. The meeting was forced to admit that Conway would need much firmer evidence for his allegations.

Sir Hugh told the meeting that each and every one of them was in very grave danger. They did not have strongholds where they could take refuge (like Vaux or Browne), while they had too many enemies in Calais 'that will be glad to destroy and murder us all'. Moreover, it had been written that Henry's reign would last no longer than Edward IV's – which had been little more than twenty-two years – but did not specify his source.

Terrified the conversation might be reported to the king, Conway's hearers angrily refused to believe the prophecy, protesting their loyalty to Henry VII and the Tudors. Norton told him to burn the book in which the prophesy was written, adding that he hoped its writer would come to a bad end. 'I pray you, leave off this prophesying about the king,' said Sir Richard, who added that Conway was talking about things he himself had never heard of before. 'My prayer is that I live day neither hour longer than the king's grace, and [that] his children shall have and enjoy the realm of England.'

In response, Conway insisted that he was only mentioning such matters for the good of the king and his children, as well as for the safety of Calais. Nothing would ever be achieved without open and honest discussion. There could be no security so long as 'The Lady Luse' was in the castle: 'for the castle is the key of this town: he that is therin being of a contrary mind may let men enough in one night to destroy us all while we shall be in our beds sleeping'. Elizabeth Lucy – 'The Lady Luse' – was the wife of Sir Anthony Browne, lieutenant of the castle or citadel of Calais. A niece of the late Warwick the Kingmaker (her father, the Marquess Montagu, had been killed at the battle of Barnet in 1471), she had her own ideas about the succession. Once King Henry was dead, continued Conway, 'she being in the castle here and Edmund de la Pole her cousin at his liberty . . . she would help him in his cause with all her power and . . . let him come into this town by the postern [gate] of the castle, to the destruction of us all'.

Sir Hugh was saying that even now – nearly twenty years after Bosworth – Calais remained full of irreconcilable Yorkists who had never accepted the Tudor regime. He and his colleagues must never relax their guard in case King Henry should die unexpectedly. He also added that Calais was on the opposite side of the Channel to Kent, where he knew Suffolk had powerful supporters, such as Sir Richard Guildford.

Sir Richard Nanfan declared unctuously – for the third time and no doubt for the record – that he prayed to God he would not live to see the king's death, but whatever happened they must ensure that Calais stayed in the hands of 'my lord prince'. With luck they could 'destroy all the captains and ringleaders that be of ill and contrary mind'. It should be easy enough to manage the others.

Flamank then summarizes everything he has so far reported, while insisting that the Nanfans and Norton could all give the king a much better account of the discussion. He undermines his credibility, however, by adding that he has heard both Norton and William Nanfan mention that Sir Hugh Conway had said several times that there would be no more popes in Rome after the present one, and no more kings in Ireland after Henry VII. He finishes by describing a conversation in which the treasurer confided to him how he had suggested to both Sir Richard and Norton that, since it was so difficult to find out what was happening in England, it would be a good idea to employ a reliable man 'to lie about the court . . . he may all times send us [news] how the world goeth'. Conway was ready to pay half the cost, 'for God knoweth how suddenly a change may [be]fall'.

Without doubt, the report was deliberately biased against Sir Hugh Conway, perhaps an attempt by Flamank and Norton to secure his dismissal. He is portrayed as hopelessly unbal-lanced, to the point of hysteria, while references to his dislike of Lord Daubeney may have been invented to cause bad blood. Conceivably, Sir Richard Nanfan, who made all those carefully noted professions of loyalty, was the document's real author, even if he did not write it himself.

What made the report convincing was that during the pre-vious year Sir Richard Guildford had been denounced by another spy as ready to welcome Suffolk. A former controller of the household, Guildford had been with Henry in Brittany and fought for him at Bosworth. Although probably unfounded, the accusation was given just a little substance by his being heavily in debt and facing ruin. The king gave him the benefit of the doubt, however, although in 1505 he had him arrested and sent to Fleet prison for not keeping proper accounts when Master of the Ordnance. Guildford's career was over. Next year he went on pilgrimage to Jerusalem where he died. Reservations about his loyalty may well have had something to do with his downfall.

When the reliability of key supporters such as Guildford was in doubt, it is no wonder Henry VII went in fear of Suffolk.

# 16

# Winter 1505–6:
# An Ill Wind

'And then it was agreed between the King and the Duke
of Burgoyne that Edmund de la Pole should be sent home
again, and so he was.'

*Chronicle of the Grey Friars of London*[1]

Even before the deterioration in Henry VII's physical health, a
lack of mental equilibrium could be discerned. As already suggested, one symptom was a feverish obsession with Edmund
de la Pole. It appears that his secret agents, carefully briefed,
had been in touch with the White Rose, doing their best to
persuade him to come home. No doubt they used every induce-
ment, promising that all would be forgiven. In his wretchedness,
Edmund convinced himself that this was possible. After all, the
Emperor Maximilian had suggested it, assuring him he would
work for such an outcome. Towards the end of January 1506 he
made up his mind to negotiate with the king. A stream of pom-
pously phrased letters shows that he thought he was negotiating
from a position of strength and could dictate terms.

On 28 January 'the right excellent prince, My Lord Edmund, Duke of Suffolk', as he styled himself, solemnly commissioned his trusty and well-beloved servants, his steward Thomas Killingworth and John Griffiths, to go to King Henry and inform him of their master's wishes. His father's duchy was to be restored to him, together with all his father's estates, and also the town of Leighton Buzzard which Edward IV had forced the family to lease to the canons of Windsor. His wife, his daughter and his brother Richard were to recover all their legal rights. His brother William de la Pole was to be set at liberty, as well as every gentleman who had been imprisoned on his account. Sir George Neville's lands were to be restored to him. Edmund also asked Henry to help him recover his liberty should Philip try and keep him a prisoner by force. However, at the time he wrote his letters, Edmund was unaware of what had happened to his gaoler, the archduke.[2]

At the beginning of the month, Archduke Philip had set off by sea for Spain. Heir to the Habsburg domains and the Holy Roman Empire, and – as Duke of Burgundy – ruler of the Low Countries, he had married Princess Juanna – Katherine of Aragon's elder sister – who was the heiress to the Spanish throne. Since the death of his mother-in-law Queen Isabella, he had called himself King of Castile, much to the fury of his father-in-law, Ferdinand of Aragon. The archduke was determined to visit the country, however, and take possession of his wife's inheritance. His fleet sailed from Zealand with great pomp: when they passed Calais at night, the ships were lit by flaming torches, their guns firing salutes and their trumpeters sounding. But while still in the Channel a fierce storm blew up, steadily mounting in intensity until Philip's fleet was driven off course. Each vessel had to run for safety before the wind.

In England, the worst tempest within living memory began at noon on 15 January 1506, 'the hideous wind which endured upon an xi days following, more or less in continual blowing'.[3]

In London it ripped tiles off roofs, demolished entire houses and toppled the weathercock off the steeple of old St Paul's cathedral. It was far worse at sea. Although her cannon were thrown overboard, for a moment Philip's ship went gunwale under, while he was knocked off his feet by a huge wave and had to cling to the rigging. Eventually she struggled into Melcombe Regis in Dorset, opposite Weymouth. The archduke was lucky to escape with his life. A novice sailor, he had suffered miserably and insisted on going ashore to recuperate, despite his courtiers' warnings.

According to Polydore Vergil, on learning of Philip's arrival Henry VII was delighted, 'scarcely able to believe his luck when he realized that divine providence had given him the means of getting his hands on Edmund de la Pole, Earl of Suffolk, who had been the leader of the conspiracy against him a few years previously'.[4]

He immediately sent the Earl of Arundel to bring Philip to London, with an escort of 300 men-at-arms bearing torches, as it was a hard winter and the roads were covered in snow. The archduke was the king's prisoner, however sumptuously he might be entertained and despite being made a Knight of the Garter. Henry had a well-deserved name for being the toughest bargainer in Europe, and eventually Philip signed a treaty of alliance, which ended the latest commercial dispute between England and Flanders with an agreement so favourable to England that it became known in the Low Countries as the Evil Treaty – the *Intercursus Malus*. Above all, the archduke reluctantly agreed to hand over Edmund de la Pole.

The king agreed to do much more than spare Edmund's life. Adrian de Croy (one of Archduke Philip's household) told the emperor that Henry had given his master a written promise 'sealed with his own seal' that the earl should be pardoned unconditionally and that his estates would be restored to him.[5] Venetian sources confirm this. But by pure chance the promise disappeared, after being entrusted to a man who was apparently poisoned by King Ferdinand's ambassador in Flanders – for reasons that had nothing to do with Henry.

There was no question of the archduke being allowed to leave until Suffolk had been handed over. As quickly as possible, Philip's officers went to Mechlin, where by now the earl was confined, and on 16 March he was brought to Calais. According to Vergil, Edmund was not especially worried, confident that Philip would soon persuade Henry to forgive him and give back his estates. Escorted across the Channel to Dover a week later by Sir John Wiltshire and six men-at-arms in full armour from the Calais garrison, the White Rose was at once taken to London where his illusions were immediately dispelled. He disappeared into a cell at the Tower, probably tethered by a chain, despite Henry's promises and even though Vergil described it as 'honourable confinement'.[6]

The king ordered Edmund to be interrogated, hinting at torture if he did not cooperate. In the event, he gave full details about his followers and any steps they had taken to forward his cause. Among names he supplied were those of Lord Bergavenny and Sir Thomas Green of Greens Norton in Northamptonshire, who were arrested and taken to the Tower for questioning. Nothing could be proved, however, because Edmund had not accused them of plotting but merely included them among his supporters. Although Bergavenny was soon released, Sir Thomas fell ill, dying in the Tower. Vergil comments that King Henry suspected that in both cases the earl was not telling the truth – conceivably, he named them for the sake of revenge, but it is more likely he did so to give the impresssion he was cooperating and to avoid torture.[7]

Suffolk implicated two other magnates, however, whose treatment was so severe as to imply there was evidence they had been ready to rise for him. The *Chronicle of Calais* tells us what happened to the Marquess of Dorset and Lord William Courtenay, 'which were both of kin to the late Queen Elizabeth and her blood' and had been in the Tower for a long time. In

October 1507 the pair were taken across the Channel, where they were 'kept prisoners in the castle of Calais as long as King Henry VII lived and should have been put to death if he had lived longer'.[8]

For by then the king was a very sick man indeed. During the last three years of his life he fell ill annually, always in the spring, a progressive collapse in his physical health that was accompanied by an unmistakeable decline in mental powers. As early as 1502 Vergil noticed he was treating his subjects much more harshly and saying he wanted to frighten them into loyalty.[9]

Despite the apparent security of his regime, with the current White Rose firmly under lock and key, Henry did not feel safe. There are indications that, after decades of fighting off Yorkist pretenders, his paranoia had grown so intense that he began to see his own son and heir as a potential rival. Ironically, the hope of the Tudors was kept under close surveillance, guarded so strictly that he was all but under lock and key. (Perhaps his father, no mean judge of character, realized that his son was a very dangerous young man.)

The end of Henry VII's reign was a thoroughly unhappy time for England and not just for the king. Driven by increasing avarice, Henry used the bonds he had developed to deter poten-tial rebels (ruinous fines hanging over their heads) to screw money out of all and sundry. By now, his principal ministers were two ruthless young careerists, Sir Richard Empson and Edmund Dudley, both brutal extortioners. 'As for Empson and Dudley's mills, they did grind more than ever, so that it was a strange thing to see what golden showers poured down on the King's treasury,' comments Bacon. 'Belike he thought to leave his son a kingdom and such a mass of treasure as he might choose his greatness where he would.'[10]

Although the rich of whatever political hue suffered – blame-less country gentlemen with large estates and rich city aldermen were favourite targets – there are indications that those who had long-standing Yorkist links were singled out in particular. Dudley, awaiting execution after Henry's death, wrote a 'Petition', citing victims of the late king's extortion. Among them were the Earl of Northumberland whose father's loyalty had always been suspect; the Abbot of Furness, a friend and neighbour of Sir Thomas Broughton; and William Catesby of Northampton, the son and heir of Richard III's henchman.[11]

Meanwhile, the fate of the Yorkist pretender, the White Rose, could not have been unhappier. At any moment he might be taken from the Tower and executed as a traitor – there was no need for a trial since he had been condemned to death during his exile. At some time in 1507 his faithful steward Killingworth sent a 'memorial' to Emperor Maximilian in which he says that, should the King of England die, then 'the lord Duke Edmund will be in the greatest danger [*maximo pericolo*]'.[12] All Europe knew that Henry VII's health had been giving cause for alarm.

The king died on 21 April 1509. He had succeeded in keeping his throne by unremitting vigilance, never able to relax for a moment and enjoy what he had won, because of the threat from the White Rose. On his deathbed, however, Henry revealed to his son that he felt guilty about certain acts of injustice that he had committed during his reign, particularly the Earl of Warwick's death, and he asked him to restore Warwick's sister Margaret to her inheritance.[13]

# PART 2

# Henry VIII and the White Rose

# 17

# Spring 1509:
# A Yorkist Tudor?

'The Rose both White and Red
In one Rose now doth grow.'

John Skelton, 'A Laud and Praise made for our
Sovereign Lord the King', 1509[1]

In a poem extolling Henry VIII's coronation, perhaps with a certain exaggeration, Thomas More spoke of a new Messiah. Yet no monarch had ascended the throne in such tranquility since Henry VI in 1422. The new ruler could claim to be the heir of York, as indeed he was in most Englishmen's eyes, and on more convincing grounds than the Tudors' dubious pretensions to represent Lancaster. 'Of Kingès line most straight his title doth record,' wrote Skelton pointedly in his own *Laud*. Hall called him the 'flower and very heir of both the said lineages', stressing his White as well as his Red Rose blood.[2]

Henry even looked like his maternal grandfather, King Edward. A handsome giant, well over six foot tall – in an age when most men were little more than five – vigorous, athletic, he possessed the same superb presence and magnetic personality. Above a long, slender throat he had a delicate, sensitive and almost girlish face framed by long, thick, auburn hair – contemporaries said it might have belonged to a pretty woman. An undistinguished portrait of 1513, which is attributed to an unknown court artist but is possibly by a French painter, shows the same, unusual, strikingly handsome looks. Yet it has to be said that his eyes are on the small side, with a bird-like watchfulness, while his odd little mouth – scarcely wider than the space between his nostrils – already has the same tight lips of later years.

In June 1509, a fortnight before his coronation, the king married his brother's widow, Katherine of Aragon. Although nearly seven years older than her new husband, she was still only twenty-four, as dignified and intelligent as she was beautiful, adaptable and sympathetic, with an instinctive understanding of her adopted country. Most of England was in ecstasies over the attractive young couple who presided over so glamorous a court. Not yet eighteen, the king gave himself up to pleasure and Queen Catherine remembered the early years of her marriage as a time of continuous feasting.

Henry's loyal chronicler Edward Hall, who captures the idyllic existence of his court at the start of his reign, writes:

> On May day then next following, in the second year of his reign His Grace being young and willing not to be idle, rose in the morning very early to fetch May or green boughs, himself fresh and richly apparelled, and clothed all his knights, squires and gentlemen in white satin, and all his Guard and Yeomen of the Crown in white sarcenet,
>
> . . . And so went every man with his bow and arrows shooting to the wood, and so repaired again to the court, every man with a green bough in his hat, and at his returning many hearing of his going a Maying were desirous to see

him shoot, for at that time His Grace shot as strong and as great a length as any in his guard. . . .

From thence the whole court removed to Windsor, [King Henry] then beginning his progress, exercising himself daily in shooting, singing, dancing, wrestling, casting of the bar, playing at the recorders, flute, virginals, and in setting of songs, making of ballads, and did set two goodly Masses, every one of them five parts, which were sung often times in his chapel and afterwards in divers other places . . . And when he came to Woking there were kept both jousts and tourneys: the rest of this progress was spent in hunting, hawking and shooting.[3]

In addition, there were banquets and also masques in the Italian fashion – the first ever staged in England.

At the same time, Henry had intellectual interests. 'You might well say he is an all round genius,' Erasmus (soon to become the most famous scholar in Europe, who had been summoned to court) told a friend. 'He never forgets to study and whenever he finds himself free from matters of state, he reads or discusses – he is very fond of discussions – with unusual courtesy and complete good temper. He seems more like a companion than a king.'[4] As well as a humanist fascinated by ancient Greece and Rome, Henry enjoyed theology, his favourite reading being the works of Thomas Aquinas.

For all the euphoria, some people saw the new king as another usurper, despite his Yorkist blood. In the absence of printed histories there was no easily accessible acccount of how the Tudors had acquired the throne, but everyone knew they were parvenus: as late as 1541 a tailor of Colchester told a bawdy story about Owain Tudor seducing Henry V's widow and founding the family fortunes.[5] In any case, older courtiers could remember Edward IV and Richard III. A question mark still hung over the dynasty.

From the start Henry was aware of this, even during the honeymoon with his subjects. Historians sometimes call Edmund de la Pole the last Yorkist pretender, yet it was never the king's view. Although at this stage he seemed the ideal Renaissance Man, cultivated and learned, he was haunted by a terror of rivals, real or imaginary, that persisted until the last days of his life. Had he sensed his vulnerability when a child? Had he read Flamank's report? Or others in the same vein?

His uneasiness showed itself at once. Although there is a striking contrast between the young Henry VIII and the monster he became in middle life, they were the same man – highly strung, moody and pathologically suspicious. (In more ways than one he resembled Edward IV who killed his brother Clarence in a butt of malmsey, had his brother-in-law the Duke of Exeter thrown overboard at sea and ordered Henry VI's murder.) Admittedly the new king took some time before getting into his stride and turning into England's Ivan the Terrible. But the two hated ministers who had levied his father's taxes, Dudley and Empson, were immediately thrown to the wolves. Charged with treason, they were tried and condemend on false evidence, then executed, although in law they had committed no crime – the first of Henry's legal murders.

When a general pardon was proclaimed on 30 April, eighty people were omitted.[6] The royal clemency did not extend to the White Rose. At the top of the list of those excluded were Edmund de la Pole and his brothers Richard and William. Among the others were Sir George Neville and old John Taylor, that steady Yorkist, who had been one of the brains behind the 'Duke of York' and who, according to the pardon, was 'still in ward in the Tower'.

The Yeomen of the Guard were reinforced by a new force, the Band of Pensioners or Spears. (It still exists, as the Honourable Corps of Gentlemen at Arms.) 'This year [1509], the King ordained fifty Gentlemen to be Spears, every [one] of them to have an archer, a demi-lance and a costrel, and every spear to have three great horses to be attendant on his person.' (A demi-lance was a foot soldier with a half-pike, a costrel a servant with a sword.) Unlike the yeomen, the Spears were recruited exclusively from the upper gentry as their equipment was so expensive: 'they and their horses were apparelled and trapped in cloth of gold [and] silver and goldsmiths' work, and their servants [were] richly apparelled also'.[7] Although on campaign they served as a military unit, off duty these gentlemen were indistinguishable from other courtiers while forming a bodyguard in the modern sense – ready to deal with any would-be assassin.

Similarly, Knights of the Garter were asked to replace their oath to defend the priestly College of Windsor. Instead, they took a new oath in which they swore to fight for Henry's 'honours, quarrels, rights, dominions and cause' – a phrase that tacitly included his claim to the throne against pretenders.[8]

Insecurity can be seen, too, in the way he tried to win his Yorkist kindred's support during these early years. The Earl of Warwick's sister, Margaret Plantagenet, had been married off to the son of a half-sister of Henry Tudor's mother, Margaret Beaufort, who insisted on the match, although it would have been wiser to send the girl into a nunnery. Her husband was Sir Richard Pole of Medmenham in Buckinghamshire (no relation of the de la Poles), a committed Tudor henchman, who had died in 1504, leaving her in reduced circumstances.

According to Margaret's son, Reginald Pole, Henry VIII felt guilty about Warwick's death. Almost as soon as he came to the throne he gave Margaret an annuity of £100. In 1513 he even granted her petition to reverse Warwick's attainder, presumably after instructing her to petition, and then created her Countess of Salisbury (one of her brother's titles) in her own right, restoring many of her Neville mother's family estates. He did so, however, on condition she forgave any injuries done to her by his father, by which he could only have meant her brother's killing. Margaret's eldest son was later created Lord Montague, a Neville title. In 1516 she was invited to become one of the godmothers to the Princess Mary, Henry's daughter, and shortly after, appointed governess of the princess's household.

Although omitted from the general pardon, the husband of Catherine Plantagenet (one of the late Queen Elizabeth's sisters) Lord William Courtenay – who by now had become Earl of Devon – was soon released from the Tower. He did not enjoy his inheritance for long, dying in 1511. However, his son Edward, a grandchild of Edward IV, was created Marquess of Exeter. Another supporter of Suffolk to be set free was the Marquess of Dorset, whose marquisate was restored to him.

Yet one day Henry was to turn on his White Rose cousins. Despite the amiability he showed during the early years of his reign, he had already revealed his merciless streak. A well-known Yorkist, John Parleben, putting too much trust in rumours of the new ruler's good nature, had unwisely come home and tried to obtain a pardon. Described by the Privy Council in October 1510 as 'one of the most errant traitors and railers against the King's father beyond the seas', he was immediately arrested, Henry giving express orders that Parleben should never receive a pardon even if one had already been issued and sealed.[9] Presumably, he swiftly ended up on the gallows.

Eager to cut a figure on the European stage, Henry hoped to revive the Hundred Years' War and make good his Plantagenet ancestors' claim to the throne of France. A first expedition of 12,000 troops to conquer Guienne in 1512 ended in abject failure. Leaving the English soldiers in their camp on the coast of Guipuzcoa, King Ferdinand cynically used them to distract the French while he conquered southern Navarre, and they succumbed to the local wine before being struck down by dysentery. Finally they mutinied, insisting on being shipped home.

Nevertheless, encouraged by his new minister, Thomas Wolsey, at midsummer 1513 Henry VIII invaded France with an impressively large army that included the Yeomen and the new Bodyguard, who both fought as units on the campaign. Marching out from Calais, in August he routed a small French force that his cavalry caught by surprise, so swiftly that the engagement was called the 'battle of the Spurs'. He went on to capture the little town of Thérouanne and in September, after a siege lasting only a week, the city of Tournai.

The Scots took advantage of Henry's absence to invade Northern England, but the seventy-year-old Earl of Surrey annihilated them at Flodden, James IV himself being among the dead, along with the better part of the Scottish nobility. (In reward, Surrey was restored to his family dukedom of Norfolk.) Delighted by his own successes in France – however modest they may have been, they were the first English victories over the French for nearly a century – the king came home in triumph, more popular than ever with his subjects.

Yet when Louis XII had responded to the English invasion by giving Edmund de la Pole's brother Richard an important military command, Henry had feared an anti-Tudor coup were he himself to be taken prisoner. Just before crossing to France, he gave orders for Edmund's execution. There was no need for a trial as an Act of Attainder had condemned the earl to death in 1502. Taken from his cell to Tower Hill, he was discreetly beheaded on 4 May 1513.[10]

Edmund's elimination prepared the way for another, more formidable, White Rose.

# 18

# 1513–21:
# A King over the Water

'But Richard his brother, being an expert and politic man, so craftily conveyed and so wisely ordered himself in this stormy tempest that he was not attrapped, either with net or snare.'

Edward Hall, *The Union of the two Noble and Illustre Famelies of Lancaste and Yorke*[1]

Foreign envoys were charmed by the friendly way Henry VIII gossiped and joked with them, as a flattered Venetian embassy reported in 1515. But roars of laughter and back-slapping were a good way of concealing his real thoughts. Among these was a lasting obsession with murdering Edmund de la Pole's brother Richard. Frustratingly, royal agents found that they were pursuing a very elusive quarry indeed.

This obscure cousin frightened the king as much as Warbeck had frightened his father. Richard had been in exile since 1500 when he was a youth of about nineteen. Few Englishmen can have set eyes on him, while the tenants and retainers on the old de la Pole lands in East Anglia and the Thames Valley had long ago been given new lords. Yet beyond any question, the king feared Richard, convinced there must still be a strong Yorkist underground, the size of which, characteristically, he overestimated.

Left behind at Aix-la-Chapelle in 1504 as security for the debts of Edmund (not then been caught by Henry VII), in a desperate letter, Richard begged his brother 'humbly' ['ombully'] to send him money.[2] In another overwrought letter, he said he was pestered in the streets of Aix, not only by Martyn, landlord at *Le Pot*, but also by other creditors. The king had written to the burgesses, saying that if they handed him over, he would pay well. People were warning him not to go into the streets because if he was murdered, Henry would pay his killers, although Richard suspected he had been told this to frighten him into returning to England. He swore that if Edmund could get him out of the mess, 'You will find me your loyal brother, come what may'.[3] Two days later, Edmund, who had no means of helping him, told Killingworth that 'my brother [is] like to be delivered to King Henry, or else to be driven by force to forsake me, or else to be slain in the town of Aachen by the bourgeois'.[4] In January 1506 Richard was still writing in the same vein: 'And here I lie in great pain and poverty for your grace, and no manner of comfort I have of your grace or none other: nor none is coming, so far as I can see. Wherefore I pray God to send me out of this world.'[5] After Edmund had been handed over, Richard's situation seemed hopeless. Almost miraculously, he was saved by the recently appointed Bishop of Liège, Everard de la Marck (later Cardinal de Bouillon), who paid his debts and sent him as far out of Henry's reach as possible, to the Hungarian court at Buda. Unlike Edmund or Killingworth, the bishop knew how to make the most of the de la Poles' kinship with the late Queen Anne of Hungary who, as a Foix-Candale, had been the young man's cousin. Arriving in August 1506, he was warmly welcomed by Ladislas II and given a pension.

The de la Poles' steward was still at Aix, nominally in Richard's service, and in August 1506 Thomas Killingworth of London, 'gentilman', was offered a full pardon by Henry VII, despite his recent attainder. It stipulated that 'whenever the King shall please to examine him alone or cause him to be examined by someone of his council upon any matters concerning the King's Majesty or the security of his realm, he shall declare all.' What Henry wanted was the steward's cooperation in identifying and tracking down Yorkists at home and abroad – including Richard de la Pole.[6]

Killingworth ignored the offer, however. The following month he obtained a passport from Everard de la Mark to stay at Liège and other cities under the bishop's control, escorted by four servants armed with swords, daggers and lances. He needed a passport so that he could accept Richard's invitation to visit Hungary, arriving in March 1507. Richard promptly sent him to Constance, where an Imperial Diet was meeting, to ask for the emperor's protection for the de la Poles.

The steward wrote in dog-Latin to the emperor, begging him to secure Suffolk's release, mentioning Henry's offer but swearing he would stay a faithful servant. 'I await a reply, Lord Caesar.'[7] Reminding the Emperor Maximilian of his promise to help Suffolk and his brother, Killingworth says, 'I have served my said lord duke for 20 years, which is no small period of time.' He adds, 'And to serve my said lord duke I have left wife, friends and possessions, which may no doubt look contrary to nature, yet the ill fortune of the said lord duke grieves me.'[8] Later, he told Maximilian that the French might try and persuade King Ladislas to hand over Richard to them, for use as a bargaining counter with England. He suggested that Richard might be hidden in some Austrian castle.[9]

Killingworth sent a final letter to Maximilian in early summer 1507, saying he owed 53 florins to his landlord at Aix, besides 12 florins to others. 'I am ill, in the greatest possible want and poverty as I have no money left and do not know where to turn for it except to Your Sacred Majesty.' He also warned the emperor against Sir Edward Wingfield, who had recently arrived at the imperial court. After a last plea for money Killingworth disappeared, perhaps dying as a beggar on the streets of Aix. (Somehow Henry's agents got hold of his correspondence.) He had given everything for the Suffolk brothers – they must have possessed some fine qualities to inspire such loyalty.

For young Richard, bred in East Anglia and the Thames Valley, Hungary and its Magyar language were no doubt bewildering – presumably he communicated in French or Latin. Tudor agents soon learned of his arrival and his links with the Foix-Candale: he had become more dangerous, even though he could not be an immediate threat while his brother Edmund resided in the Tower. Henry VII made repeated demands for him to be sent back to England, but by now he was a favourite of King Ladislas, who refused. (Normally, known as 'King All Right' by the nobles, he agreed to everything.) De la Pole's pension was paid until Ladislas's death in 1516. His protector was also King of Poland and Bohemia, and it is possible that Richard accompanied him to Prague in February 1509, while he probably went to Maximilian's court at Freiburg – late in 1510 the emperor wrote to Margaret of Savoy (his regent in Flanders), urging her to try and persuade the English king to pardon 'the young Suffolk'.

It is likely that, by then, Richard was with the French army in Italy. Because of the war between France and Spain, military skill was a sure way to Louis XII's favour, and Richard may have served under his fire-eating cousin Odet de Foix-Grailly, Vicomte de Lautrec. If so, he experienced some very fierce fighting. Judging from Louis's later confidence in him, the tough young Englishman had been noticed by the king who realized he was a born soldier. We know for certain that in 1512 he served in Navarre, a little kingdom stretching across the Pyrenees from Béarn to Tudela, with his Foix cousin Katherine III as queen, which had been invaded by Ferdinand of Aragon. Those who fought in the campaign to restore her included some of the period's most famous soldiers, such as the Chevalier Bayard. They were unsuccessful, however, and within a few weeks it became clear that Katherine had lost all her territories south of the Pyrenees.

When hostilities broke out between France and England the same year, a Venetian reported that Louis XII was planning to restore 'the son of the deceased sister of the King [Richard III] killed by the late King', by which he meant Edmund de la Pole, who was still alive.[10] He did not mean Richard, as is sometimes supposed, since he could not usurp his elder brother's right to the throne; to do so would deny the law of succession on which the de la Pole claim was based.[11] However, Louis gave Richard a pension of 36,000 crowns and a command. It seems he was in touch with his brother in the Tower. During 1512 a French spy at the English court was said to have brought back letters from the Suffolk family, which may mean messages from Edmund. The following year a Milanese wrote that Edmund de la Pole had been executed for corresponding with Richard about organizing a rebellion.[12] About this time, Henry VIII began to worry about the presence in France of 'our rebel Richard de la Pole'.[13]

Richard had cut an impressive figure during the Navarrese campaign, forming friendships with the Dauphin François and the Chevalier Bayard, and leading a regiment of landsknechts, freebooters marching to shawms and drums, followed by wives and children, thieves and prostitutes, robbing and raping as they went. Always in a state of semi-mutiny, they were not easy to command, but the White Rose knew how to get the best out of them. 'Your rebel, Richard de la Pole, was in the said wars, captain of the Almains, where there your said rebel and his company received most hurt and loss of men than any other,' the English ambassador John Stile reported to Henry VIII in January 1513.[14]

Richard began calling himself Duke of Suffolk and White Rose in the summer of 1513, after his brother's death when

Louis recognized him as King of England. Although he fought against his countrymen at the siege of Therouanne in July, commanding a force 6,000 strong, a handful of Yorkists joined him. Among these was the 'Bastard of Stanley', the son of Henry VII's chamberlain, whom no one in England dared to employ because he had spent fourteen years in the Tower. Richard gave him a job, as gentleman porter at twenty crowns a year. In January 1514 Cardinal Bainbridge, in Rome, reported that he had arrested two members of his household, one of them being Reginald Chambre formerly of the Calais garrison, for planning to join Richard.[15]

In February 1514 King Henry bestowed the duchy of Suffolk on his favourite, Charles Brandon. If a gesture of friendship towards an old friend, it was still more an act of spite, even of fear. For by now he had come to appreciate that the latest White Rose was likely to be much more dangerous than his brother Edmund.

'The French King this year [1514] appointed to Richard de la Pole, traitor of England and banished the realm, 12,000 lanceknights to keep Normandy, and also to enter into England and conquer,' says Hall.[16] Spending so much money on such a large force means that Louis believed that an invasion could succeed, and that he had real respect for the White Rose's ability as a soldier. Richard took his troops to Normandy, but when they began terrorizing the locals he moved them to St Malo in Brittany. John, Duke of Albany, the Scottish regent who was in France, agreed to welcome them to his own country from where they could invade across the Border. By June everything was ready and it appeared that another battle of Stoke lay ahead. This time the Yorkist army consisted of veteran professional soldiers under a battle-tested commander. All that they would face were inexperienced levies under the Duke of Norfolk (Surrey), whose recent victory at Flodden had been over ill-disciplined and badly led opponents.

Richard was about to sail when suddenly King Louis made peace with Henry VIII. The invasion was abandoned and the

White Rose had to leave France. Louis's solution was to send him to Metz, just over the border, while the Dauphin gave him a large sum of money. Metz was an imperial city within Lorraine so King Louis wrote to its council asking them to welcome Richard. When he arrived there in September 1514 – with sixty horsemen and a guard of honour sent by the Duke of Lorraine – he was made a citizen, and a local gentleman, the Chevalier Baudoiche, lent him an elegant mansion for his residence, a 'pleasure house' which was named Passe Temps.

When Louis died early in 1515, Richard's French pension was confirmed by the new King of France, his old crony the Dauphin – now Francis I. Richard continued to live at Metz, then a beautiful city, where he gathered a small court including musicians who had played for his brother, and who were clothed in a livery of blue and grey. The most interesting was a singer called Petrus Alamire, who was also a music scribe with a highly successful business in Flanders patronized by several European courts. Another old friend of his brother Edmund with whom he re-established contact was a Flemish merchant named Claus Bakker, who became a useful agent for the Yorkist cause.

From Metz Richard could keep an eye on what was happening in northern France, where the English still occupied Therouanne and Tournai. In February 1515, the garrison at Tournai, led by a Davy Appowell, mutinied over arrears of pay, threatening to lynch their commander, old Sir Sampson Norton from Calais. Order was restored by Lord Mountjoy, but there were too many mutineers to punish.[17] On 25 February, accompanied only by his cook and a page, Richard had left Metz secretly, riding from dawn to dusk. The agents thought he did so from fear, yet could not explain what he was afraid of.[18] Fear seems unlikely, since soon he was back at Metz. As his wild gallop brought him within a day's ride of Tournai, the answer may be that he had hoped to take command of the mutineers, but that order had been restored before he reached the town.

Just as his father's agents had done with Perkin, Henry VIII's spies ferreted out all they could about the new White Rose. Their employer must have been disturbed to learn that Richard was treated as an equal by princes and liked by his troops, and that his Foix-Candale cousins were able to open so many doors for him. More worrying still, was his friendship with King Francis.

Although Henry VIII prided himself on his piety and morality, he had no reservations about a murder, deciding that assassination – quick, discreet, final – was the best way in which to dispose of his rival. A small, folding crossbow (easily hidden in a cloak) should do the job, or a poisoned stiletto, or even a gun: only recently the 'great' Earl of Kildare had been killed in an ambush by a bullet from an arquebus. There was a slight problem however, which was finding a reliable assassin.

Sir Edward Poynings and the Earl of Worcester (Lord Chamberlain) were put in charge of the operation, reporting to Wolsey. That men of such high rank were given the task shows the importance Henry set on it. Sir Thomas Spinelly, English ambassador in Flanders, bribed a member of Richard's household to spy on his master – the singing scribe, Petrus Alamire, who signed his reports with the musical notation '*La mi re*'.

Soon an assassin was hired, a petty Flemish nobleman called Percheval de Matte. Stalking his quarry, he sent in detailed reports on the White Rose's activities: how he exercised his horses in the fields outside Metz with the local gentry, hunting the hare in all weathers, how he was nearly arrested over a huge debt to a German lord but rescued by a loan from a prince of Lorraine.[19] Despite all this impressive intelligence work, Matte made no attempt to kill Richard so Poynings engaged another professional cuthroat, a soldier called Captain Symonde Francoyse, yet he, too, failed to deliver.[20]

In February 1516 the French authorities caught an English desperado, Robert Latimer, who confessed to being sent by King Henry to assassinate Richard. Widely reported, the incident did more than reveal Henry's readiness to commit murder.

It showed all Europe how terrified he was of a rival whom in public he pretended to despise.

These attempts on the White Rose's life should be seen against a background of growing hostility between France and England. In 1515 Francis I had won a stunning victory over the Swiss at Marignano, conquering the duchy of Milan which then became part of France. Although Maximilian and his grandson, the new Habsburg King of Spain (the future Emperor Charles V), were horrified, Henry VIII's attempts to humble the French resulted in nothing but a waste of English money: he was betrayed or let down in turn by the Swiss and Charles V. The new situation enhanced Richard de la Pole's standing as pretender.

Evidence of support for the Yorkist cause emerged at Tournai in February 1516 when a leader of the recent mutiny, John Packman, was brought back to England after being caught in Flanders. He had been with the White Rose or people close to him. Questioned by Lord Mountjoy, Packman said that Richard was in touch with East Anglian merchants – men from Suffolk and Norfolk, who remembered when the de la Poles were the region's leading magnates. Packman added that Richard had gone to meet the Black Band, a regiment of German land-sknechts in French service led by Robert de la Marck, known as the 'Devil', who was a kinsman of his old friend the Bishop of Liège. A few months later, Packman was duly hanged and gutted as a traitor – more for his Yorkism than for mutiny.[21]

There were rumours early in 1516 that the White Rose was preparing to invade, with not only French backing but also Spanish, Scottish and Danish. (His agent Claus Bakker was at the court of the new King of Denmark, Christian II.) When Francis I came back from Italy in March he invited Richard to visit him. Derick van Reydt, Richard's steward, told the banker Leonardo Frescobaldi, how warmly his master had been received by the French king and queen, and by Francis's mother, Louise of Savoy – when Richard complained of his fate, Francis promised to help him regain his throne and gave

(*right*) Henry VII as a young man, either just before or just after the beginning of his reign. Mid-sixteenth century drawing by Jacques de Boucq. (A sixteenth century copy of a contemporary sketch.) *(Bridgeman)*

(*left*) Henry VII c. 1505 when still in his forties, prematurely aged by illness and insecurity. *(Bridgeman)*

(*left*) 'Richard IV'
– Perkin Warbeck –
whom many believed
to be the Duke of York
(the younger of the
'Princes in the Tower').
*(Photo, author's collection)*

(*right*) Fra' John
Kendall, Grand Prior
of the Knights of
St John, who was
secretly accused by
his secretary of having
been in contact with
Warbeck and plotting
to murder Henry VII.
*(Photo, author's collection)*

Young, handsome and charming, c.1513. Anon. *(Bridgeman)*

## Henry VIII

In his prime. A copy at Chatsworth of Holbein's portrait in a lost fresco at the Palace of Whitehall. *(Photo, author's collection)*

Old, ill and merciless, 1540s. Portrait medal by Steven van Herryck. *(Photo, author's collection)*

Penshurst Place was a favourite residence of Henry VIII's victim, the Duke of Buckingham, and gives us some idea of his vast wealth and magnificence. *(Bridgeman)*

ET DEI SET FIDENS CHRISTI REGISQVE MINISTER CONSTANS VIR PROMPTVS PECTORE FRONTE MANV
VIX IN AMICICIA TALIS VIX NASCITVR HEROS PLVS PATRIE FIDVS PLVS PIETATIS AMANS

(*above*) Thomas Cromwell, Henry VIII's chief minister. Convinced that the White Rose families were a danger, he destroyed them in 1538 by inventing the so-called 'Exeter Conspiracy'. Early seventeenth century copy of a portrait by Holbein from The National Portrait Gallery. *(Photo, author's collection)*

(*left*) Bishop John Fisher, beheaded in 1535 for refusing to accept Henry VIII's break with Rome. He encouraged the plan to replace the king with Mary and a Yorkist king consort. *(Photo, author's collection)*

(*right*) A young Katherine of Aragon, *c.* 1504–5. Her failure to give Henry VIII a male heir heightened his sense of insecurity and fear of Yorkist conspiracies. (*The Trustees of the 9th Duke of Buccleuch's Chattels Fund*)

(*left*) The Lady Mary (Mary I) in the 1540s. Bastardized by her father, there are hints that during the 1530s she was ready to replace him on the throne and take a Yorkist husband as her consort – Reginald Pole. (*By kind permission of Viscount De L'Isle from his private collection at Penshurst Place, Kent, England*)

Cardinal Reginald Pole (1500–58), Clarence's grandson. During the 1530s the Yorkists hoped to make him king consort. Henry VIII saw Pole as a dangerous rival and sent assassins to Italy to kill him. *(Photo, author's collection)*

(*left*) Margaret Plantagenet, Countess of Salisbury. Daughter of Edward IV's brother, the Duke of Clarence, she was the last Plantagenet. In 1541 Henry VIII had her beheaded without trial as part of his campaign to exterminate the White Rose families. (*TopFoto*)

(*right*) Henry Howard, Earl of Surrey (1517–47), beheaded by Henry VIII who suspected he was planning to seize the throne – the only 'evidence' being that he had added the coat of arms of a Saxon king of England to his heraldic achievement. (*Photo, author's collection*)

him money.[22] Reports of this sort made uncomfortable reading for King Henry.

In June 1516 Sir Thomas Spinelly paid sixty gold florins to Jacques de Eesebeke, for services 'in the matter of *Blancherose*'. Jacques found lodgings overlooking Richard de la Pole's mansion at Metz, and kept him under surveillance, sending reports to Sir Thomas that must have made Tudor hair stand on end when forwarded to the king. Eesebeke described Richard riding a mule, with Francis I riding pillion behind and swearing to help him gain the English throne, and how Francis had said that a 'Marquis' (the Margrave of Brandenburg?) was eager to aid the Yorkist cause. Four French thugs paid 4,000 gold crowns by '*Blancherose*' were coming to England to set fire to Henry's palace and murder him, said Eesbeke – he knew this from a man in Richard's confidence. Also, Anthony Spynell, a 'marvellous great enemy' of the king, was receiving a salary from the French to spy on him.[23] As Sir Thomas Spinelly had a relative called Anthony – possibly the same person – this item may have embarrassed him.

No less sensational information was received by Wolsey in autumn 1516 from Alamire. He had been with Richard in Germany when his employer received a message from his steward Derick van Reydt, to say that King Francis wanted him to bring as many troops as he could find to France. Officially, these were reinforcements for the French garrison in Italy, but Alamire suspected they might be used to invade England, as Derick had confided in him at the Frankfurt fair, 'Now is the time that [the] White Rose, Duke of Suffolk, has longed for'. Alamire claimed he had done his best to dissuade his employer from invading, saying they had insufficient money and recalling what had happened to Perkin and Lincoln. 'Alamire, you tell me strange things,' had been the reaction of Richard, who added that if he asked King Henry for a pardon, as Alamire suggested, not only was he unlikely to get one but the request would cost him King Francis's friendship.[24]

In November the musician reported that Sir George Neville, his master's 'ancient friend . . . formerly Admiral of the English Sea', had joined the White Rose at Metz and was travelling with him to France. Two unknown Yorkists had visited Metz and given money to Richard before going home. Alamire also said his employer was planning to ship troops to Scotland.[25] He did not mention that there was another English knight at Metz, in Richard's household, Sir William Pounder.

It was hard for Henry's spies to keep track of Richard as he was always on the move, secretly meeting King Francis in Paris, raising troops in Germany or Switzerland, visiting Italy, or staying with Robert de la Marck. Once again they tried to kill him. In February 1517 the Earl of Worcester arrived at Tournai to coordinate operations and in the same month, English agents persuaded Sir William Pounder to desert the White Rose. Coming to Tournai, he surrendered to Worcester, saying he had been imprisoned by Richard for refusing to join him. He told all he knew in return for a pardon. While he confirmed that the White Rose was visiting Paris for discussions with Francis I (always at night), revealed details of French troop movements and identified a French spy working in England, Sir William's defection did little to alter the situation.[26]

In spring 1517 Alamire reported that Christian of Denmark had offered Richard 20,000 troops. He also said an Englishman had come with letters 'from some lords in England', but that de la Pole was suspicious and would not give him a written answer. The singer added that Thomas Stanley had been despatched to England to discover the truth about the letters, although he had not got much further than the coast.[27] This was a lie because Richard and Stanley had by now parted company, and Alamire was a double agent, who regularly sent in false information.

Angry at not being paid his wages as gentleman porter, the Bastard of Stanley had begun spying for Henry. One night Richard burst into his room with some servants, shouting, 'Thou false traitor! Long hast thou been a spy in my company – thou shalt before thou depart show who sent thee hither!' The servants bound his two great toes together with a cord which they twisted, ordering him to confess. It broke and while they were looking for another cord he escaped, finding refuge in a nearby friary. Stanley then approached Dr Cuthbert Tunstall, who was at Bruges on a diplomatic mission, offering information about the White Rose in return for a pardon and a safe conduct home. He claimed that Robert Latimer, arrested after being sent to England by Richard to contact Yorkist sympathizers, had lied about his mission. (Latimer was the assassin hired by Henry in 1516.)

Despite spending so much money on spies and informers, it became abundantly clear that King Henry's agents were unable to eliminate the White Rose. Wolsey, in overall charge of the operation, realized that he had failed dismally. He needed to find a means of placating his master, something that would distract him. Suddenly an opportunity presented itself.

# 19

# 1519–Autumn 1520: The Duke of Buckingham

'Suspicions among thoughts are like bats amongst birds: they ever fly by twilight.'

Sir Francis Bacon, *Essays – Of Suspicion*.

From the start, King Henry distrusted England's great nobles, continuing his father's policy of appointing as his ministers new men who came from modest backgrounds. Methodically, he reduced the magnates' influence in the same way that Henry VII had done, excluding them from any real power while parading them on great occasions as if they were pieces of court furniture. Like his father, he was secretly afraid that some great nobleman might suddenly rise up against him and revive the Wars of the Roses or, at the very least, might try to seize the throne should he die young.

Still hoping that Queen Katherine was going to bear him a son and heir, he cannot have failed to note the worrying rumours about a threat to an infant king north of the Border. In 1515 the Duke of Albany returned from exile in France to become Regent of Scotland for his two-year-old cousin, James V. 'Many were alarmed by the prospect, knowing how strong is the lust for power,' Vergil tells us. 'As the duke was of King James's blood and would inherit the realm should he die, there seemed to be a real risk that driven by the desire to reign he might arrange for the child's death.' One Scottish noble warned the queen that the little king's life was in danger after being put in the care of a man who desperately wanted the throne – 'entrusting a sheep to a wolf'.[1] Although in fact the duke proved to be an excellent regent, the Queen of Scots was Henry VIII's sister, and the king was aware of her concern. It was an uncomfortable reminder of how vulnerable a son of his might be in a similar situation.

Beyond any question, England's leading magnate was 'The right high and mighty prince, Edward, Duke of Buckingham, Earl of Hereford, Stafford and Northampton', as he styled himself. Edward Stafford (or Bohun, a surname he preferred) had been born in 1478 and when his father's revolt against Richard III was crushed had spent two years in hiding disguised as a girl. After Bosworth his title and estates were restored to him but, while he was appointed to great ceremonial offices by Henry VII and given a high profile on state occasions, he was deliberately excluded from any sort of political power.

Until 1513 the only surviving duke in the realm and the greatest landowner in the whole country with estates in 24 shires (that included 12 castles and 124 manors), Buckingham was hereditary Lord High Constable of England, an office inherited from his Bohun forebears that, in theory, made him commander-in-chief of the king's armies. His father had been beheaded for rebelling against Richard III, his grandfather and great-grandfather had been killed in battle. Descended from many men who had fought by William the Conqueror's side at Hastings, inheritor of a score of lesser peerages whose titles he did not bother to use, this giant pachyderm of a magnate embodied the old nobility. Such a man was scarcely to be overawed by a Tudor, even though that Tudor was his crowned and anointed sovereign, and the king knew it.

Edward Stafford may not have had any Yorkist blood, but he certainly possessed Plantagenet blood, being descended from Edward III through the female line, from the heiress of Edward's fifth son, the Duke of Gloucester. His claim to the throne was as good as the king's. The men at the secret conference in Calais in 1504 had seen him as the most likely successor to Henry VII, and after Queen Katherine's failure to produce a son he was regarded throughout Europe as the most likely successor to Henry VIII. In 1519 the Venetian ambassador, Sebastian Giustinian, reported that 'should the King die without male heirs, the Duke could easily get the crown'.[2] Henry was well aware of such gossip.

In 1510, while Queen Katherine was pregnant, the king strayed. His reputed mistress was Lady FitzWalter, the former Lady Elizabeth Stafford, who was Buckingham's sister.[3] To avert suspicion from Henry one of his courtiers, Sir William Compton, pretended to pursue her. A lady-in-waiting was so outraged that she explained the situation to the duke, who shortly afterwards found Sir William in his sister's apartments. Furious, he snarled, 'Women of the Stafford family are no game for Comptons, no, nor for Tudors either.' It was a blunt reminder that in his eyes the Tudors were parvenus. Shortly after the ensuing recriminations, the king angrily rebuked Buckingham, who left court. Lady FitzWalter's husband dragged her away for a spell in a convent, which suggests that he believed she had been unfaithful. But Henry appeared to forget the incident.[4]

Stafford lived with staggering opulence and display, never going on a journey without a 'travelling household' of sixty horsemen. His full household numbered between 130 and 150, all of whom ate and lodged at his expense. On the feast of the Epiphany 1508 he had given dinner to no less than 459 people, and he often entertained on a similarly sumptuous a scale. He dressed in priceless silks, velvets and furs (including

Russian sables), and in cloth of gold or silver, sewn with a multitude of little family badges in gold, notably the Stafford knots and the Bohun swans and antelopes and the Bohun motto, 'God and the Swann'.

For many years Stafford had been building a new castle-palace with two courtyards at Thornbury in Gloucestershire. Although never completed, enough remains to give us some idea of how splendid he intended it to be, especially the large and beautiful oriel windows. It had a garden with a huge orchard criss-crossed by alleys, with summerhouses in the trees, thirteen fishponds and a park containing 700 deer. While intended to be defensible against troops without artillery, it was very much a great house as well as a castle, with large, luxurious rooms. Much of what survives is where the duke and his wife, Alianore Percy, daughter of the fourth Earl of Northumberland, spent most of their time, with the duchess's apartments on the ground floor.

Thornbury was merely one of Stafford's palatial residences, and others he used most included Bletchingley in Surrey, Penshurst in Kent and Newport in Monmouthshire. He also owned the castles of Tunbridge in Kent, Kimbolton in Huntingdonshire, Maxstoke in Warwickshire, Stafford in Staffordshire, and Brecon in Wales (where he was Prince of Brecknock). His London 'inn' or mansion was the Red Rose, near the church of St Lawrence, Pultney, just off Candlewick Street. During the summer of 1519 King Henry, together with the entire court, spent several days as his guests at Penshurst. (This is the only one of the duke's houses that still conveys something of his magnificence.)

The duke was not without some good qualities. He got on well with many of his kindred. After his son married Ursula Pole, the Countess of Salisbury's daughter, her brothers spent so much time with Buckingham that they were mistaken for his nephews. He was genuinely religious, an admirer of the Carthusians, and at their behest he paid the expenses of a boy at Oxford who wanted to become a priest.[5] Despite his litigiousness he had a sense of justice – we know that he had been deeply shocked by the Earl of Warwick's execution. And, as he would one day prove, he also possessed both dignity and courage.

On the other hand, he was a difficult man, not merely proud and hot-tempered but aggressive and revengeful, always at law over some dispute. A contemporarary portrait shows a heavy, unmistakeably obstinate face. He was constantly falling out with his own household, sometimes arresting and imprisoning them illegally, confiscating their goods and chattels, instituting nearly fifty court cases against former employees.[6] He suspected everybody of trying to cheat him, possibly because he knew he was running seriously into debt; his estates had been badly run for generations. By the end of his career he was being forced to sell large amounts of land.

Buckingham quarrelled as much with equals as he did with servants. In a legal battle over an adjoining estate at Thornbury, he stated that Lord Berkeley's wife was a witch and that Berkeley would end up feeding pigs, the job for which he was best fitted, adding that his lordship's only other qualities were greed and coveting what did not belong to him.[7] During a long-running feud – as usual, over land – with Thomas Lucas, a former solicitor general, he sued for libel, alleging that Lucas had declared 'he set not by the Duke two pins' and that Buckingham 'had no more conscience than a dog'. Although the duke won the case, he was awarded a derisive £40 out of the £1,000 he had claimed in damages.[8]

As a landlord he was notably harsh, ruthless over rents and a relentless 'encloser' of land – at Thornbury alone a thousand acres – which involved the destruction of dozens of little farms and reduced the farmers to beggary. Wherever possible he brought back serfdom: his officials methodically investigated his tenants' ancestry, reclaiming them as 'bond men' if their forebears had been serfs and enforcing the old, feudal bond service. In Wales, where because of years of neglect his estates were in chaos and rents seldom paid, such measures provoked armed resistance.

Henry had felt uneasy about him for a long time. In 1513 he created his friend Charles Brandon Duke of Suffolk, partly to stress that the de la Poles had forfeited their duchy, but also to deprive Buckingham of his status as England's only duke. The king began to worry increasingly about Buckingham's wealth, power and royal blood, a worry that was fuelled by his own lack of a son. For Warwick's curse struck again and again. Apart from a daughter Princess Mary, born in 1516, all his children by Katherine of Aragon died in early infancy and the man most likely to succeed him was Buckingham. Henry's worries were understood only too well by his new minister, Thomas Wolsey.

Keen on enjoying himself, disliking the drudgery of administration, the king entrusted the affairs of state to Wolsey. The architect of Henry's splendid victory in France, Wolsey had been appointed almoner (chief chaplain) in 1509, although he did not become a member of the council for another two years. 'A fine looking man, he is very learned, unusually persuasive, exceptionally able and quite inexhaustible,' reported the Venetian envoy.[9] The last of England's great ecclesiastical statesmen, a superb administrator and diplomat, Wolsey made himself indispensable, and in 1515 he became Lord Chancellor. During the same year – already Archbishop of York, Bishop of Lincoln and Tournai – he was created a cardinal at Henry's request.

Although humbly born (the son of an Ipswich butcher), he was unpleasantly arrogant with all save his king and queen. Skelton conveys his bullying manner in the law courts:

> . . . in the Chamber of Stars
> All matters there he mars,
> Clapping his rod in the board,
> No man dare speak a word:
>
> For he hath all the saying without any renaying.
> He rolleth in his records,

And saith, 'How say ye, My Lords?
Is not my reason good? . . .'
He ruleth all the roost
With bragging and with boast . . .
At the Common Pleas
Or at the King's Bench,
He wringeth them such a wrench
That all our learned men
Dare not set their pen
To plead a true trial
Within Westminster Hall.[10]

He was just as overbearing outside the courts.

In 1515 Polydore Vergil wrote to a friend at Rome that Wolsey had grown so tyrannical and so heartily disliked by most Englishmen that he could not last much longer. Vergil's letter was intercepted by the cardinal's men and he spent several months in the Tower until Pope Leo interceded for him. Other critics received similar treatment. No one loathed Wolsey more than the old nobility, who detested the way he lorded it over them. But Wolsey was able to discover exactly what his master wanted and make it happen. For nearly two decades Henry VIII would not hear a word against him.

The king was glad to have a strong man at his side. The cardinal was more than just a wise adviser. Not only did he relieve Henry of chores and business, but his network of spies watched for the slightest signs of disaffection. Here was someone who could be relied on to keep Henry safe from the White Rose and Richard de la Pole. Yet Wolsey knew he must produce some sort of result if he was going to soothe the king's chronic insecurity. His own future depended on it. While he might not be able to eliminate Suffolk, he could at least demonstrate his loyalty and ingenuity by inventing another 'great traitor' and then destroying him. Providentially, a perfect candidate for the role played into his hands.

Despising Wolsey as an upstart, the Duke of Buckingham was infuriated by his pretentious behaviour, grumbling at having to be 'subservient to so base and uncivil a fellow'.[11] Nor did he bother to conceal his disapproval of the cardinal's conduct of foreign affairs, unaware that these were in fact the king's own policies. He complained bitterly about the Field of Cloth of Gold in 1520, where Henry met Francis I: not only was he opposed to an alliance with France, but he took a violent dislike to the French king – a dislike that was reciprocated. He also begrudged having to spend so much money on equipping his retinue. He was embittered, too, that a great noble such as himself should not be allowed more influence in the royal council. There were rumours that he wanted to assassinate Wolsey.[12] However, despite having friends who shared his views, Buckingham was in no way the head of a faction.

Such an alarming state of anarchy existed in Buckingham's Welsh lordships that the king became concerned that the crown had lost control of the region. In 1518 Henry sent the duke a formal rebuke, complaining that bonds for good behaviour were not being enforced because of 'your default and negligence'. As a result, 'many and divers murders, rapes, robberies, riots and other misdemeanours have been of late and daily be committed . . . to our no little displeasure'.[13] The situation was so bad that English fugitives from justice, often violent criminals, were taking refuge in the Welsh Marches.

The splendour of Buckingham's hospitality at Penshurst in 1519, which cost him the enormous sum of nearly £1,500, was another reminder of his semi-regal pretensions. The scale of the princely entertainment offered to the guests may well have irritated King Henry, who in any case must have felt unhappy at seeing the royal arms of England quartering those of Stafford so prominently displayed, whether carved over gateways or on the stained-glass windows – a public statement of the duke's Plantagenet descent. This was the same year that Buckingham's son Henry married Ursula Pole,

Clarence's granddaughter, which brought Yorkist blood into the family.

The old aristocracy's exclusion from office and hatred of Wolsey would have made many of them welcome a conspiracy led by the duke. They knew how popular he was[14] and that, if he wanted, he might perhaps bring down the cardinal and even King Henry. The magnates sensed the Tudors' vulnerability, aware that more than once it had looked likely that the de la Poles might replace them. But Buckingham's pride, touchiness and difficult character made it impossible for him to be a leader.

A firm believer in the curse brought upon the Tudors by the Earl of Warwick's execution, Edward Stafford thought it highly probable that one day he or his son would be king. Yet it is extremely unlikely that he ever thought of speeding up the process. This can be seen from the record of a meeting he held with some of his council at Thornbury after dinner (late in the morning) on 26 October 1520. Those present were Master Thomas Wotton, dean of his chapel; Mr George Poley, his almoner; Dr Jenyns, his surveyor particular; Thomas Moscroff, his counsellor in physic; Mr John Delacourt, his chaplain; and Thomas Cade, his receiver-general.

When they sat down, the duke told them that while he had asked them to bring their ledgers, he did not intend to discuss business. Perhaps they were surprised to see him wearing a beard, he continued. It was because 'I make a vow unto God that it shall never be shaven until such time as I have been at Jerusalem.' If he could obtain royal permission to go to the Holy City, it would make him happier than if the king gave him £10,000. Mr Poley, Mr Delacourt and Sir William Curteys, his Master of Works, had promised to go with him. In his absence, the council would run his estates. But while he hoped to get permission for his pilgrimage fairly soon, he did not think he would be able to set off for another two years.[15]

This scarcely sounds like the behaviour of a man who was plotting a rebellion.

# 20

# Winter 1520–Spring 1521: 'A Giant Traitor'

'There's mischief in this man.'

Shakespeare, *King Henry VIII*, Act 1, scene 2

About the year 1520, when Henry VIII was just over thirty, a sculptor, probably Petro Torrigiano, made a painted, terracotta bust of him. The king has shaved off his beard, revealing a jovial, handsome face. Yet looking at it, one begins to understand Sir Thomas More's comment to Cromwell, 'For if the lion knew his own strength, hard were it for any man to rule him.'[1] Here is someone dangerously unpredictable, with all the unpredictable ferocity of a big cat lying beneath the leonine charm. Even those who knew Henry well did not know when he was going to pounce or on whom.

Shakespeare's account of Buckingham's downfall in *Henry VIII* is in many ways surprisingly accurate. The play tells the story as a tragedy, which was exactly how contemporaries saw it – an innocent man becoming the victim of unjust suspicions produced by a fevered imagination. But whether or not Cardinal Wolsey was responsible is hard to tell. Vergil, admittedly biased, says that, 'boiling with hatred for the Duke of Buckingham', Wolsey had been fanning Henry's suspicions about him since 1518.[2] Branding the duke as a traitor would distract the king's attention from the cardinal's failure over Richard de la Pole.

Early in November 1520 one of Henry's servants, Sir William Bulmer, came to court wearing a prominent 'Stafford knot' badge on his doublet which signified he had entered Buckingham's service as well as the king's. Enraged, Henry prosecuted Bulmer in the Star Chamber, although he was eventually forgiven. The king was no less furious with the duke, to such an extent that Buckingham thought he was going to be sent to the Tower. Always a prey to imagination, Henry, by now, had grown to hate him no less than did Wolsey. Still lacking an heir – it was clear Queen Katherine would bear no more children – he began to suspect Buckingham of having designs on his throne. He wrote to the cardinal, ordering him to keep close watch on the duke as well as on other peers.

In theory Buckingham could muster a private army of 5,000 men, although in practice he would have been hard put to find 500. At the end of November 1520, shortly after the Bulmer affair, he announced his intention of visiting his Welsh estates during the next year with three or four hundred armed retainers, in order to restore order: he also asked the cardinal for the king's permission for his men to take 'harness' (armour) with them – to be worn only if needed. Plenty of people could remember how the duke's father had gone to Wales when he revolted against Richard III, and while Henry may not have anticipated a rebellion, he was unsettled by the news. Then, towards the end of 1520, a letter, whose signature has disappeared, reached Cardinal Wolsey, suggesting there was a chance of plausibly charging Buckingham with treason.

After the Bulmer affair, Buckingham had become very uneasy about his relations with Henry and Wolsey. In November 1520 he commissioned his chancellor Robert Gilbert to order a gold cup with a cover as a New Year's gift for the cardinal, a conciliatory gesture that indicates he sensed some sort of danger. He tried to make allies, instructing Gilbert at about the same time to take a letter to the Duke and Duchess of Norfolk, telling them he had 'as great trust in them as any child they have'.[3]

Ironically, the person most responsible for Buckingham's ruin, if indirectly, was someone who saw a great deal of good in him and had known him for many years. This was the man he called 'my ghostly father' – meaning his confessor and spiritual adviser – Dan Nicholas Hopkyns, a Carthusian monk of Hinton Charterhouse in Somerset. (Carthusians were hermits living in community.) Dan Nicholas specialized in prophecy, perhaps inspired by the works of Savonarola, who had given 'foreknowledge' a respectable name. Loneliness, lack of sleep and fasting may have persuaded a man not really suited for the Carthusian life that he was able to see into the future.

Dan Nicholas had impressed Buckingham by predicting in 1513 that 'if the King of Scots came [into this realm] he would not go home again'. 'I . . . asked him whether he had knowledge therof [by] prophecy, but he said to [me], "Nay, *Ex Deo habeo*" – 'I have it from God', recalled the duke. The monk proved to be right – James IV died at Flodden. Hopkyns convinced himself that Henry VIII was going to die without sons and that Buckingham would become King of England. If Dan Nicholas had not encouraged Buckingham's dreams, and had he not spoken of them, the duke might have survived. Shakespeare in *Henry VIII* may be wrong in calling Hopkyns a 'devil-monk' because of his role in Buckingham's ruin but he is right in saying that he 'fed him with his prophecies'.[4]

Just before leaving for the Field of Cloth of Gold in 1520, the duke had sacked his surveyor Charles Knyvet, who was also his cousin, from the stewardship of some of his estates because he was ill-treating the tenants. Deeply resentful, Knyvet made damaging allegations about his former employer that circulated far and wide. They reached the ears of whoever wrote the letter mentioned above.

It is often assumed that the writer belonged to the ducal household at Thornbury. Yet the familiar, if respectful, tone suggests he is more likely to have been a colleague of Wolsey, while clearly he was a lawyer used to questioning suspects, as well as someone with a good knowledge of politics during the previous reign. The obvious candidate is the Lord Privy Seal, Dr Thomas Ruthal, Bishop of Durham, an oily prelate noted for avarice, whom a Venetian observer once described as 'singing treble to Wolsey's bass'. What makes this identification almost certain is that it was Ruthal who interrogated and groomed the witnesses for Buckingham's trial. As an ally of the cardinal, he naturally welcomed any information that might harm the duke.

In his letter, the writer says that Wolsey already knows Knyvet. He reports that the man wants to enter royal service, which will enable him to reveal all he knows without fear of the duke, and has promised that if he joins, 'Then will I speak, by St Mary, for it toucheth the King indeed'. The writer adds, 'And so, if it please your grace, of likelihood some great matter there is, or else is Charles [Knyvet], a marvellous, simple, insolent body.'

Commenting that the late Henry VII would have handled the case cautiously before acting, he advises the cardinal to send for Knyvet and ask why he has left the duke's employment after all the good work he did for him, especially when he is a kinsman. He should also remark how he has heard from other employees whom Buckingham has dismissed that 'in his fumes and displeasures' the duke often rages against the king and Wolsey. Then he should order Knyvet to tell all he knew without hiding anything, while promising to protect him against Buckingham. If he refuses to repeat what he has told others, then the cardinal must terrify him by showing displeasure.[5]

His colleague had stumbled on just what Wolsey needed. After questioning Knyvet, he realized he had found the perfect tool with which to play on the king's fears and bring down the duke. Even better, there was no need for him to show his hand during the last act. Unluckily for Buckingham, two powerful allies who might have defended him, his brother-in-law the Earl of Northumberland and his son-in-law the Earl of Surrey, would not be able to help him. The former was under a cloud – a few years earlier, he had been imprisoned for abducting a ward – while Surrey, towards whom the king was better disposed, was away in Ireland.

On 8 April 1521 a royal messenger arrived at Thornbury with a message from King Henry, asking the duke to come to him at Greenwich Palace. Unsuspecting, Buckingham set out with his usual entourage, never dreaming he would never see his beautiful house again. But soon he noticed he was being followed by armed men, who billeted themselves at the inns where he and his men slept en route. Only after spending a night at Windsor did Buckingham gain an inkling of what might be in store. During breakfast in the castle on 16 April he saw a royal pursuivant, Thomas Ward, loitering near his table, and enquired sharply what he was doing. Told it was on the king's orders, he was so shaken that his face turned ashen and he could not finish his breakfast.

Buckingham and his household nonetheless continued their journey along the Thames. He rode for some of the way before boarding his great barge. Just after Westminster he landed, to call on Wolsey at his magnificently palatial inn, York Place, to be told that the cardinal was seriously ill and unable to receive him. Defiantly, he answered, 'Well, yet will I drink of my lord's wine ere I pass', which he did before returning to the boat, en route for the city where he meant to go to his mansion off Candlewick Street.

As the ducal barge approached London Bridge a flotilla of wherries suddenly shot out from the shore to intercept it, a hundred Yeomen of the Guard jumping on board. (Had they waited any longer, the need to 'shoot the arches' of the bridge

would have made boarding impossible.) The Yeomen were commanded by their septuagenarian captain, Sir Henry Marney, who
told Buckingham he was under arrest. He was taken ashore, to
be marched to the Tower under escort.

Knyvet was already in another part of the Tower, together
with the duke's chancellor Robert Gilbert, his chaplain John
Delacourt and Dan Nicholas Hopkyns. The four had been
brought to London some days before the duke had been invited
to visit the king at Greenwich. Here they were interrogated by
Bishop Ruthall, who also groomed them to appear as witnesses.
Knyvet proved so cooperative that throughout the trial he was
politely referred to as 'Charles Knyvet, Esquire', while the others
were terrified into saying what the prosecution wanted – they
may have been threatened with torture. On 8 May their former
patron was indicted for high treason at the Guildhall.

The gravest charge in the indictment, that he had intended
'to exalt himself to the crown', was based on his relationship with Dan Nicholas. Since 1512, by letter or through his
chaplain Delacourt, the Carthusian had been promising the duke
that Henry VIII would have no sons and he 'should have all'.
In 1514 Buckingham had visited the charterhouse at Hinton,
and when the monk told him he would be King of England
the duke replied, 'he would be a just prince'. In 1517 his chancellor Gilbert had brought a message from Hopkyns that there
would be a 'change', before next Christmas and Buckingham
'should have the rule of all England'. When this did not happen, Buckingham had again visited Hinton in person in 1518,
to be reassured that he would be king. He told Dan Nicholas he
was right in warning Delacourt to keep it secret under the seal
of confession: 'if the King knew of it, he should be altogether
destroyed'.

According to Robert Gilbert, the ducal chancellor from
Thornbury, on his master's orders he had bought cloth of gold
and silver and silks, to bribe members of the Royal Guard into
joining his cause. In 1518 Buckingham had sent him to London

to obtain a licence to raise troops in the West Country, and permission to equip them with weapons and armour for use in Wales, since the duke had the intention of 'fortifying himself against the King'. Later, Buckingham informed Gilbert he was waiting for a better time for a rebellion, which could succeed if the 'lords of the kingdom' would tell each other what they really thought. He had said that everything done by the late king had been wrong and he was always grumbling about what the present king was doing. He had also told Gilbert he possessed a copy of an Act of Parliament legitimizing the Duke of Somerset (and the Tudor claim to the throne) but would not give it to Henry 'for £10,000'.[6]

Robert Gilbert's deposition has survived and much of it is in the indictment. However, a good deal was omitted as it was too embarrassing, such as his claim that the duke believed the Tudors had brought a curse upon themselves: he '[did] grudge that the Earl of Warwick was put to death and say that God would punish it by not suffering the king's issue to prosper'. Buckingham, Gilbert told his interrogators, thought that Wolsey had asked an evil spirit for help in keeping Henry's favour, besides procuring women for him, and that the private lives of both Henry and his minister were so abominable that they deserved to be punished by God. He had constantly remarked that the cardinal wanted to 'undo' (ruin) every nobleman in England.[7]

The evidence given by Charles Knyvet was no less lurid. In May 1520, when they were at the Red Rose in London, discussing the imminent Field of Cloth of Gold, the duke had apparently commented that something unpleasant was likely to happen to Henry in France because 'a certain holy monk' had told his chaplain Delacourt that 'neither the King nor his heirs should prosper' and Buckingham must do his best 'to obtain the love of the community of England because I . . . and my blood should prosper and have the rule'. Knyvet had warned Buckingham that the monk might be deluded by the Devil and that it was dangerous to meddle with this sort of thing but, clearly delighted by Hopkyns's prophecy, the duke had replied that it could not possibly do him any harm. He also said that had the king died of a recent malady, he would have beheaded the cardinal at once, and that he would rather die than go on being ordered about all the time.

In September 1520, 'walking in his gallery at Bletchingley' with Lord Bergavenny (one of his sons-in-law), Buckingham had complained of the king's councillors and said that should Henry die, then 'he meant to have the rule in England, whoever would say the contrary'. He warned that if Bergavenny repeated this remark, he would strike him over the head with his sword. In November, at East Greenwich, Buckingham had told Knyvet that during the row over his employing Bulmer he had thought for a moment that he might be sent to the Tower, and had decided that if Henry gave the order for this, he would do what his father had meant to do to Richard III – kneel before the king and stab him. Placing his hand on his dagger, said Knyvet, 'This he swore by the blood of Our Lord'.[8]

Another charge – made by others too – was that after the king's most recent illness, when the duke had declared that 'if it had happened well' (meaning if Henry had died) he would have chopped off the Lord Cardinal's head, he had also said how, given the chance, he would do the same to the king. Anyone acquainted with Buckingham and his temper knew that such outbursts meant very little. But they were taken with the outmost seriousness by Henry, who personally examined the four witnesses. According to a note written on the back of a letter by the royal secretary Richard Pace, the king, after examing them, became convinced that Buckingham was going to be found guilty and would be condemned by the Lords. Pace added that the crisis was so grave that Parliament was going to be summoned to deal with 'the matter'.

On 13 May 1521 the duke was taken to Westminster by barge for his trial, under strong guard, amid fears that his retainers might attempt to rescue him. Had he escaped, there could have been another battle of Stoke. Scaffolding was errected in Westminster Hall for the seventeen peers who were to be his jurors. They were presided over by his son-in-law's father, the old Duke of Norfolk, once a trusted henchman of Richard III.

'Sir Edward, Duke of Buckingham, hold up thy hand,' he was told by the crown attorney, after being led to the Bar with the Tower axe carried before him. 'Thou art indicted of high treason, for that thou traitorously hast conspired and imagined as far as in thee lay, to shorten the life of our sovereign lord the King. Of this treason, how wilt thou acquit thee?' 'By my peers,' replied Buckingham. When the indictment had been read, he said angrily, 'It is false and untrue, and conspired, and forged to bring me to my death.'[9]

Buckingham then defended himself against the charges with surprising eloquence. In response, the depositions made by the four witnesses were read out, Knevet reading his own. When the duke then demanded that all the witnesses be produced, they were called but, very unfairly, he was not allowed to cross-examine any of them. However, he was permitted to make another speech in his own defence, lasting for an hour and creating a considerable impression.

The jury retired, 'conferring a great while'. Eventually, each peer gave his verdict to Norfolk, who wrote against each name, '*Dicit quod est cupabilis*' ('he says he is guilty'). Knowing the king was determined he should die, not one of them dared to dissent. Then they returned to Westminster Hall, each repeating their verdict. 'The Duke was brought to the Bar, sore chafing, and sweat marvellously.' After a long silence, with tears rolling down his face, old Norfolk informed the defendant he had been found guilty of high treason, then read out the statutory sentence for a convicted traitor:

> You shall be led to the King's prison and there laid on a hurdle and so drawn to the place of execution, and there

to be hanged, cut down alive, your members to be cut off and cast into the fire, your bowels burned before you, your head smitten off, and your body quartered and divided at the King's will, and may God have mercy on your soul.[10]

Although both verdict and sentence may no doubt have been technically sound according to the law of the land, morally they amounted to murder. A recent American biographer of Buckingham has argued that sixteenth-century England always accepted such decisions without question.[11] However, this was simply not true, as, for example, had been amply demonstrated by the revulsion at Warwick's fate. 'If all the patterns of a lawless prince had been lost in the world, they might have been found in this king,' Sir Walter Raleigh later observed of Henry VIII.

'You have said as a traitor should be said unto, but I was never none,' the duke told the court calmly. 'But my lords I nothing malign [you] for that you have done to me, but the eternal God forgive you my death, and I do [too].' He added, with the curious fatalism of Tudor victims of state, 'I shall never sue to the King for life, howbeit he is a gracious prince.' Buckingham ended by saying, 'I desire you, my lords, and all my fellows to pray for me.' Then he was taken back to the Tower, the axe displayed with its edge towards him where he sat in the barge. Shakespeare refines movingly the words attributed by Hall:[12] 'When I came hither, I was lord high constable, And Duke of Buckingham: now, poor Edward Bohun.' (*Henry VIII*, Act II, scene 1)

His son-in-law Lord Bergavenny (once Edmund de la Pole's boon companion) was committed to the Tower for not having reported the duke's alleged threats against the king. This made him guilty of the crime called 'misprision of treason' and he was only released on payment of a huge fine. This so impoverished Bergavenny that, years afterwards, the imperial ambassador would comment sardonically that he had 'lost all his feathers'.

The Carthusians of Hinton wrote to the Lord Chamberlain, asking that Dan Nicholas should be sent to some other charter-house, 'there to be punished for his offences as long as shall please the King's noble grace'.[13] According to tradition, poor Hopkyns died from grief. Nothing more is known about the other witnesses.

On 17 May 1521 Buckingham was escorted by 500 troops to Tower Hill, where he was beheaded, dying on the block with notable courage despite a messy execution that took three strokes of the axe to cut off his head. As had been done with Warwick and Suffolk before him, his corpse – reunited to his head – was buried in the church of the Austin Friars. Even Hall, a fanatical supporter of everything done by King Henry, admitted that many of the watching crowd (who may have included Hall himself) were in tears.

At the next Parliament an Act of Attainder was passed, disinheriting Buckingham's heirs and confiscating his estates. Yet another indignity had already been inflicted, the duke's posthumous 'degradation' from the Order of the Garter. His garter-plate and banner with the arms of England (the display of which gave Henry so much offence) were taken down from over his former stall in St George's Chapel at Windsor. Then the heralds solemnly kicked the insignia out of the chapel before throwing them into a ditch.

More than a few of Buckingham's contemporaries felt sorry for him. Having read the chronicles of Hall and the Elizabethan historian Stowe, Shakespeare hints at this pity, although he shifts most of the blame for his destruction from Henry on to Wolsey. While there was not the slightest sign of protest, the incident contributed to the king's growing unpopularity. Some of his subjects began to realize he was no longer the young god whom they had worshipped at his accession in 1509 and that they had an alarmingly ruthless ruler.

Edward Stafford's only 'crime' lay in speaking of the possibility that Henry VIII and his children might die young, and that he would inherit the crown.

# 21

# Winter 1524–5:
# A White Rose Dies

'The White Rose died on the field of battle – I saw him lying
dead with all the others.'

Macquereau, *Histoire générale de l'Europe*[1]

In October 1518 a new peace between England and France put
plans for a Yorkist invasion on hold once again. More discour-
agement came in June 1520 after Henry VIII and Francis I had
an exceptionally amiable meeting at the Field of Cloth of Gold,
although the French king continued to pay the White Rose a
lavish pension. When the Chevalier Baudoiche asked for the
return of his mansion (perhaps because Richard had seduced his
daughter), the canons of Metz cathedral gave Richard a lease
for life at a low rent for a château called La Haulte Pierre near
St Symphorien on condition he refurbished it, which he could
afford to do in splendid style. Undoubtedly, his standing at the
French court remained high. In 1518 Francis had acquired a
strong-minded new mistress, the Comtesse de Châteaubriant.

Born Françoise de Foix and sister of Marshal Lautrec, she was Richard's cousin and an invaluable contact.

Never for a moment did he lose sight of his ambition to take Henry's place on the throne. In September 1519 a priest named Edward Allen was arrested at Leicester, accused of being one of Richard's spies, suspicion being further aroused when servants of Lord Hastings and Sir Richard Stanley brought Allen expensive food in prison – a haunch of venison – although there was no evidence to implicate their employers. The authorities were also worried about the Marquess of Dorset, but unable to find any solid proof that he supported the White Rose.

Rumours persisted that Richard was on his way with an invasion fleet. In August 1521 a totally unfounded story circulated that, accompanied by the Duke of Albany, he had landed at Dunbar and, joined by Scottish troops, was marching south towards the Border, although after their bloody humiliation at Flodden the Scots were in no mood to risk another war. Even so, during the following year Wolsey was to complain of Albany's support for the White Rose, declaring that King Francis was encouraging him. The cardinal was more than justified. About midsummer the same year, King Francis commissioned Derick van Reydt to tell Duke Frederick of Holstein-Gottorp that should the English attack France or Scotland he intended to give Richard an invasion fleet.[2] Later, he suggested that Frederick's daughter should marry Richard if he succeeded, and Frederick was so excited that he sent his secretary to Paris to discuss the idea.

At home, Yorkist sentiment was far from dead, even though most of those who still retained it were usually wise enough not to advertise the fact. In May 1521, however, the parson of Rampisham in Dorset, Robert Sherard, told a parishioner called Agnes Clyfton that the king was unworthy of his crown – 'the father of Henry VIII was a horsegroom and a keeper of horses', who had no more right to the crown than Agnes because 'he came to the throne by dint of the sword'.[3] During the previous month Lord Mounteagle had arrested his own (bastard) son, together with another parson and a soldier called John Goghe (or Strydley), for planning to go abroad and join the White Rose. Goghe had boasted of meeting Richard de la Pole at Rouen, saying he was 'a valiant man, worthy to be a great captain'.[4] Admittedly, these two were obviously a most unsavoury pair, the priest accompanied by his young mistress and Goghe bragging of his success as a blackmailer.

The Duke of Buckingham's execution that spring had horrified many of the courts of Western Europe, besides damaging Henry's popularity at home. In August 1521 a Hanse merchant, Perpoynte Deventer, informed the English authorities that the Lieutenant Governor of Boulogne had asked him if he knew the duke's son, commenting that a Yorkist invasion from Scotland would certainly find 50,000 supporters in England. Deventer said, too, that he had met the Duc de la Trémouille, the French king's Lord Chamberlain, who told him that if Henry declared war the White Rose would cross the Channel. In addition, the Duc de Vendôme had told Deventer that France and Denmark were planning to help Richard raise a revolt in areas with estates that had formerly belonged to Buckingham.

In the meantime, the White Rose acquired a mistress at Metz, a certain Sebille who was considered the loveliest young woman in the city – 'tall, straight and slender, and white as snow', according to the chronicler Philippe de Vignolles. She was the wife of a rich goldsmith, Mâitre Nicholas, employed by Richard, who sent him on a mission to Paris so that he could seduce her. In the autumn of 1520 she fled to La Haulte Pierre to live with him, prudently bringing with her the pick of her husband's jewels. Shortly after, Richard was acosted in the streets of Metz by the incensed Nicholas with a band of friends. Richard drew his dagger and, when the goldsmith ran for his life, threw it after him. The city council intervened, and Richard offered to give her up, on condition her husband did not beat her. Nicholas refused, hiring German assassins to kill him, but he escaped. Eventually, Sebille rejoined Richard and for the next three years they lived together at Toul in a house lent to them by the Cardinal of Lorraine.[5]

The romance did not make Richard lose sight of his goal in any way. In May 1521 he wrote to the Margrave of Brandenburg, replying to an offer of assistance. Addressing the Margrave as 'dearly beloved lord and uncle', he asks him to promote 'the most favourable understanding of our affair with our uncle of Holstein' – the affair being an invasion of England – and thanked him for being such a good friend. Chancellor of the Empire and a man of great influence, the Margrave was a useful ally.

In May 1522 another war broke out between England and France. Henry VIII, whose grasp of international politics seems to have been unrealistic at the best of times, began to see the looming conflict between Francis and the Emperor Charles V as an opportunity to revive the Anglo-French kingdom of his predecessor Henry V. He would reign over north-western France, including Paris, and be crowned at St Denis, while the emperor as Duke of Burgundy could rule the north-east. The Duke of Bourbon, who had recently rebelled against Francis, would graciously be allowed to have the country's central provinces.

Understandably, this made the French king take Richard de la Pole even more seriously, and once again a Yorkist invasion of England became a distinct possibility.

The situation was complicated, however, by a civil war in Scandinavia from where help for the White Rose might otherwise have been expected. Christian II of Denmark was being challenged for the Danish throne by his uncle, Duke Frederick of Holstein-Gottorp. Richard kept in touch with both sides until Frederick overthrew Christian in 1522. His success boded well for Yorkism, as the new King of Denmark was convinced that the White Rose would triumph over the Tudor.

At the end of 1522 two White Rose agents were caught in England, busily trying to recruit troops for their leader by offering higher wages than those paid by King Henry. They had already enlisted over a hundred men.[6] At the start of 1523 the authorities arrested another agent, Simon Jones from Monmouth. No doubt under torture, Simon admitted that since spring the previous year he had been in England working for the 'Roose', who had instructed him to sound out Lord Stafford, Buckingham's son, and the Earl of Derby. Stafford had just seen his father beheaded and his inheritance confiscated, while Derby had received slightingly few favours from the Tudor regime, but there was no evidence that Jones had managed to contact either of them.[7]

During the next two years, stories that a new English civil war was about to break out circulated all over Europe. In May 1523 Charles V was told that a bishop had been sent to the Tower for involvement in a Yorkist plot; 'a hundred thousand pounds' found in his possession were intended to finance a rising. While there was no truth in the tale, it indicates that at the very least a handful of reasonably well-informed people were expecting a Yorkist revolt.[8] There were also unfounded reports that the Duke of Albany was going to invade over the Scottish Border.

In autumn 1523, 10,000 English troops got within 50 miles of Paris, but withdrew when the French repulsed the Spanish advance in the south. The English stayed in Picardy, however, where Richard led his landsknechts against them. Early in May 1524 he wrote to the French queen mother, Louise of Savoy, that he was disappointed his English opponents had retreated, since both he and his men would have shown that all they cared for was to live and die in her son's service. He also told her, in the same letter, 'all that I possess in the world comes from you'.[9]

Shortly afterwards, the English commander Sir William Fizwilliam demanded reinforcements on the grounds that 'this wretched traitor is in the field' and that his German troops were the best in the French army – a grudging testimony to Richard's reputation as a soldier.[10] In the same month, FitzWilliam sent the Calais pursuivant on a parley to the French commander, Charles de Bourbon, Duc de Vendôme. When the White Rose entered the tent during the parley Vendôme told the herald, 'Behold

your King!' Terrified, the man began shouting that Richard was
no such thing, until Vendôme told him to hold his tongue.[11]

Francis I had been serious enough in asking Richard to lead
an expedition, advancing 200,000 livres. In 1522 the French
responded eagerly when James, Earl of Desmond (a kinsman of
the Foix) sent an envoy to their king, informing him he wanted
to drive the English out of Ireland: in June 1523 the Comte
de Foix-Candale arrived at the earl's great castle of Askeaton in
what is now Co. Limerick and signed a treaty with Desmond,
who promised to rise against Henry VIII in support of Richard's
claims. Even though the earl's main motive was hostility towards
English rule, it appears that Yorkist sentiment was still alive in
Ireland.[12] Throughout the summer of 1523 Venetian observers thought there would be an expedition against England 'led
by the White Rose', but in the autumn the republic's government told its ambassador at Rome that the invasion had been
called off.[13]

As late as February 1524 Richard was still hoping to take
troops across the Channel, encouraged by the new King of
Denmark. He needed massive sums of ready cash to hire his
indispensable German landsknechts, and pay their wages on
time. Unfortunately for Richard, the only man who could lend
him the money was Francis I, who then decided to concentrate
all his resources on another front.

In April the French forces in northern Italy were routed at
Sesia and at midsummer the Duc de Bourbon invaded south-
eastern France with imperial troops, at first carrying all before
him, only to be driven back into Italy along the Riviera in head-
long retreat. Richard was among the French army that pursued
Bourbon. Crossing the Alps, in October 1524 King Francis
invested Pavia, which he besieged throughout the winter, despite
unceasing rain and outbreaks of disease that decimated his men.
The king and his nobles stayed in local castles or villas, however,
so Richard, who was in command of the infantry, must have
been reasonably comfortable. His men included the famous

Black Band, 5,000 landsknechts under their captain, Georg Langenmantel and François, Count of Lambec – the Duke of Lorraine's nineteen-year-old brother.

The decisive confrontation between the French forces and an imperial army that had recently arrived to relieve Pavia took place on 25 February 1525. Among the enemy's reinforcements were 15,000 pikemen and arquebusiers commanded by the great Swabian soldier of fortune, Georg von Frundsberg – the 'Father of Landsknechts'. During the final stages of a confused but ferocious battle, the French were wiped out by Frundsberg's arquebusiers, who shot them down from behind trees or bushes, and in one of the worst defeats ever suffered by a French army, King Francis was taken prisoner. The French right wing, the Black Band under the command of the White Rose and François de Lorraine, was overwhelmed in a pincer attack on both flanks by numerically superior forces led by Frundsberg himself. Richard and François fought to the death.

The pair were interred in a fine tomb in the cloister of a church at Pavia. The White Rose's enemy the Duc de Bourbon, whom he had known in Paris, attended the funeral wearing mourning. An exile himself, who had also lost everything in his native land, the Frenchman felt a certain sympathy. When news of Richard's death reached Metz, the cathedral's canons instituted an annual Requiem Mass for the repose of his soul. He left a daughter called Marguerite whose mother was a Flemish lady, said by some to be the daughter of the Chevalier Baudoiche who had lent him his mansion. Brought up at King Francis's expense, a good marriage was arranged for her and she became a lady-in-waiting to his sister, the Queen of Navarre. Clearly, Francis remembered his old comrade in arms with affection.[14]

According to an eighteenth-century historian (who does not give his source), when King Henry was woken at Whitehall before dawn on 9 March to be given the news of the battle of Pavia, he jumped out of bed, fell to his knees and thanked God. 'My friend,' he told the emperor's messenger, 'you are like the

Angel Gabriel, who announced the coming of Christ.' Then he called for wine to be brought. After this, in response to repeated questions by the king, the messenger, who had himself fought in the battle, described how Francis I had been disarmed and taken prisoner. He went on to describe the slaughter of the French army. 'And Richard de la Pole?' demanded the king. 'The White Rose died on the field of battle,' answered the messenger. 'I saw him lying dead with all the others.' 'God have mercy on his soul!' Henry cried exultantly. 'All the enemies of England are gone – give him more wine.'[15]

Bonfires blazed in every London street and conduits flowed with wine; during a High Mass at St Paul's the *Te Deum* was sung. Although Pavia had ruined his pro-French policy, Wolsey himself celebrated the Mass in the Sarum rite, the most splendid in all Western Christendom, with twenty ministers in gold vestments at the altar. Officially, the service was to thank God for the defeat of a ruler who was at war with England. But it was also a thanksgiving for Richard's death. Having known the depth of Henry's terror, the cardinal understood his relief.

Richard de la Pole possessed all the qualities needed in a sixteenth-century king. A gifted commander who impressed Francis I enough to be entrusted with half the French army at Pavia, he was Henry VIII's most formidable rival. Had he succeeded in invading England with his *landsknechts*, he might well have ousted the Tudor. One can understand why the king had been so wary of him.

# 22

# 1525–35:
# The White Rose Party

'From off this briar pluck a white rose with me.'

Shakespeare, *King Henry VI*, Part 1, Act II, scene 4[1]

For some years after Richard de la Pole's death Henry VIII's insecurity was less evident. During the early 1530s he still appeared healthy and athletic, if putting on too much weight and developing heavy jowels, hidden by his red beard. In manner he continued to be the gracious Renaissance Man he had seemed at the start of his reign, while he had developed a truly awe-inspiring presence. Beneath, lay a megalomaniac self-confidence, which was fed by awareness of his power over everyone around him.

Yet he was becoming increasingly worried about the succession. Although Queen Katherine was barren, he had sired an illegitimate son whom he was considering making his heir. The chronicler Hall describes how 'Henry FitzRoy' came into the world:

The King in his fresh youth was in the chains of love with a fair damsel called Elizabeth Blount, daughter to Sir John

Blount, Knight, which damsel in singing and dancing and in
all goodly pastimes exceeded all other, by the which goodly
pastimes she won the King's heart, and she again showed
him such favour that by him she bore a goodly manchild, of
beauty like to the father and mother.[2]

In 1525, when the boy was six, he was officially acknowledged as
Henry's son and given the semi-royal dukedoms of Richmond
and Somerset, his father granting him a coat of arms that he
designed personally. Henry contemplated making him King of
Ireland, even obtaining a papal dispensation for him to marry
his half-sister Mary. He grew up to be a handsome, intelligent
and high-spirited youth with a strong resemblance to the king,
who became devoted to his 'worldly jewel'.

Yet while Richard de la Pole may have been the last man to
challenge openly the Tudors' right to the throne of England,
and although it was forty years since the Yorkist cause had gone
down at Bosworth, this did not mean that nostalgia for the
House of York had died out. The White Rose was still alive.
The king knew that, should enough Englishmen decide to reject
his rule, there were Yorkist pretenders in waiting.

Henry Courtenay, Marquess of Exeter, born in 1496,
belonged to one of the few great Lancastrian families to survive
the Wars of the Roses; his grandfather had fought for Henry
Tudor at Bosworth. However, Henry's father, who had married
one of King Edward's daughters, had been accused of supporting the White Rose and sent to the Tower where he remained
until 1509. His earldom of Devon was inherited by Courtenay,
who was also heir presumptive to the English throne if the Lady
Mary's claims were disallowed – and no woman had ever occupied the throne. Significantly, in 1519 Charles V's first minister
suggested that Courtenay should marry one of the emperor's
nieces.[3] For the moment, however, this did not arouse any fears
on King Henry's part, as Courtenay appeared timid and lacking
in ambition.

At this date, the king had complete confidence in Henry Courtenay, who became a member of the Privy Council in 1520 and accompanied him at the Field of Cloth of Gold. He was made a Knight of the Garter the year after, taking the Duke of Buckingham's stall in St George's Chapel – and a sizable chunk of his lands – and was created Marquess of Exeter in 1525. For many years he was very much one of Henry's innermost circle.

The other family who had Yorkist blood were the Poles, consisting of Margaret, Countess of Salisbury, and her four sons: Henry, Lord Montague, and Arthur, Reginald and Geoffrey Pole. Like Courtenay these nephews of the Earl of Warwick seemed happy enough to live under a Tudor king so long as he remained well disposed towards them. After all, Margaret was the person closest to both his queen and his daughter. Yet the fact remained that had Richard III stayed on the throne and died childless, his successor in blood was Warwick whose heirs were the Poles: if Bosworth had not taken place, they might have been ruling England. Moreover, when the king 'restored' the countess they had been children, but now they were grown men. It was also relevant that in those early days King Henry had reason to expect the queen would still give him a son.

Not only was the countess's daughter Ursula Pole married to the Duke of Buckingham's heir, but her sons were close friends with the Staffords, a dangerous link when the duke fell. Lord Montague was sent to the Tower with his father-in-law Lord Bergavenny, both accused of 'misprision' – failing to report Buckingham's remark that should Henry die he would make himself king. Arthur Pole was told to leave court. Henry, his imagination out of control, had decided they must be implicated in the duke's non-existent plot and told the Venetian ambassador that the Serene Republic should not treat Reginald Pole (who had recently arrived in Venetian territory to pursue his studies) too respectfully in case he turned out to be disloyal like his brothers. But then the king recovered his equilibrium and the Poles quickly regained favour.

It was the women of these families, the Countess of Salisbury and the Marchioness of Exeter, who gradually transformed the White Rose cause into a faction. They were motivated by loyalty to Queen Katherine, forming part of what is sometimes called the 'Aragonese' faction. We know a fair amount about Lady Salisbury, but comparatively little about Lady Exeter. Born Gertrude Blount in 1502, she was the daughter of the fourth Lord Mountjoy, whose family had always served the Tudors faithfully, and of his Spanish wife who was once one of Katherine's ladies-in-waiting.

Katherine of Aragon had become very popular, inspiring not just loyalty but affection in all who came in contact with her. Endearingly, amid the splendours of Tudor court life, she made her husband's shirts. One imagines her as short and dumpy, with a radiant, heart-warming smile. But although she was intelligent, humorous and companionable, at the end of 1525 or the beginning of 1526 the king stopped sharing her bed. Forty when he was thirty-two, she had lost her looks and, crucially, she could not give him an heir: her three sons had died very quickly. If Henry recalled Warwick's curse that God would not allow Tudor male children to live, he saw it as a curse on Katherine's marriage to Prince Arthur, not on himself. Despite legitimizing Bessie Blount's son, he needed a lawfully begotten heir who would ensure his dynasty's survival.

The Church could annul a wedding and the king was convinced he had found grounds in a text from Leviticus warning that it was sinful for a man to marry his brother's wife: if he did, they would be childless.[4] When the queen insisted her marriage to Arthur had never been consummated, Henry refused to believe it. The real reason why he wanted a divorce, however, was because he had fallen in love with Anne Boleyn (no beauty but a devastatingly attractive brunette), who refused to become his mistress. The king's 'great matter' dragged on, partly because Katherine was the emperor's aunt and the pope did not wish to offend him, especially after imperial troops occupied Rome in 1527.

Henry's subjects were shocked by his behaviour. The 'common people daily murmured and spoke their foolish fantasies,' admitted Edward Hall. 'But the affairs of Princes be not ordered by the common people.'[5] They were outraged at the prospect of the Lady Mary being bastardized, just as Edward IV's children had been bastardized by King Richard. The queen's defenders included Thomas Warham, Archbishop of Canterbury and John Fisher, Bishop of Rochester (who published seven books and a flow of tracts on the subject), and three other bishops, together with the London Carthusians and the Observant Franciscans, as well as the Lord Chancellor, Sir Thomas More. Among many other supporters were the Courtenays and the Poles, although they were wise enough to keep their opinions to themselves.

An especially influential defender was Elizabeth Barton, a young 'holy woman' in the tradition of Margery Kempe and Julian of Norwich, who in earlier times might have been canonized. A former servant girl born in 1506, after being cured of a serious disease by a vision she believed to be miraculous, Elizabeth had entered a Benedictine nunnery at Canterbury, where she continued to see visions that made her famous all over England. Whether she was a hysteric or a saint, the 'Nun of Kent' was revered. Summoned twice to the royal presence, she told Henry he would incur speedy damnation if he divorced his wife and married Anne Boleyn. He tried to buy her off, promising to make her an abbess despite her youth, but she declined the offer.

To a certain extent Elizabeth was manipulated by her confessor Dr Edward Bocking, a monk of Christchurch, Canterbury and one of the queen's most fervent advocates; she spoke in similar vein to Thomas More, Archbishop Warham and Bishop Fisher – who wept for joy on hearing her – and other influential clergy. In addition, she published a number of what must have been luridly sensational books which the authorities later destroyed. The gist of her message was that, within a month of marrying Anne, King Henry would not only lose his crown and die miserably, but he would go to Hell: she had been granted a vision of the spectacularly nasty place being prepared for him. A Franciscan friar, Richard Rich, repeated her revelations about the king to Lady Salisbury and Lady Exeter, who almost certainly believed in them.[6]

In 1531 two Cornish gentlemen named Kendall and Quyntrell, supported by armed friends, declared they were ready to rise for the Marquess of Exeter, whom they said would become king if Henry married Anne Boleyn, 'or else it should cost a thousand men's lives'.[7] It was also alleged that Exeter's servants – presumably Kendall and Quyntrell – were claiming he 'shall wear the garland at the last'.[8] In consequence, Exeter was banished from court. He may even have been sent to the Tower on suspicion of treason but, if so, he was soon released. Henry VIII was still sane enough to realize that the Marquess was temperamentally incapable of plotting against him.

The royal divorce dragged on for six years, discussed by all England, the king growing more determined than ever. Pressure was brought to bear on the outspoken Bishop Fisher, a fiery preacher and indefatigable pamphleteer, who was threatened with physical violence more than once as well as with arrest. In 1531 someone fired a gun at his London residence. Undeterred, in the end, he became the only man who dared to defend the queen's marriage in public.

Even so, Henry was shocked when Fisher's cook, who had almost certainly been bribed by the Boleyn family, made a crude attempt to poison the bishop, by putting a white powder (arsenic) in the soup served at dinner. Several of the bishop's guests died in agony at the dining table, while he himself suffered from excruciating stomach pain: luckily he had only swallowed a mouthful. However convenient his death might have been, the king gave his immediate assent to an Act of Parliament that was macabre even by sixteenth-century standards – perhaps he feared a smilar attempt on his own life. In Hall's words, 'whosoever did poison any person should be boiled to the death'. The chronicler goes on to relate with relish how Fisher's cook 'was boiled in Smithfield . . . the Wednesday following, to the terrible example of all other'.⁹

In May 1533 Archbishop Cranmer annulled Henry's marriage to Katherine and very soon afterwards Anne Boleyn became Henry's wife. At the end of the month she was crowned queen. During the procession to her coronation at Westminster Abbey by her friend the Archbishop, men in the crowds refused to take their hats off, and the 'goggle eyed whore', as they called her, grew increasingly unpopular as time went by. On one occasion the congregation of a London church walked out when the priest prayed for Queen Anne. Reports from Justices of the Peace throughout the country came flooding in, that men of all classes were saying the king was no better than a lecher and that they would never accept any queen other than Katherine.

In July the Nun of Kent was arrested. As soon as Parliament met, which was early in the following year, she was attainted and declared guilty of treason, together with nine of her closest associates (Dr Bocking and another monk from Canterbury, two friars, two parsons and some laymen). The bill of attainder did away with the need for a trial, which might have proved troublesome as it was by no means certain that a jury would find them guilty. All were duly hanged at Tyburn in April 1534, the men drawn and quartered. Elizabeth escaped burning, which was the normal penalty for women found guilty of treason, but her head was stuck up with the others on Tower Bridge.

Sir Thomas More and Bishop Fisher had also been accused of supporting her. More escaped by pretending he had always thought of Elizabeth as 'a wicked woman'. Fisher, who openly accepted that her visions were genuine, was convicted, but only of failing to inform the authorities – for misprision. This was not a capital offence and he avoided any punishment by pointing out that the nun had told the king exactly what she had told him.

Elizabeth Barton's political significance tends to be overlooked, yet Henry VIII had been in no doubt about the danger she posed.[10] Hall devoted six pages of his folio chronicle to this 'new found saint and hypocrite called the Maid of Kent', quoting from her attainder. She was charged with saying 'there was a root with three branches and till they were plucked up it should never be merry in England'. The root had been Cardinal Wolsey, while the branches were the king, the Duke of Norfolk and the Duke of Suffolk (Charles Brandon). The attainder claimed that the nun's followers had decided that, after marrying Anne Boleyn, Henry was no longer king in the eyes of God, and they had tried to bring others round to their opinion. They had wanted to sow 'a secret rupture and grudge in the heart of the King's subjects' over the divorce, and to start a rebellion.

One of those executed, Henry Gold, a Kentish parson, had been specifically charged with secretly visiting 'the Lady Katherine, Princess Dowager' (the ex-queen) in order to recruit her help in replacing Henry on the throne with his daughter, the Lady Mary, who 'should prosper and reign in this realm and have many friends to sustain and maintain her'.[11] The charge contained the kernel of what became the White Rose group's long-term plan, although wish list is perhaps a better description than plan. This was to overthrow Henry, make Mary queen and give her a husband with Yorkist blood, who would be king consort.

The scheme ignored the Marquess of Exeter's own chances of elbowing Mary aside in the event of Henry's death, which seemed far from distant in view of his regular bouts of ill health. Yet while there are hints that until the birth of the future Edward VI Exeter hoped he might inherit the throne, he would almost certainly have accepted a White Rose solution. On the other hand, incapable of plotting, he would do nothing to help the Lady Mary replace her father, dutifully serving the king as one of the commissioners for Queen Katherine's formal deposition in 1533 – and, three years later, for her successor's trial. Meanwhile, Lady Salisbury and Lady Exeter remained in secret contact with the so-called 'princess dowager', not daring to visit her because her household was full of spies.

# 23

# 1533–4:
# Rebellion?

'Your Majesty should try every means possible to have near you, or somewhere under your control, the son of the Princess's Governess, the daughter of the Duke of Clarence, to whom in the opinion of many people here the realm should belong.'

Eustache Chapuys to Charles V, 27 September 1533[1]

England was shaken to the core by Henry VIII's divorce from Katherine of Aragon, and by the questioning of spiritual certainties that resulted from the king's religious policies. Secular traditions were questioned almost as much. Sitting in seven sessions between 1529 and 1536, the 'Reformation Parliament' enacted new laws that increased the crown's powers enormously. An administrative revolution had been imposed by Henry's chief minister Thomas Cromwell, who bribed, bullied and cajoled MPs into passing the necessary bills. Sometimes the king himself came and addressed both Houses.

Courts were set up to control England's landowners more firmly. The Court of Wards and the Court of General Surveyors were staffed by high-handed officials, and similar courts were established for Wales and the Welsh Marches. The crown's new intrusiveness, its meddling with day-to-day life, did not endear it to ordinary people. Men were encouraged to report disloyal comments by neighbours to the local justices of the peace, who were ordered to send denunciations to London without delay. Cromwell's spies seemed to be listening at every keyhole.

The Henrician revolution, the creeping 'increase in governance', unsettled everybody – nobility, gentry and common folk. There was unease all over England. Many people began to hope that King Henry would soon be succeeded by his daughter Mary who, despite the grim reputation she later gained, enjoyed extraordinary popularity in the 1530s. However, the king had no intention of letting a girl follow him to the throne, bringing an end to the Tudor dynasty.

Among those who helped to revive the cause of the White Rose was a most unlikely Yorkist – Katherine of Aragon. A friend of Lady Salisbury and Lady Exeter, the former queen warmly encouraged the Yorkist cause. In her eyes the heir to the English throne was her daughter Mary, and she was determined to ensure her succession. No woman had ever ruled Katherine's adopted country, but she did not see this as an obstacle: her mother and her sister had both been sovereigns. Should the king beget other children, then Mary must fight them. A consort who represented the House of York would be a vital ally in such a situation and in consequence the aims of the 'Aragonese faction' coincided with those of the White Rose families.

Aware that her marriage to Prince Arthur had been the cause of Warwick's death, Katherine suffered from a guilty conscience, believing 'Divine justice had punished the sin of her father King Ferdinand'. It was Lady Salisbury who first explained the situation to her. Years later, the countess's son Reginald Pole wrote that the queen felt 'very much bound to recompense and requite us for the detriment that we had received on her account'. By 'detriment', he meant his uncle Warwick's murder. With so many of her children dead in infancy, Katherine was understandably inclined to share the belief that the earl's killing had brought a curse upon the Tudors.[2]

'You can have no conception of just how strongly people here want Your Majesty to send troops,' Eustache Chapuys, the imperial ambassador, wrote to Charles V in the summer of 1533. A subtle cleric from Savoy in his mid-forties, an exceptionally able lawyer whose experience included presiding over legal tribunals and interrogating witnesses, and also a scholar who was yet another of Erasmus's innumerable friends, Chapuys had been carefully selected for his post by the emperor. King Henry took a great liking to the new envoy, frequently chatting with him and never guessing during his long stay in England that he was a dedicated enemy.

Almost modern in his skills as an intelligence gatherer, Chapuys listened to opinions as widely as possible, from broad-ranging circles, knowing how to make his contacts trust him and talk freely.'Every day I am approached . . . by Englishmen of distinction, education and intelligence, who inform me the late King Richard was never hated as much as is this King by his subjects,' he reported.[3] Exceeding his instructions in a way that would have shocked the emperor had he known of it, Chapuys methodically encouraged and coordinated this hostility, creating a very dangerous situation.[4]

Since 1531 (after being told he and his friends would be thrown in the Thames if they continued to oppose royal policy), John Fisher, Bishop of Rochester had been in close, if discreet, touch with Chapuys. Although a conservative theologian and an ascetic – he kept a skull on the altar when saying Mass – Fisher was also a keen humanist who had been taught Greek by Erasmus. He had gained an international reputation by his eloquent attacks on Martin Luther, while at the same time he was an admirer of Savonarola (whose ideas had seen a revival during the 1520s), realizing that the Church was in urgent need of reform. Alone among English bishops, Fisher understood where Henry's policies were heading and that nothing short of his deposition could save England from what would one day be called Protestantism. Moreover, he realized the potential strength of the White Rose–Aragonese faction.

This frail, bony-faced ascetic became one of the king's most formidable enemies. In autumn 1533 Chapuys twice quoted him as wanting the emperor to send troops (and, by inference, depose Henry), a deed that he said would please God more than any crusade against the Turk. On the second occasion the bishop advised prompt action, assuring the ambassador that the majority of Englishmen shared his views and expected Charles V to intervene: they preferred an invasion to a trade embargo that might cause a far worse upheaval – a small seaborne force should be enough to topple King Henry. 'Innumerable people from all walks of life keep on telling me this, to such an extent that they are almost deafening me,' added Chapuys.[5]

Chapuys also advised Charles to have Reginald Pole at his court, or somewhere else under his control, as so many people in England saw him as the rightful successor to the throne. The ambassador emphasized that the young man and his brothers had many relatives and allies among the English nobility, besides a large party of supporters – which surely meant Yorkist sympathizers. Among the allies was the Marquess of Exeter, who begged Chapuys to ask the emperor to come and rescue the country from Henry.

The ambassador also named as a potential ally Lord Bergavenny (Edmund de la Pole's old friend) whom he had recently met at court.

One of the most powerful, wise and prudent lords of England, [he] is ill-pleased with the King because he detained him so long in prison with the Duke of Buckingham, his father-in-law, who left therin his person, while Bergavenny left his feathers – that is to say, a great part of his revenue, which he will be glad to get back again by any means and revenge himself.

Chapuys grumbled that they had been unable to talk properly because Cromwell had walked as close behind them as possible, trying to overhear their conversation.[6]

Chapuys explained that Katherine of Aragon wanted Reginald to marry Mary, because of his Yorkist descent. Although she expressed surprising affection for Henry on her deathbed (she went on making his shirts to the end), Katherine was convinced he ought to be deposed. Whatever happened, she wanted her daughter to succeed him. She was a little worried about cutting out Exeter as he was the next male heir to Edward IV after Henry, but the ambassador cited the bastardization of King Edward's children in 1483 by Bishop Stillington, acting on behalf of Richard of Gloucester. Again and again, Chapuys stressed Reginald's right to the throne.[7] Whether or not the ambassador was familiar with the saga of the White Rose under the Tudors, it certainly appears that he had talked to a canon lawyer with Yorkist sympathies.

The Lady Mary was of course crucial. Only seventeen in 1533, yet highly educated, even erudite, and already with a political sense, she knew that her father's divorce meant the loss of her inheritance. Even so, many saw her as their next ruler. Very different in aspect from the sour, pinched figure of later years, she was an attractive girl, possessing some of her father's Yorkist good looks, with strong features – apart from a snub nose – and red-gold hair, and something of her mother's warmth and dignity. We know from her household's accounts for this year that her guests included Reginald's brothers Lord Montague and Sir Geoffrey Pole, the Earls of Oxford and Essex, and Lord Sandys, all men who disliked Henry's policies. Among women visitors were Lady Bergavenny, the Countess of Derby and Lady Kingston, whose husbands held similar opinions.[8] No doubt

Mary was surrounded by Cromwell's spies, and careful not to discuss her future in public.

Bishop Fisher's plan was not unrealistic; it was potentially as great a threat as any faced by Henry VII. Nothing so menacing had ever emerged before, while it was supported by far more magnates than were to take part in the Pilgrimage of Grace: in 1533 a larger percentage of peers and gentry were ready to rise in revolt than had supported York against Lancaster in 1461 and brought down Henry VI.

Cromwell sensed something very dangerous was at foot without being able to identify what it was. This may have been the reason for a number of otherwise inexplicable attacks on several peers who were known to be friends of the Lady Mary. In 1534 Lord Dacre of the North was falsely accused of having had treasonable dealings with the Scots, while in 1535 Lord Bray was charged with dabbling in alchemy (not even a crime) and Lord Darcy was forbidden to leave London. Although omitted from the charges listed in Fisher's attainder, Cromwell claimed after his execution that the bishop had been trying to start a rebellion.[9]

But however many people may have hated King Henry and wanted the rebellion to happen, it never took place. Threatened by the Lutheran princes in Germany, with his long-running struggle against France and his never-ending war on the Turkish front, the emperor simply could not afford to waste valuable troops on helping the Yorkists who, while they might be able to find a candidate for the throne, all too obviously lacked a military leader. Had they possessed someone such as Richard de la Pole, matters might have taken a very different turn. The only possible candidate, Lord Darcy, was too ill and too old for the role, and in any case he had never been an outstanding soldier.

The biggest deterrent was Henry himself, who cowed opponents by his terrifying personality and political skills. Visits to both Houses of Parliament, where he listened to debates for hours on end, and their members' readiness to pass the bills he wanted, gave him a misleading aura of popularity. Opponents were further demoralized by a fear that Cromwell's agents were spying on them, knowing that the slightest hint of disloyalty would result in immediate arrest and probably ruin. Despite this, some Yorkists – especially Darcy – still persisted in hoping against hope for a rising.

Encouragingly, across the Irish Sea during the summer of 1534 the FitzGeralds rose after hearing a false rumour that the Earl of Kildare, currently imprisoned in the Tower, had been executed. The earl's son, popularly known as 'Silken Thomas', sent an embassy to Charles V, offering to rule Ireland as a fief of the Holy See if the emperor would support him with troops to fight the 'English schismatics'. Even though the rebels murdered the Archbishop of Dublin, the rising was welcomed in England with noticeable warmth, much to the alarm of Henry VIII and Cromwell, Chapuys commenting cheerfully that certainly 'it made a very good beginning'.[10] However, despite for a moment threatening Dublin itself, the FitzGeralds were defeated. Silken Thomas and his five uncles were captured through treachery, to be hanged at Tyburn two years later.

'A year ago I wrote to Your Majesty the same thing,' Chapuys wrote on 3 November 1534, replying to a query from Charles about a letter from the Spanish consul at Venice, which he enclosed in cypher. (The consul was suggesting that Reginald Pole might be able to take over England, and save Queen Katherine and Princess Mary from King Henry.) Chapuys repeated that Katherine was most anxious for her daughter to marry Pole, insisting the English would at once show strong support for him, 'especially as there are innumerable good personages who hold that the true title to this Kingdom belongs to the Duke of Clarence's family'. He urged an immediate invasion. Affairs were in such a state, he said, that everyone in England would welcome an imperial army, 'especially if the said Lord Reynold were in it'.

Chapuys then mentioned Reginald's younger brother, Sir Geoffrey Pole, who often came to see him – rather too often thought the ambassador, who had warned him to keep away for fear of attracting the attention of Cromwell's spies. 'He does not cease, like so many others, to beseech me to write to Your Majesty of the facility with which this King might be conquered, and that all the people look for nothing else.' Chapuys had been careful to mention Reginald to Geoffrey on only one occasion: 'long ago, I told him that Reginald would do better to beg for his bread than come back to all the trouble over here, where he might easily be given the same treatment as the Bishop of Rochester or worse.' But he was shrewd enough to realize that Sir Geoffrey was a lightweight, dangerously unstable and indiscreet, if an extremely useful source of information.[11]

Two elderly but formidable peers, who had been young men when Richard III was king, became more influential with the White Rose party at this time. Steady supporters of Queen Katherine, both would have liked to see the deposition of the present monarch. One, already mentioned, was Lord Darcy de Darcy, KG.

Born in the 1460s, Darcy was a fierce old veteran of ancient family from Templehurst in Yorkshire, ennobled by Henry VIII. For many years the steward to the young Earl of Westmorland, whose widowed mother he married, as Warden of the East Marches he had seen plenty of fighting on the Scottish Border. A Northener to his fingertips, Darcy was called the 'Key to the North' because he understood its people so well.[12] Although he had signed a petition to the pope for Henry's divorce, he was horrified by it, as well as by the king's religious policies, which he attributed to his new minister Thomas Cromwell – the 'vicegerent'. In 1532 at a private meeting of notables held by the Duke of Norfolk, Darcy insisted that the pope was the supreme judge in all spiritual matters, later telling the House of Lords that Parliament had no right to meddle with religion.

The second important recruit was John Hussey, whose father had been a judge in Edward IV's day. Now in his sixties, he himself had first risen to prominence by helping to put down Lord Lovell's rising in 1486. A former henchman of Messers Empson and Dudley, Hussey had then made himself so useful to Henry VIII that he had been rewarded with large grants of land and created a peer. He was sufficiently trusted to be appointed chamberlain to the recently bastardized Lady Mary in 1533, after which he and his wife had become indignant at the girl's shabby treatment.[13]

During the summer of 1534 Lord Darcy and Lord Hussey dined together at Hussey's house in London, with Darcy's friend, Sir Robert Constable of Flamborough – a wealthy Northern magnate who was a Knight of the Body to the king although his father had fought for Richard at Bosworth. The main topic discussed was their shared revulsion at a sermon given by the chaplain to an evangelical Yorkshire landowner, Sir Ralph Bigod, in which the priest – a keen follower of the New Learning – had attacked the cult of the Virgin Mary. All agreed that they could never be heretics but were going to live and die as Christian men.[14]

On another occasion, in the garden of his house at Sleaford in Lincolnshire, when discussing the appearance of heresy in Yorkshire, Hussey confided to an acquaintance, that although the new doctrines did not appear to be making much progress there, 'a few particular persons' were nonetheless hoping to make the king bring them in, to such a point that one day it would clearly become necessary to take up arms in defence of the Catholic Faith, because the situation 'will never mend without we fight'.[15]

By autumn both Darcy and Hussey were in touch with Eustache Chapuys, urging him to persuade the emperor to invade England where his troops would be certain of an enthusiastic welcome, especially in the North Country where, so Darcy claimed, there were at least 600 lords and rich gentlemen who shared their opinions. In September Darcy proposed to the ambassador that Charles should send a small expedition up the Thames to rescue the Lady Mary, who was then at Greenwich, while his own men would free Queen Katherine from Kimbolton. In addition, he asked to be given a small force of arquebusiers and money to pay them, so that he could start a rising as soon as he was able to obtain permission from the authorities to return to Yorkshire. The English were so discontented with Henry's regime that they would rush to join the revolt. Even if both Darcy and Chapuys exaggerated, this was the first suggestion of armed action by the White Rose since the death of Richard de la Pole.

Lords Darcy and Hussey were far from alone among English peers in hoping for a revolt that would topple Henry VIII. The Earl of Northumberland's doctor brought Chapuys a secret message from his master, saying the king was about to lose his throne. (Once betrothed to Anne Boleyn, the earl had fainted when she was condemned to death, while he had other reasons for hating Henry.) A similar message arrived from Darcy's brother-in-law, Lord Sandys, the Lord Chamberlain and Deputy of Calais, who had a considerable reputation as a soldier. Other peers must have thought the same way without caring to inform Chapuys, for example the earls of Derby and Essex, and perhaps the Lords Dacre of the North and Bray. It was the same mood of discontented neo-feudalism that, in the previous century, had helped to bring about the Wars of the Roses.

At about this time, 'the good old lord' (Darcy's name in the imperial code book) presented Chapuys with an enamelled gold pansy and, as that well-informed ambassador must have known, the pansy was the badge of the Pole family. At Christmas Darcy sent him a magnificent sword, which Chapuys interpreted as meaning the time had come for an armed rising. The old warrior was the sort of man who spoke to everyone in his neighbourhood, of every class, and he realized that the North was seething with indignation: if the commons rose in sufficient numbers, the gentry and clergy should be able to take command. But just as Richard de la Pole, Perkin Warbeck and the Earl of Lincoln had known – and Henry Tudor in 1485 – Darcy realized that foreign troops and foreign money were needed if there was to be any chance of success.

The Emperor Charles was not convinced of the viability of Darcy's plan, however. While he wanted his cousin Mary to inherit the throne and disapproved of Henry VIII, he was equally anxious to avoid the Anglo-French alliance that would almost certainly result if he meddled too much in English affairs. He therefore did nothing, although he told his ambassador to encourage 'the good old lord'. But while the authorities had no inkling of Darcy's intentions, they were suspicious of him because of his open opposition to the king's policies and he was not allowed to return home until the summer of 1535.

# 24

# 1535–6: The Lady Mary and the White Rose

'The finger of God in those men's blood.'

Reginald Pole, *Apologia to Charles V*[1]

In 1536 during a tournament at Greenwich the king, who had put on weight in recent years, fell heavily from his horse. For several hours he remained unconscious so that there were grave fears for his life. He never jousted again. He also gave up hunting, and instead had deer driven past a stand from where he could shoot them with a bow.

Earlier falls may have inflicted cumulative brain damage of the type suffered by boxers. Since 1519 his concentration had been hindered by headaches that became increasingly severe, while he was tormented by a sore on his leg, an ulcerated vein or a bone infection. When he ceased to take exercise after his fall, his already gross body swelled to a truly vast size, making him

feel even more ill. It affected his temper, his furious rages causing him to aim blows at anyone within reach: Cromwell was
beaten about the head at least twice a week. Yet this ferocity – he
became the only English monarch to burn women alive for
treason – owed more to an already unbalanced temperament
than brain damage. The collapse of his health did not so much
change his personality as aggravate an innate savagery.[2]

Even before the fall, he had been fearsome enough. His religious revolution had gathered pace after the Act of Supremacy
of 1534 completed the break with Rome and created him
'Supreme head on earth of the Church of England'. Gifted with
an insight denied to previous English monarchs, Henry had
realized during the impasse over his divorce that the Bishop of
Rome possessed no more authority outside his diocese than any
other bishop, and that the provinces of York and Canterbury
formed a separate Church. Anyone who disgreed with this revelation risked losing his life.

A new Treason Act proscribed the death penalty for anyone
who should 'deny' the king any of his titles, or who stated in
writing or by word of mouth that he was 'a heretic, a schismatic, a
tyrant or an infidel'. (A testimony to what many people thought of
Henry VIII and his policies.) Also denounced in the Treason Act
was anyone who declared 'our sovereign lord' was 'a usurper of
the crown'. Generally overlooked, this can only refer to Yorkists.[3]

England soon realized that it had become a very dangerous
place. In April 1535 three Carthusian priors were executed at
Tyburn with spectacular cruelty for refusing to accept Henry
as head of the Church. Opposition or criticism infuriated him.
When Pope Paul III made Bishop John Fisher a cardinal in
May as a reward for his uncompromising loyalty to Rome, the
enraged king had him beheaded the next month – although he
did not carry out his threat of sending Fisher's skull to Rome so
that it could wear the red hat.

Sir Thomas More, the former Lord Chancellor, a brilliant
scholar and writer who was admired not just in England but

all over Europe, followed the bishop to the scaffold in July. Once upon a time he had been among Henry's closest friends. They were keen astronomers and had watched the stars together from the roof of Greenwich Palace. The king had liked to arrive unannounced at his house in Chelsea, to dine and then stroll around the garden with him arm in arm. However, because of his reputation Sir Thomas was capable of rallying massive opposition, so that it made political sense to eliminate him.

While the pair undoubtedly died for their consciences, the king's decision to kill them was prompted by more than their loyalty to Rome. Where Fisher was concerned, Cromwell was only stating the facts when he told Sir John Wallop to tell Francis I they had been executed because of 'their treasons, conspiracies and practises secretly practised as well within the realm as without' – for planning 'the destruction of the King'. Although Cromwell could not produce any evidence, by now he had plainly learned something about Fisher's attempts to start a rebellion. As for More, even if he had not been actively involved he would certainly have approved whole heartedly of Henry's replacement by the impeccably Catholic Lady Mary.[4]

Behind the executions, the White Rose party saw a message from on high that Henry was too wicked to remain King of England. Devout Catholics, both Lady Salisbury and Lady Exeter must already have been shocked by the spread of the 'New Learning'. The break with Rome horrified them. Attributing it entirely to Henry's passion for Anne Boleyn, they felt, as Elizabethan papists would put it, that the reformed Church of England had come out of the king's codpiece.

Although Bergavenny's death in June 1535 was a heavy blow for the White Rose, Lord Darcy remained determined to overthrow Henry. It says volumes that for many months the authorities would not let him return to the North. They knew he was planning something but could not discover what. While detained in London, Darcy sent an aged kinsman to Chapuys, probably Dr Marmaduke Waldby, a prebendary of Carlisle, who told the ambassador he was going to see the emperor and find out if he really meant to help them – if not, they would rise by themselves. Warned that such a mission might alert Henry's government, the old man answered that once Darcy was back in the North Country there would be no need to worry. Yet when Lord Darcy finally went home he reluctantly decided that he could do nothing without imperial assistance.

The Lady Mary was widely pitied for being disowned by her father and kept away from her mother. It was said that the new queen was constantly urging Henry to have the 'Princess Dowager' and her daughter put to death, and that she was humiliating Mary in all sorts of petty ways: ordering a lady-in-waiting to box her ears, trying to have her made a servant to the little Princess Elizabeth. Mary had become a key figure in the White Rose programme and a latent threat to the king.

As it was, Henry grew increasingly irritated by Mary's refusal to accept the Acts of Supremacy and Succession. At the end of 1535 Lady Exeter warned Chapuys that she had heard that the king was telling his councillors he was tired of all the trouble the princess dowager and her daughter were causing him, and meant to do something about it when Parliament met, which sounded as if he was thinking of getting rid of them by legal murder. It may have been no more than bluster, but it frightened their friends. 'The Marchioness swears this is true as the Gospel and begs me to inform your Majesty and prays you to have pity on the ladies,' reported Chapuys.[6]

Chapuys had grown devoted to the ex-queen and her daughter, and not merely because they were his master's kindred. In dispatches he stressed how popular Queen Katherine remained, not only among the upper classes but with the common people, who were constantly risking their lives to cheer her. He invariably referred to Henry's new consort as the 'whore' or the 'concubine' and called her daughter Elizabeth 'the little bastard'. He himself was only too anxious for Emperor Charles to rescue

Katherine and Mary, yet at the same time had grown nervous about recommending an invasion.

Chapuys spent several days with the princess dowager at Kimbolton Castle, just before she died in January 1536 – expressing her sadness that she could not see her husband for a last farewell. Even her daughter was not allowed to visit her. The king and Queen Anne greeted the news of her death with unseemly delight, dressing in yellow as soon as they heard, instead of wearing mourning. 'God be praised!' cried Henry. 'We are free from all suspicion of war' – by which he meant that Charles V was unlikely to invade England now that his aunt was dead. No doubt the White Rose folk thought so too and that there was no longer even a faint hope of being rescued by the emperor.

The King's tournament fall took place shortly after this, making him more dangerous than ever. Despite her rejoicing at Katherine's death, by now Anne Boleyn was terrified of him, and with reason. On 29 January she suffered another miscarriage, producing a stillborn male child. Not only had she lost her looks and grown painfully thin but, far worse, she had failed to bear the long-desired son and ensure the succession. Moreover, Henry had belatedly discovered, after their marriage, that she was really a rather horrible woman – vindictive, arrogant, domineering and vile-tempered. In any case, he had half fallen in love with one of her ladies-in-waiting, Jane Seymour.

Besides anatagonizing her uncle Norfolk and a whole host of other courtiers, Anne was stupid enough to make an enemy of Thomas Cromwell, who decided his survival depended on destroying her. Somehow, he learned she had not been a virgin when Henry married her and this discovery had angered the king, especially after her long refusal to become his mistress. Together with Norfolk, for once his ally, Cromwell planted misgivings about her fidelity in the perennially suspicious mind of Henry, who in April set up an official commission to investigate Anne's private life. Cromwell seized the opportunity to fabricate a list of scabrous accusations.

On 2 May Queen Anne was sent to the Tower, and that evening, bathed in tears, Henry told the Duke of Richmond and the Lady Mary that she had been planning to poison them. Later, he claimed that since her marriage Anne must have committed adultery with at least a hundred men. His lack of balance is apparent from Chapuys's description of how, after giving vent to frenzied outbursts about being betrayed, he passed his evenings in joyous musical parties on the river in a gilded barge filled with ladies, returning to Greenwich or York House during the small hours of the morning, in an age when most men and women rose at 4 a.m.

A fortnight later, Anne was tried at the Tower before an audience of over 2,000, to be found guilty of preposterous charges of adultery with four lovers and of incest with her brother, despite her convincing rebuttals. She was even accused of plotting her husband's death, together with her alleged paramours. (The five unfortunate men had already gone to the scaffold.) Her sentence was burning or beheading, at the king's pleasure. Henry graciously settled for the latter. She went to the block on 19 May, less than three weeks after her arrest, dying under the sword instead of the axe with admirable courage.

Within under a fortnight her husband had married her former lady-in-waiting Jane Seymour. A pale, gentle, mouselike blonde from an old but undistinguished family of Wiltshire knights, not very clever, the new queen was a tranquil-tempered, good-natured and kindly young woman, who upset nobody.

England rejoiced for days on end at 'the ruin of the concubine'. Everybody believed that now both Anne and Katherine were dead, Henry would return to Rome, while they were delighted by the prospect of the Lady Mary recovering her position. If Chapuys is to be believed, even Queen Jane suggested to Henry that Mary should be reinstated, only to be told she was a fool for asking such a favour. But it was clear that 'the concubine's little bastard' (the future Queen Elizabeth) would also be excluded from the succession.

Even so, Lord Hussey and his wife remained convinced that Mary was going to regain her position as heir to the throne. Had Lady Hussey known about the dreams of the White Rose party, devoted to the Lady Mary as she was, she would certainly have been in sympathy with them. Visiting her in June, she was heard referring to Mary as 'the princess', by which she meant Princess of Wales, and was promptly arrested, while her husband was dismissed from his post as the girl's chamberlain. Sent to the Tower for interrogation, Lady Hussey was not released until the end of September, her health seriously damaged. The king thought she had been encouraging his daughter's refusal to accept the Act which disinherited her.

By now Henry was so infuriated by his daughter's obstinacy that he threatened to have her executed. In the end, Chapuys persuaded the isolated, humiliated, girl – who was suffering from constant bouts of painful ill health – to give in and to acknowledge her father as head of the Church. Finally, she accepted that she had become a bastard, even if it meant renouncing her loyalty to Rome and her mother's memory. Otherwise she would have gone to the scaffold – some of the council were urging the king to put her to death.

In the ambassador's view, her treatment was intended as a warning to her supporters. Besides Lady Hussey, others who had hoped for Mary's reinstatement were questioned, among them Lord Exeter and the Treasurer Sir William FitzWilliam, who for a time were not allowed to attend meetings of the council, together with the Master of Horse Sir Nicholas Carew and some gentlemen of the Privy Chamber. Soon a new Succession Act stipulated that the throne must be inherited by Jane Seymour's children or whoever the king should name in his will. The Act was aimed at the Aragonese–White Rose faction, of whose aims Cromwell and the king were by now well aware.

The fact remained, however, that Queen Jane was still childless. The Lady Mary's submission to her father did nothing to lessen her popularity, but only increased the pity that people felt for a young princess so cruelly and unjustly bullied into renouncing her inheritance. She remained a rallying point for supporters of the old religion, who at that date included most English men and women. Everybody was delighted when Queen Jane at last prevailed, and in December 1536 Mary was summoned to court although her right to succeed to the throne would not be restored until 1544. They looked forward more than ever to the day when she would replace Henry as their sovereign. Ironically, a Tudor had become the White Rose families' greatest asset.

# 25

# Summer 1535:
# A New White Rose?

'I am sure [the Lady Mary] will never consent to marry anyone in this country, save perhaps Master Reginald Pole, now
at Venice, or the son of Lord Montague.'

Eustache Chapuys on the Lady Mary,
8 July 1536[1]

Reginald Pole (called 'Reynold' by his family) had been born in
1500, the third son of Sir Richard Pole and Margaret, Countess
of Salisbury, and therefore a nephew of the Earl of Warwick.
His elder brother, created Lord Montague by Henry VIII, was
married with children, which was why the White Rose party
placed their hopes in an unmarried younger son as a husband
for the Lady Mary: Montague would certainly have made
no difficulty about renouncing his own claims to the throne.
In any case, Reginald was a most suitable choice for a king
consort. His abilities had long been recognized, in particular
by Henry VIII.

At a very early age Reginald decided to enter the Church. He attended the small Carthusian school at Sheen, and possibly one run by Benedictines at Canterbury, before going up to Magdalen College, Oxford when he was thirteen, where he was given a taste for humanist learning by such brilliant tutors as Thomas Linacre and William Latimer, who later ensured that he became a friend of Sir Thomas More. The king took genuine interest in his progress, paying £12 a year towards his education – the only member of the nobility whom he ever favoured in this way. At eighteen the highly promising young man was ordained as a deacon, Henry granting him the deanery of Wimborne Minster and a prebend of Salisbury Cathedral, which provided him with further income.

When Reginald was twenty-one, the king encouraged him to go to Italy and pursue his studies, subsidizing them lavishly. He spent six years at Padua, one of the most distinguished universities in Europe (known by its students as the 'Bo'), installing himself in Palazzo Roccabonella. Here he was taught Greek, reading Plato and Aristotle, besides acquiring a mastery of elegant Ciceronian Latin from the great Pietro Bembo. During his time at the university, Reginald became known to Erasmus, still reckoned the leading intellectual of the day, who corresponded with him and regarded him as a friend. In 1523 he was elected to a fellowship at Corpus Christi College, Oxford, which provided him with yet further funds, supplemented by a clutch of benefices, such as Harting rectory in Sussex. In 1525–6 he made a lengthy visit to Rome, where he acquired influential friends.

In 1527 he returned to England, to live in a little house (built by Dean Colet of St Paul's) in the garden of the Carthusians at Sheen. Here, by his own wish, he led a solitary, studious life that was dedicated to scholarship, concentrating on theology and adding Hebrew to his languages. Further signs of royal favour followed – the deanery of Exeter and a canonry of York Minister.

Despite his seclusion, Pole sometimes visited Cardinal Wolsey's palace of York Place, where one day he was accosted by a vulgar-looking, middle-aged man with a round, thin-lipped, porcine face and sharp, very watchful, eyes. This was Thomas Cromwell, who in those days was just one of Wolsey's minor officials. Reginald always remembered their conversation. Cromwell asked him what qualifications were needed by men who advised rulers, but Pole guessed that the real object was to discover what he thought about the king's divorce, which was still dividing the Privy Council.

Cromwell had been born near Putney during Richard III's reign. His father was said by some to have been an armourer although Chapuys believed he was a blacksmith, while Pole records contemptuously, with more accuracy, that he was 'a man of no pedigree; and that his stepfather earned his living as a fuller [cloth-maker]'. Yet the great nobleman with royal blood and the upstart from the back streets had at least something in common, which was Italy. As a young man Thomas had worked in Venice as a bookkeeper for a merchant of Reginald's acquaintance and, after a spell as a clerk at Antwerp, he returned to fight as a mercenary. (One source says he was serving with the Duke of Bourbon's army when it sacked Rome.) He then came home to be a scrivener, a combination of solicitor and money-lender, without much success, before entering Wolsey's service.

In answer to his enquiry about what advice a counsellor should give a king, Reginald was carefully noncommital, replying that it must be to act honourably. Cromwell then gave him the benefit of his own ideas on the subject. If he really wanted to succeed, a prince should concentrate on getting exactly what he wanted, without letting himself be hampered by scruples – although outwardly, of course, he should make a show of being absolutely devoted to religion and virtue. Years after, Pole told Charles V that had Thomas Cromwell been Nero's adviser he would certainly have approved of the emperor's decision to murder his own mother.

Seeing the horrified look on Pole's face, Cromwell told him he was handicapped by his lack of experience of the real world, having wasted too much time studying philosophy. He recommended a book by a modern writer who did not fool about like Plato by describing dreams, but provided rules for politicians that worked. Cromwell offered to send him a copy if he promised to read it. (This was Machiavelli's *Il Principe*, which Reginald later read, observing that it must have been 'written by the Enemy of the human race himself' – meaning Satan.) They said goodbye amiably, remembered Pole, who commented that Cromwell only survived Wolsey's fall by buying friends with money he had made from dissolving some small monasteries for the cardinal, adding, 'He was certainly born with an aptitude for ruin and destruction'.

It has been suggested that this meeting with Thomas Cromwell was a figment of Pole's imagination, yet there is no reason for doubting his account in his *Apologia* to Emperor Charles V. Admittedly, he is rather unfair to Cromwell, who had his own ideals – such as blind loyalty to his sovereign.[2] It is significant that Cromwell, the political opportunist looking for useful contacts who might advance his career, spared so much time talking with such a little known figure – he recognized ability when he saw it.

Aware of the quality of his cousin's mind and his growing reputation in academic circles, the king hoped to make use of his gifts. Reginald had gone to Paris in 1529 to study at the university, and the following year he was asked to obtain – with the help of hard cash – judgments from the canon lawyers at the Sorbonne that Henry's marriage to Katherine was invalid. Although Pole obeyed his instructions, securing helpful ammunition for the king, privately he did not agree with the Sorbonne's interpretation.

Soon after Reginald returned to England, the king sent the Duke of Norfolk to offer him the archbishopric of York, in succession to Wolsey who had just died. When he declined, he was summoned to an audience with Henry, who received him alone in a private gallery at York House and asked his opinion on the divorce. Pole had come full of answers in favour, but instead found himself arguing against it. This was not surprising as his mother was the queen's best friend. He recalled how the king grew red with fury and clapped his hand on his dagger, then left the gallery, banging the door. Afterwards, Henry said he had been so angry that he thought of killing him there and then.

Some months later Reginald wrote a letter to Henry, in which he explained as tactfully as he could, why he did not think the royal marriage invalid. He pointed out that the king's father, Henry VII, and the queen's father, Ferdinand of Aragon, had both approved of it. Another reason he gave was that if Henry had heirs by different wives it might lead to the same sort of rivalry that had existed between York and Lancaster – the Lady Mary was extremely popular in England and the emperor was certain to support his niece's claim. The king showed the letter to a new adviser, an obscure Cambridge don called Thomas Cranmer (who had recently gained the royal favour by arguing that the marriage was invalid. 'This man, I trow, has got the right sow by the ear,' Henry commented delightedly when he heard his argument.) Cranmer warned him that Pole's letter must never be made public because it made such a good case for Katherine.

During the spring of 1532 Reginald left England again, still on friendly terms with the king and still being paid an income from his English benefices. He was just in time to avoid the dangers that threatened every critic of Henry's break with Rome. Had he stayed, he would almost certainly have ended on the scaffold like Thomas More and John Fisher. Before setting off, Reginald had a meeting with another kinsman, the Marquess of Exeter, of which he was to give an account in a letter to Exeter's son in 1553. 'Lord Cousin Pole, your departure from the realm at this present time shows in what a miserable state we find ourselves,' the marquess told him. 'It is to the universal shame of all us nobles, who allow you to absent yourself when we ought most to avail ourselves of your presence, but being unable to find any other remedy for this we pray God to find it himself.'[3] The note of deference is revealing – Exeter saw him as a leader.

After a year at Avignon, Reginald returned to Padua where he became a distinguished theologian, joining a circle of gifted young clerics whose plans to renew the Church led to the Counter-Reformation. Meanwhile, he and his friends tried to build bridges with the Lutherans and understand their point of view. Years later, his preference for compromise and lack of ambition showed themselves when he failed to be elected pope by one vote, then forbade his supporters to arrange a second round of voting that would have secured his election. These were not the best qualities for a new White Rose.

Master of the King's Jewels in 1532 and Principal Secretary in 1534, then Lord Privy Seal in 1536, Thomas Cromwell became Henry's first minister. He was also appointed 'The King's Vicegerent in Spirituals' or vicar-general in everything that concerned the Church. A political genius, he was even better than Wolsey at making his master's wishes come true; more powerful than the cardinal had ever been because of his administrative reforms and centralization of the government. Yet he never quite enjoyed Wolsey's freedom of action as Henry now played a much greater part in policy-making, if behind the scenes, content that his minister should take the blame for unpopular measures; indeed, Cromwell was blamed throughout England.

Early in 1535 Reginald Pole, studying at Padua, received a letter from his old friend Thomas Starkey, who had recently become a chaplain and a trusted confidant of King Henry. At one time Starkey had been a student with Pole at the 'Bo', and later acted as his chaplain-secretary in France and Italy. The letter contained an urgent request from the king for Reginald's opinion on the royal divorce. Henry believed that support from so respected a scholar would be particularly valuable.

Later, in October 1535, Reginald wrote to thank Cromwell for having ensured that the king still regarded him with favour, insisting that he was always ready to serve Henry 'as payment for my education'.⁴ Shortly after writing this, however, he decided that Mr Secretary was a messenger of Satan. According to Pole, when Henry had said that if Rome refused to let him divorce Queen Katherine he would abandon the idea, it was Comwell who suggested he should make himself head of the Church in England and transform any criticism of the divorce into treason.

Pole did not complete his reply until the following year. He did so in an entire treatise with the title of *Pro Unitatis Ecclesiasticae Unitatis Defensione* (A Defence of the Church's Unity), which he had written for royal eyes alone. In this little book, which is generally known as *De Unitate,* he begins by thanking Henry for having singled him out from all other English noblemen by ensuring he received a superb education. Otherwise, the work is violently critical of his former patron. He was brutally frank about the royal divorce, insisting that Henry's scruples about the validity of his marriage were a disguise for his lust. His true motive, said Reginald, was desire for Anne Boleyn. In addition, Pole suggested it was Anne herself who had come up with the idea of pretending the marriage was invalid, which was 'how the whole lying business first began'.

He did not restrict himself to the divorce. The king had 'repaid with death those who tried to teach him', said the author in the first section. During the last twenty-six years he had wrung more money out of his people and clergy than any king in five hundred: 'I know because I've seen the accounts,' he told Henry.

No one thought of pouring expensive wine into a barrel empty for a long time without cleaning the barrel first, wrote Pole, and Henry's mind was like an uncleaned barrel. He had destroyed his lords on the flimsiest pretexts, he had packed his court with vile men. His public works were pleasure-houses for himself, together with ruined monasteries and wrecked churches. His butchery and ghastly executions had turned England into a slaughterhouse for innocent people. Yet the King was the man who claimed that the Pope could not be head of the Church because of his moral turpitude.

Henry had made civil war inevitable by disinheriting the Lady Mary, Pole continued, because so many English noble families would fight for her rights. Why for the past three years had Henry been taking these rights away from a daughter who had been his heir for the past twenty? What sort of a parent was it who could confiscate a lawfully begotten child's inheritance and give it to one begotten of a concubine? If the king's father came back, would he not be astonished to find that Pole – a nephew of an innocent man [Warwick] whom he had sent to his death because he was too near the throne – was having to defend the Tudor succession? After all, Pole belonged to the same man's family.

He went on to say that the present king was more dangerous for Christendom than the Sultan of Turkey, and that his kingdom ought to be taken away from him. Even if the emperor had been fighting the Turks and on the point of conquering the Bosphorus, Reginald would have asked Charles to make his ships alter course for England, where 'there is a worse enemy of the Faith and a greater heretic than any in Germany'. His final gibe was to remind Henry of what had happened to Richard III.[5] A little surprisingly, he ended by offering to submit to the king if he would take his advice.

Pole wrote so emotively because he believed the previous pope, Clement VII, had been too weak in dealing with Henry. Instead of listening politely to his threats, Clement should have excommunicated the king early on in the divorce dispute. The treatise was designed to remedy the pope's mistake. Reginald insisted on sending it despite his friend Cardinal Contarini's attempts to dissuade him. Later, he explained he had sent it to Henry, 'just after he got rid of the woman who was reckoned to be the cause of this calamity for the whole kingdom [Anne Boleyn], for though he had bought her at such a price, his love was soon sated and turned into hatred. Everybody expected a change for the better.'[6]

However, Reginald had altogether misread Henry. Quite apart from the abuse, it was particularly unwise to compare him with Richard III, while in view of the king's increasing girth, likening the royal mind to a barrel was no less tactless. Only Luther had been so rude to Henry, in his diatribe against 'Junker Heinrich', but he was a German – no Englishman had ever dared to address the king in such a way. What made it worse was that Pole, a man whose scholarship was admired by the king, owed his education to royal generosity. Yet Reginald saw his book as an appeal, not a denunciation, begging Henry to change his misguided ways – as 'your friend, your physician, your former favourite'.

The book arrived in June 1536. Although the king did not read it at once and it was given to a committee of scholars to study, he obtained a good idea of what was in it from a synopsis by Richard Moryson, one of Cromwell's experts. Both the king and the new Lord Privy Seal realized the impact it might have on public opinion.[7] Graciously, Henry invited Pole to return home, where more learned men than he would be able to put his own point of view. Reginald declined, privately quoting the parable of the fox refusing an invitation to visit the lion's cave after noticing that no animal that did so ever came out. In writing his treatise he had hoped the king might still be redeemable, but by now Pole was convinced that Henry really was a monster. As for the king, he realized there was a new White Rose.

# 26

# Autumn 1536:
# The Pilgrimage of Grace

Christ crucified!
For thy wounds wide
Us commons guide.
Which pilgrims be
Through God's grace
For to purchase
Old wealth and peace.

*The Pilgrims' Ballad*, 1536[1]

Henry VIII's religious policies, implemented by Thomas Cromwell (his 'Vicegerent in Spirituals' who oversaw all clerical matters), caused widespread indignation. Most Englishmen objected not so much to repudiating the pope as to closing down monasteries and convents, and abolishing customs of great antiquity. Laws introduced by Parliament suggested that the crown intended to intrude into every aspect of life, while in all counties there seemed to be commissioners or government spies, or both. The surprising efficiency of Tudor administration contributed to the climate of suspicion. (In 1535 an investigation known as the *Valor Ecclesiasticus* took only five months to inform Mr Secretary Cromwell of the income of every single clergyman in the kingdom, from bishops down to parish priests and chantry chaplains.)

During the coming explosion, the Northeners would sing a wistful doggerel written by a Lancashire monk, a verse from which is quoted above. Again and again, the ballad makes it clear that they wanted things to remain as they always had been, whether worldly or spiritual; the king's men should stop meddling and leave them in peace.[2]

In April 1536 a number of rebels were executed in Somerset, while 140 other persons in the same county sued for pardons after making unlawful assemblies. Almost nothing is known about this rising, but it anticipated far more dangerous disturbances in the North and we can safely assume that it was about religion.[3] Many of the nobles and gentry were angry and resentful, and not just the 'commons', but were too frightened to take action.

In particular, there was real anger in the North Country at the closure of the smaller monasteries, which had been popular because they had supplied not only careers for younger sons and unmarriageable daughters but rudimentary social services: some basic education, a certain amount of accommodation for the elderly, hospitality to travellers, and above all food and clothing for the destitute. In addition, they had built roads, bridges and sea walls that nobody else in the area could provide. In the opinion of Robert Aske (about to play a leading role in the subsequent upheaval), their suppression was a serious loss for the communities in their neighbourhood: 'the abbeys was one of the beauties of this realm to all men and [to] strangers passing through . . . gentlemen were much succoured in their needs with money, their young sons there succoured, and in nunneries their daughters brought up in virtue'.[4]

The proposed new registers of births, marriages and deaths caused almost as much disquiet. There were rumours that swingeing new taxes were to be introduced on every baptism, wedding and funeral, that church plate and ornaments would be confiscated, and that many parish churches were to be closed down. It was said, too, that there would be fines on eating goose, chicken or white bread.

In Lincolnshire these unsettling rumours appeared to be confirmed by the appearance during the autumn of three bodies of commissioners in the north-east of the county: one charged with closing down smaller monasteries, another with inspecting the clergy and a third with (supposedly) imposing a new tax called the 'subsidy'. Early in October 1536, led by a cobbler, the people around the market town of Louth rose in protest, attacking any government officials they could catch. The Bishop of Lincoln's unpopular chancellor was beaten to death with staves, while another man was (wrongly) reported to have been blinded, sewn in a newly flayed bullhide and then baited to death by dogs. Although the report turned out to be untrue, it showed the wild uneasiness of the times.

Local gentry and priests joined the revolt, with gentlemen putting on 'harness' (armour). Others sympathized but were frightened to take part. Lord Hussey supported the revolt although the extent of his involvement is unclear: if he did take an active role, he was incapable of providing leadership. Within a few days, 10,000 men had taken up arms (bows or scythe-blades on poles) and drawn up a petition. On 6 October they occupied Lincoln. They declared they would not pay any new taxes, demanding the restoration of the monasteries, the removal of heretical prelates such as Cranmer and the dismissal of Cromwell from the royal council.

Henry reacted quickly. He ordered the mustering of an 'Army Royal' to protect London in case the rebels marched on the capital. If they did not come south, the army was to head north and disperse them. The troops assembled at Ampthill in

Bedfordshire, under the Duke of Suffolk. A letter from the king reached Lincoln on 10 October, angrily threatening 'the rude commons of one shire, and that one of the most brute and beastly of the whole realm' with severe punishment.[5] Simultaneously, a herald arrived, repeating the threats and insisting there was no truth in the rumours of new taxes or church closures. Next day, lacking a proper leader, the gentry decided the situation was hopeless and persuaded the rebels to disperse. So did the Army Royal, which had got as far as Stamford, forty miles from Lincoln. Although many rebels went home reluctantly, everything quietened down very quickly. The Lincolnshire rising was over.

But within a few days the trouble flared up elsewhere, on a larger scale. Starting at Beverley in the East Riding of Yorkshire on 8 October, it then spread north-west, to Kirby Stephen in Westmorland and Penrith in Cumberland, as well as south-west into northern Lancashire along the Ribble valley. The rumours in all these areas were the same as those that had circulated in Lincolnshire, and so were the protests. To some degree Lord Darcy was behind the disturbances. How much is unknown, but it certainly appears that he was encouraging men to rise in defence of Catholicism. It is likely, too, that he still had every intention of destroying Henry VIII.

Unluckily for Lord Darcy – and for the White Rose party – the leadership passed into the hands of a one-eyed Yorkshire gentleman named Robert Aske from Aughton in the Derwent valley, an eloquent lawyer in his thirties with an oddly naive streak, who had been marginally involved in the Lincolnshire rising. While Aske wanted changes to the king's policies, he never contemplated deposing him, instead turning the rising into a crusade which he christened 'The Pilgrimage of Grace for the Commonwealth'. The pilgrims were divided into military-style companies, with a daily roll-call. Their basic aims were to defend the Church against heresy and rescue the king from his advisers – bishops such as Thomas Cranmer and Hugh Latimer, and above all from his minister Cromwell.

Darcy realized it would be impossible to play the White Rose card. The Lady Mary was popular with the pilgrims, but as heir to the throne: they had no wish for her to replace her father while he remained alive and followed Aske's line that this was a pilgrimage to save the king from his evil ministers. Afflicted by long-standing health problems – a hernia and a chronic bowel complaint – Darcy confined himself to trying to maintain what influence he could over the rising. A few weeks later, with breath-taking insincerity he declared: 'For my part I have been and ever will be true both to King Henry VII and to the King our Sovereign Lord, and I defy him that will say the contrary for, as I have ever said, one god, one faith, one king.'[6]

Aske, the 'Chief Captain' as he styled himself, did not have complete control over the rebels so that the Pilgrimage was not fully coordinated. Eventually there were nine armies under nine lesser 'captains'. They included a 'Captain Poverty' in Richmondshire whose name indicates that worries such as a fear of enclosures played a role. But the overriding motives were undoubtedly religion and discontent with the government.

On 16 October thousands of armed pilgrims marched into York, and Aske sent the mayor a list of five 'Articles', which was addressed to the king. The first complained of the suppression of religious houses. Three days later the rebels took Hull, while on 17 October the people of Pontefract rose and invested the castle. Inside were Lord Darcy, constable of the castle, and the Archbishop of York with local knights and gentlemen. After a show of resistance, Darcy opened the castle gates on 21 October, his tactics being to run with the hare and hunt with the hounds, although his sympathies were entirely with the pilgrims. Together with his friend Sir Robert Constable, he joined the leadership, becoming second only to Robert Aske. Throughout, he maintained his pose as a bluff, simple, honest man – 'Old Tom'.

After the fall of Pontefract Castle, badges of the Five Wounds of Christ suddenly became plentifully available to the pilgrims.

These displayed two hands and two feet pierced by nails, surrounding a bleeding heart on a chalice – a device Lord Darcy's men had worn during a would-be crusade against the Moors in 1511. Secretly, he hoped that foreign troops were going to reinforce the pilgrims' army. Aske's loyalty to Henry infuriated Darcy as he knew the king's treacherous, revengeful nature – leaving such an enemy on the throne was madness. But at least the Chief Captain was keen to have the Lady Mary's right of succession restored, a key part of the White Rose programme.

Even though none of the great Northern magnates were involved, it must have seemed to King Henry and Cromwell that the entire North Country supported Aske; so large an army had not been seen throughout the Wars of the Roses. 'This matter hangeth like a fever, one day good, another bad,' wrote a member of the council to Cromwell on 15 October.[7] The king had no clear picture of what was happening, but suspected that Darcy must be behind it. The army intended for Lincolnshire had returned home. With considerable difficulty, the king assembled two new forces to send north, one commanded by the elderly Earl of Shrewsbury and the other by the Duke of Norfolk. Irregularly paid and ill-fed, these troops were inclined to sympathize with the pilgrims.

As a youth Lord Shrewsbury, who brought 7,000 men, had ridden to Bosworth with King Richard,[8] although in 1487 he had fought for his supplanter at Stoke against the Earl of Lincoln. Throughout Henry VII's reign he had been called on to muster his household men and tenants in emergencies, but had never acquired any experience of commanding troops in battle. Ironically, he, too, detested Cromwell. So did the Duke of Norfolk, an equally unexperienced general whose own force numbered about 5,000. Like Shrewsbury and no doubt most of his own men Norfolk secretly shared the pilgrims' views, but he was much too frightened of the king to disobey him.

Apart from uncompromising spirits such as Sir Robert Constable, the pilgrims' leaders did not want a war although there was a moment on their march to Doncaster when battle was only averted by torrential rain. By now they were 30,000 to 40,000 well-armed men, officered by gentry. 'Lord Hussey sent me word that the rebels are sufficiently well appointed, and in a condition to fight the royal army, since they are numerically stronger by one third,' Chapuys reported to the emperor on 5 November. 'Besides abundance of provisions of all kinds they have a tolerably large sum of money, but they still want some help in men either from Flanders or from Spain and are confident that Your Majesty will assist them.'[9] Chapuys did not realize that by now the pilgrims had missed their opportunity.

The Duke of Norfolk's levies, not yet reinforced by Shrewsbury, were outnumbered and demoralized. Most would probably have run for their lives rather than fight. Had the 'Army Royal' been defeated in the North Country, it is difficult to see how King Henry could have kept his crown. An invasion of imperial troops with Pole at their head, which many observers thought more than likely, would have completed his ruin. When Norfolk realized just how large an army he was facing, he secured a truce on 27 October – and saved his master's skin.

Little was heard from the Lord Cromwell of Wimbledon (his sonorous title since the previous summer), who was largely responsible for causing the crisis and whose head the pilgrims were demanding loudly. Seemingly terror stricken, he kept in the background as far as possible. There is a note of hysteria in the very few surviving letters he wrote during the crisis.

Lengthy negotiations began. Two of the pilgrims' leaders, Sir Ralph Ellerker and Robert Bowes (a barrister), took a petition to Henry at Windsor. In a long letter in reply, the king promised that if they could prove, as they alleged, 'certain of our Council to be subverters both of God's law and the laws of this realm . . . we shall proceed against them'. He ended by promising every pilgrim a full pardon with the exception of ten ringleaders, commenting with unquenchable self-satisfaction,

'Now note the benignity of your Prince'. Throughout his reply Henry congratulated himself on the good government he had given his people for the last twenty-eight years.[10]

Norfolk tried hard to win over Lord Darcy. 'I cannot do it in no wise, for I have made promise to the contrary, and my coat was never hitherto stained with any such blot,' was his reply to an invitation to betray Aske and his fellow pilgrims.[11] In November, expecting the negotiations to fail, he gave his kinsman, old Canon Waldby from Carlisle, £20 for expenses and sent him to the Low Countries to ask the regent for 2,000 landsknechts and 2,000 arquebuses. But Darcy then changed his mind, cancelling Waldby's journey.

In any case, Henry had taken care to deflect foreign intervention, by offering the Lady Mary's hand in marriage to the sons of both Charles V and Francis I, ignoring her recent 'bastardization'. Neither of these rulers wanted to drive the English king into an alliance with his greatest rival. At the same time, their ambassadors in London, methodically fed misinformation by Cromwell, were reporting that the king would soon crush the rebellion, regardless of any help from abroad.

Henry sent Sir Ralph Ellerker and Robert Bowles back to the North with his reply. On 18 December, they reached Darcy's house at Templehirst, where the 'captains' had assembled. Wrongly, the king had decided they must be tired of being under arms, especially with winter approaching, and that his promise of a pardon for nearly everybody would ensure the swift collapse of the Pilgrimage, just as it had ended the trouble in Lincolnshire. He was therefore astounded when the pilgrims showed not the slightest intention of going home. Despite this, he did not agree to any of their requests, merely sending them a letter that was an odd mixture of eloquence and bluster, offering little more than an insincere promise of pardons. Yet he was bound to win since the struggle had now become one of negotiation rather than civil war. The pilgrims had lost their chance by not fighting at Doncaster.

A letter from Cromwell to Sir Ralph Eure, holding Scarborough for the king, had been intercepted when a royal ship was captured. It should have warned the pilgrims not to put too much trust in Henry's pardons. 'My lord Privy Seal' had written that if the pilgrims continued with their rebellion, they would be punished so mercilessly that 'their example shall be fearful to all subjects whiles the world doth endure'.[12]

A council of captains at Pontefract drew up a manifesto. The first article showed a surprising knowledge of heresy and heretics, expressing the pilgrims' antipathy to Luther, Melancthon, Bucer and the Anabaptists, together with such home-growns as Wycliffe, Tyndale and Barnes. Nothing could have better expressed most Englishmen's loathing for the tiny little clique who were trying to force German ideas on the Church. Another article asked that all heretics, from bishops to laymen, should suffer 'condign punishment by fire', another that the Lord Cromwell and Sir Richard Rich be similarly punished as 'subverters of the good laws of the realm, and maintainers and inventers of heretics'. There were demands for the re-establishment of Rome's authority, and for dissolved religious houses to be given back to the monks and friars. A further demand was for the restoration of the Lady Mary's right to inherit the throne, 'for the Lady Mary is marvelously beloved for her virtue in the hearts of the people'.[13]

The pilgrims' articles were formally presented to the Duke of Norfolk at Doncaster on 6 December by Aske, supported by a delegation of knights, esquires and 'commons', who solemnly knelt before the duke as the king's representative. A discussion of the articles then began. Acting on instructions that he had received from Henry at the last moment, Norfolk promised every pilgrim a free pardon, announcing that Parliament would be called to discuss their demands in detail. This was a purely verbal agreement, never written down, but Aske's delegation were fully convinced that the king had given in to them and accepted their manifesto.

The gullible Robert Aske rode back in triumph to Pontefract to give the news to 3,000 pilgrims who were waiting at the market cross. The cannier among them refused to believe it, angrily threatening to raise all Yorkshire once more, but Lancaster Herald arrived from Doncaster on 8 December and read out the royal pardon, which convinced most people. Returning to Norfolk, Aske knelt and resigned his office of Chief Captain. The pilgrims took off their badges and went home.

They had been outwitted by the most treacherous monarch in English history. Henry then divided the gentry from the commons by such stratagems as inviting Aske to spend Christmas at court and presenting him with a wonderful jacket of crimson silk, but showed no sign of carrying out his promises. In the meantime, royal officials toured the North, denouncing the Pilgrimage. Just as the king had hoped, this resulted in new, smaller, risings that were easily put down. At the end of January 1537, a group of Yorkshiremen plotted to capture Hull and Scarborough, despite Aske's efforts to dissuade them, and in February Cumberland men attacked Carlisle.

These fresh revolts gave Henry an excuse for repudiating the Doncaster agreement, and he ordered the Duke of Norfolk to declare martial law in the Western Marches. The king also repudiated his promise to grant pardons. During the summer of 1537 the North Country endured a sustained reign of terror, while seventeen pilgrim leaders were taken to London for trial and execution.

Nothing could cow Lord Darcy. When examined by the Lord Privy Seal, he told him:

> Cromwell, it is thou that art the very original and chief causer of all this rebellion and mischief, and art likwise causer of the apprehension of us that be noblemen and dost daily earnestly travail to bring us to our end and to strike off our heads, and I trust that ere thou die, though thou wouldst procure all the noblemen's heads within the realm

to be stricken off, yet shall there one head remain that shall strike off thy head.[14]

'Old Tom' was beheaded on Tower Hill, Lord Hussey at Lincoln. Most of the others were executed at Lincoln or York, suffering the usual butchery except for the knights, who because of their rank were hanged until dead. Orders were given that Robert Aske, too, should not be cut down before he was dead, although his torso was hung in chains to rot on the gibbet. The only woman among them, Margaret Cheyney – Sir John Bulmer's 'paramour' – who with her lover had been found guilty on the most specious grounds, was burned alive at Smithfield – 'a very fair creature and a beautiful' according to an observer.[15]

In the meantime, given a bad fright by what he regarded as the 'horrible treason', Henry had ordered Norfolk to break the North Country. About 150 of the commons, including several monks, were hanged during a campaign of calculated frightfulness: men were strung up on trees in their own gardens, priests dangled from steeples and another woman was burned. Some hangings took place without trial, to avoid any chance of acquittal. The king rejected all appeals and if a jury found a defendant not guilty he ordered a retrial – he grumbled at Norfolk's negligence in not quartering the bodies. He announced that in the summer of 1537 he would go on a progress through the North, to accept its return to obedience, but when the time came he shirked the visit.

By any reckoning the Pilgrimage of Grace was an exceptionally dangerous upheaval: 'a formidable counter-revolutionary programme, a fundamental rejection of the Henrician Reformation'.[16] Yet there had been few signs of Yorkism. During the Lincolnshire rising someone at Stamford had demanded 'A new King'[17] while at Furness Abbey in a region once famous for loyalty to Richard III's memory, some of the monks declared that Henry VIII could not be the rightful King of England because his father 'came in by the sword', and another prophesied that 'the red rose should die in his mother's womb'. One of the brethren of Furness who spoke out was named Broughton, perhaps a kinsman of Lord Lovell's friend, Sir Thomas Broughton.[18] But that was all.

The Pilgrimage was the White Rose's only real chance of toppling the king and they let it slip.[19] Even so, Henry continued to fear the White Rose, and not entirely without reason. He knew that, had he been driven from the throne, there was only one man who could have taken his place – Reginald Pole. Judging from his bitterness towards the entire Pole family, the possibility that Reginald might still succeed in exploiting the situation was never very far from his thoughts.

# 27

# Spring–Summer 1537:
# 'Mr Pole's Traitorous Practises'

'that arch-traitor Reynold Pole, enemy to God's word and
his natural country, had moved and stirred divers great
princes and potentates of Christendom to invade the realm
of England.'

E. Hall, *The Union of the Two Noble and Illustre*
*Families of Lancaster and York*[1]

In December 1536 Pope Paul III made Reginald Pole a cardinal.
The new Prince of the Church had taken no notice of a letter
from Thomas Starkey – obviously inspired by Henry – which had
warned him that by accepting a Red Hat he would become the
enemy of his king and his country. As Henry realized only too
well, Pole had been given the hat because the pope was sending
him to help the pilgrims. Before the year was over, Reginald set
out for Flanders.

The last hope of the White Rose, Pole was a genuinely
majestic figure. Paintings show an austere, patrician face with

high cheekbones, melancholy, unusually large eyes and a long black beard. That rare Renaissance phenomenon, an Italianate English nobleman, he was impressively erudite, speaking fluent Greek and passable Hebrew. Very proud of his Plantagenet blood, he was fully aware of his family's claims. 'My mother's brother [was] the Earl of Warwick . . . who being the son of the Duke of Clarence, brother of King Edward, became, by the death of that King's sons, next heir to the English crown,' he would remind Lord Protector Somerset in 1549.[2] Yet he had no particular desire to wear the crown himself. Pole was essentially a churchman, and if called on to be king – or king consort – he would accept the role but with reluctance, and only as a means of bringing his homeland back to the Catholic fold.

'Here [at Rome] lives an English gentleman of the name of Reginald Pole,' reported a Spanish envoy in November 1536. 'His Holiness honours him much and has given him lodgings within his own palace, and over his own apartments. Though he dresses as an ecclesiastic, he is not yet in holy orders.'[3] Given such close proximity, it is likely that Paul III often discussed King Henry with Reginald, whom he had known for many years. The pope was familiar with the White Rose programme: for Mary to replace her father on the throne, possibly with Reginald as her husband. It certainly seemed a good way of bringing England back to Rome, if Henry was not prepared to do so.

At this date Catholicism was supported not just by Mary and the 'old nobility', but by England as a whole. While there may have been plenty of anti-clericalism and contempt for corrupt clergy, the vast majority of people still wanted the Mass. 'Heresy' was confined to a few tiny pockets of more or less illiterate Lollards and some small groups of 'sacramentaries' in London and East Anglia and at the universities, influenced by the new ideas from Germany or Switzerland – the only men and women who, as yet, welcomed the king's rupture with Rome with unfeigned enthusiasm. Besides the rebellion in the North and the smaller one in Somerset, an abortive rising had to be put down in Norfolk during the spring of 1537, while there were signs of open discontent in other places as well, with angry grumbling throughout the country. However, Paul III and the White Rose had two exceptionally formidable opponents in Henry VIII and Cromwell.

The pope had created Pole a cardinal so that he could go to England as a papal legate (ambassador with full powers), the Conde de Cifuentes reported from Rome. He adds, 'it was understood that the rebels wanted him and only fair that the Pope should respond to their wishes'. The mission in the bull appointing Reginald a legate was supposedly to persuade the rulers of Christendom to settle their differences so that they would be able to attend a council and plan a crusade against the Turks. However, the bull's small print empowered him to deal with other matters concerning the Church, including England's break with Rome.

In his despatch, Cifuentes mentioned that his colleague Chapuys had often written to say how important it was to send Reginald to England with money and authority to use the 'weapons of the Church'. One problem was that the mission might endanger Princess Mary's life. Another was that the new cardinal would need to travel through France, although if King Francis did not stop him this might goad Henry into quarrelling with the French, which would of course benefit the emperor. Reginald carried bills of exchange for 10,000 ducats to buy arquebuses for the rebels, and would be accompanied by Bishop Gianmatteo Giberti, Bishop of Verona.

Pole had been told the business 'might well end in his marrying the Princess', says Cifuentes, which was the reason why the pope did not let him become a priest. Although officially his job was to persuade Henry to bring England back into communion with Rome, privately he was to do as much as he could to help the pilgrims. Clearly, Paul III was a firm supporter of the White Rose programme and saw Reginald as a potential king consort.

The years 1536–8 were the most insecure of Henry's reign. Had Exeter rebelled in the West Country and Montague done so in Hampshire, the pilgrims could have marched down and occupied London, forcing Henry to flee and enabling Mary to become queen.[4] When the king crushed the Pilgrimage, he knew he had only just escaped ruin. He still felt unsafe throughout the first months of 1537.

Both Henry and Cromwell were very worried by Pole's mission, fearing that he might inflame English opinion and set off another pilgrimage by publishing *De Unitate* or the bull of excommunication issued by Clemen VII in 1533 but never promulgated, while conceivably he might even turn out to be the leader that the pilgrims had lacked. Nor was it impossible that Francis I or the emperor would provide him with troops, or that he would hire mercenaries with papal money. Danger could also come from Ireland. An Irish ship was intercepted with an Irish monk carrying letters from the FitzGeralds to Pole, and when Kildare's son fled to Europe, spies reported that Reginald had given him a place in his entourage.

The cardinal's plan was to go to London and negotiate while the free Parliament promised by the king was sitting: if Henry failed to call it, he hoped to negotiate with his envoys on foreign soil. In either case, he wanted to stir up as much English opposition as possible to the breach with Rome: he had even thought of disrupting trade between England and Flanders to arouse discontent. His ultimate aim, however, was to revive the Pilgrimage of Grace, as is clear from Paul III's bull appointing him legate.

> It may be that the Enemy of Mankind has such a hold upon the King that he will not be brought to reason except by force of arms. It is better, however, that he and his adherents should perish than be the cause of perdition to so many . . . hoping that the same people who lately took up arms to recall him to the Faith will do so again.[5]

Henry guessed at his tactics, his guess being confirmed by a secret dispatch from Rome late in 1536 and then by an envoy from Francis I in March the following year. At all costs the king was determined to stop Pole from ever setting foot on English soil in his capacity as legate, while under no circumstances would he send envoys for discussions with him in Flanders. He was simply not prepared to negotiate a matter that in his mind was non-negotiable – the king's supremacy over the English Church.

Cromwell employed an agent in the cardinal's household at Rome. This was Michael Throckmorton, from a well-known Warwickshire family, who had been given the risky job of bringing the treatise *De Unitate* to London during the summer of 1536. Arrested and put in the Tower, after swearing undying allegiance to Henry VIII he promised to spy on Pole and coax him into returning home, not as a legate but as the king's loyal subject. This apparently amiable gentleman, almost childlike in manner, was then allowed to go back to Rome. In reality, Throckmorton was among the most cunning double agents in Tudor history, one of the few who got the better of Thomas Cromwell.

In his first report, Throckmorton told the Lord Privy Seal that he was finding it hard to make his master return to England, saying it was never easy to make a great man change his mind, and that this was especially true of Reginald Pole. Tongue in cheek, Michael described Pole as honest but naive, exploited by the Roman curia. He explained that he was going to accompany the cardinal on his mission, so long as London did not object, because he could not help liking the man for his good qualities, even though he held some bad opinions, adding humbly that no man could understand the value of loyalty better than Cromwell, who from personal experience must know the wonderful comfort that it gave one. Another English agent at Rome, keeping Throckmorton under surveillance, reported that he was obviously sincere and remarked on his simplicity. Michael was gifted with a strong sense of humour as well as nerves of steel, and during Pole's mission he was to cross the Channel more than once for discreet discussions with the Lord Privy Seal, always blandly insisting that the cardinal had absolutely no intention of encouraging another revolt.

The nuncio at Paris, Archbishop Rodolfo Pio – another old friend of Reginald – refused to believe assurances by Henry's ambassadors in France that all the unpleasantness on the other side of the Channel was over. As late as April he believed the English people had been so disgusted by the way the king had tricked the pilgrims that they were going to depose him. One of Henry's ambassadors in Paris told the nuncio privately that in his opinion England would come back to Rome and Mary be recognized as heir to the throne. Pio advised Reginald to publish *De Unitate* at once – advice that was not taken since the legate still hoped he might be allowed to visit London.

Pole left Rome in February 1537, taking weeks to reach the French border. When he arrived at Paris in April, although he was treated politely Francis I refused to receive him and he had to leave France. Even so, much to Henry's fury, the French king refused repeated requests by the English ambassadors, Sir Francis Bryan and Bishop Gardiner, that Pole should be arrested and handed over. Francis also sent a secret messenger to warn him that there were plots against his life. Reginald went on to Cambrai, an independent bishopric, where he had to wait a month for permission to enter imperial territory.

He remained optimistic. From Cambrai he wrote to Rodolfo Pio that England was afflicted by a disease flowing from the head (Henry) for which there were only two remedies, either surgery or diet – by surgery he meant rebellion and by diet he meant diplomacy. He had chosen the second remedy because he believed King Francis would help him. Wrongly, he was convinced that, even if the recent rising was over, the country was not going to calm down until the problem of religion was settled. What he omits to spell out in this letter is that he hoped to destroy Henry with his diet.[6]

Friendly messages came from Queen Mary of Hungary, who governed Flanders for her brother the emperor, but no offers of assistance. Pole also learned that Henry was offering a reward of 100,000 gold crowns to anyone who brought him back to England, dead or alive. On 25 May the king wrote to Bryan and Gardiner, ordering them to make the French insist on his being thrown out of Cambrai. 'And for as much as we would be very glad to have the said Pole by some means trussed up and conveyed to Calais, we desire and pray you to consult and devise thereupon.' Bryan should hire 'fellows' to do the job.[7] In Paris the nuncio heard Sir Francis declare loudly that if Pole returned to France he would kill him with his own hands.

The cardinal soon had warning of these plans. Sent by his brother Sir Geoffrey, the messenger was a sea-captain and former pirate, Hugh Holland, who shipped wheat to Flanders. Throckmorton questioned him carefully, in case he might be an assassin, before letting him see his master. In the message Geoffrey offered to come over to the Low Countries to tell his brother how 'the world in England waxeth all crooked, God's law is turned upside down, abbeys and churches overthrown, and [Reginald] is taken for a traitor, and I think they will cast down parish churches'. At court Cromwell was saying publicly that the cardinal would destroy himself. The essence of the message, however, was that 'Mr Bryan and Peter Mewtas was sent into France to kill him with a hand-gun or otherwise as they should see best.' 'And would my Lord Privy Seal so fain kill me?', remarked Reginald. 'Well, I trust it shall not lie in his power. The King is not contented to bear me malice himself, but provoketh other against me.'[8]

A gentleman of the Privy King's Chamber who had commanded the royal artillery when Norfolk confronted the pilgrims at Doncaster, Mr Peter Mewtas turned out to be a disappointment for those who commissioned him. He may have known a lot about guns, and a red-robed cardinal was an unmistakeable target, but he and his arquebus could get nowhere within range of a quarry who, wisely, seldom if ever ventured out of doors and left off his robes when he did. It seems that Reginald's old friend Dr Thomas Starkey, risking his own life, had tipped off the Pole family about Mewtas.[9]

Sir Francis Bryan got in touch with the Knight Porter of Calais, Sir Thomas Palmer, who mounted his horse and galloped after Pole, but never managed to catch up with him. Four soldiers from the Calais garrison were then hired by Palmer to murder the cardinal, for £100 – they were to visit Cambrai disguised as horse-copers and then find an opportunity to kill him. Again, Pole was warned of the plot, possibly by Bryan himself.

After this Sir Francis and Gardiner enlisted John Hutton, the English ambassador in Brussels, who responded with enthusiasm, hoping to ingratiate himself with King Henry. He, too, was unable to find the right killers, but thought he might save face when he met a starving Welshman named William Vaughan, on the run from a manslaughter charge at home. Vaughan told Hutton that he knew a student at Louvain called Henry Phillips who would get him a post as servant to Michael Throckmorton. Phillips had confided that Throckmorton was about to sail for England with messages hidden inside hollow loaves of bread from Pole to his allies. Not realizing that Michael was Cromwell's spy, Hutton gave Vaughan money, promising to obtain a pardon for him if he sailed with Throckmorton and made certain of his arrest.

When Vaughan arrived at the cardinal's residence, Throckmorton did not like the look of the man but brought him to his master. 'As I am informed, you be banished out of your native country as well as I,' remarked Pole pleasantly, adding that he always liked meeting Welshmen as his grandfather had come from Wales. Vaughan begged for a job, saying he was penniless, to which Pole replied that he had all the servants he needed while travelling, but could offer a place if he came to him in Italy. However, after giving Vaughan a crown he told him 'to gather news' – which was employment of a sort.[10]

By this time Reginald was at Liège, installed in comfort at what was known as the old palace. His host was the Cardinal of Liège, Erard de la Marck, the same man who had rescued the young Richard de la Pole from his debtors and Henry VII's agents at Aix thirty years earlier. Sadly, we do not know if Erard reminisced about the former White Rose to his successor, but Pole says he looked after him like a father, and that during his stay he was treated with the honours due to a papal legate. The locals were ready to do anything they could to protect him, he writes thankfully in a letter of 10 June.

It was just as well. In the same letter Reginald tells how the city authorities had learned of a plot to kill him after they intercepted a letter from Hutton at Brussels which contained the words: 'If he can be killed, as we earlier discussed among ourselves, it would certainly be the gateway to being looked on with the highest favour with the King, and earn us a valuable reward.' Reginald describes how the assassin, who was an Englishman claiming to be an exile, had tried to join his household, but then lost his nerve and bolted. This does not seem to have been the Welshman Vaughan as sometimes suggested, but rather a professional killer.[11]

Although Ridolfo Pio at Paris described the behaviour of the English ambassadors as 'that of devils rather than men', their unavailing efforts to assassinate Pole bordered on farce. John Hutton's attempts were even more of a joke, and Reginald was never in any real danger. Henry had no need to kill him, however, since by the summer of 1537 it was clear the Pilgrimage of Grace had been defeated and there were going to be no more risings. In consequence, Pole's mission had become a waste of time.

Realizing that by now the situation was hopeless, Pope Paul recalled him to Rome more than once, but he insisted on prolonging his stay at Liège, just in case another Pilgrimage broke out. He did not go back to Italy until August, and then with the utmost reluctance. In a letter written from Liège, he calls the 'rulers of England' – by which he means Henry VIII and Thomas Cromwell – 'enemies of the whole human race'.[12] These may be bitter words but there is no need to doubt that this was how Reginald Pole regarded his two arch-enemies.

His campaign to recover England for Rome never stood a chance. The last, desperate risings by the pilgrims had been crushed before Pole arrived in Flanders. 'As to the danger of Mr Pole's traitorous practises, they cannot be so soon set on hand in these parts,' the Duke of Norfolk had written smugly to Henry VIII from the North Country on 2 April, 'Indeed, no part of the realm is less to be doubted.' By this he meant that the country had been so cowed that once again it was firmly beneath the royal heel.[13]

Another of Pole's handicaps had been a crippling shortage of ready money so that he was unable to hire troops – the papal letters of credit proved to be either faulty or insufficient. In June the Emperor Charles gave the Conde de Cifuentes his own, realistic assessment of the cardinal's prospects: it 'appears to us that being, as you say, so scantily provided with funds, he can scarcely be successful in his mission'.[14]

In September 1537 Cromwell at last discovered that Michael Throckmorton had been playing a double game. 'You have bleared mine eye,' he told him in an angry letter. 'I must, I think, do what I can to see you condignly punished.'[15] From then on Michael went in fear for his life. During the following summer, on a day of intense heat, a visitor to Rome ran into a sweating Throckmorton, puffing and blowing in a quilted knife-proof jacket and a steel helmet that he was wearing as protection against assassins.[16]

# 28

# Autumn 1538:
# The 'Exeter Conspiracy'

'the lord Marquess of Exeter and the Lord Montague with a sort of their adherents of mean estate and no estimation greatly have been commanded to the Tower ... their offences be not known by light suspicion but by certain proofs and confessions.'

Thomas Cromwell, letter to Sir Thomas Wyatt,
28 November 1538[1]

Yorkism never ceased to be a threat in Henry's mind. This is the only possible reason for his belief in the 'Exeter Conspiracy'. Some historians argue that his decision to destroy the Poles and Courtenays had nothing to do with their White Rose blood, yet he could not forget their claims to the throne.[2] Ambassadors such as Marillac and Chapuys, who often talked to him, speak of the 'White Rose faction' in their reports, while Marillac says that Henry used the phrase himself. The king knew that besides disliking his religious policies, its members were urging his daughter not to swear allegiance to the statutes that bastardized her. It was logical enough for him to fear that if Reginald led an invasion on Mary's behalf, the White Rose lords would join him.

In July 1536, the king's son, the Duke of Richmond, who, despite his bastardy, some thought might succeed his father on the throne, had died, probably from the tuberculosis that killed his royal grandfather. He was only seventeen. Although Henry had been very fond of the boy, instead of giving him a proper funeral he ordered the Duke of Norfolk to smuggle his body out of London in a waggonload of straw and bury it as quietly as possible in the Howards' family vault at Thetford. The reason for this heartless behaviour must surely have been that Henry feared his subjects would attribute the boy's death to the curse incurred by the Earl of Warwick's murder.

But in October 1537 Queen Jane Seymour gave birth to the son and heir for whom the king had always longed, the future Edward VI, an event greeted with magnificent celebrations that were brought to a close by her death twelve days later. By now Henry was forty-five – by Tudor standards well on the way to old age. He was determined that, if the boy succeeded when still a minor, he should not disappear like the young Edward V. With its two potential pretenders, the White Rose faction was an obvious threat. 'The King told me a long time ago that he wanted to exterminate [*exterminer*] the House of Montague that belongs to the White Rose and the Pole family of which the Cardinal is a member,' reported the Sieur de Castillon from London towards the end of the 1530s. 'So far, I don't know what he means to do about the Marquess [of Exeter] . . . It looks as if he is searching for any possible excuse that can be found to ruin and destroy them . . . I think that few lords in this country can feel safe.'[3]

Among England's richest magnates, Exeter enjoyed semi-regal status throughout the West Country. In Devon his thirty-nine manors in the Exe valley formed an estate almost as large as the Duchy of Cornwall, of which he was high steward besides being lord warden of the stannaries and where he owned another eighteen manors and castles. He had a further sixteen manors in Dorset and Hampshire. Exeter also possessed several palatial residences, the most imposing being a huge moated and castellated house at Tiverton, while his 'inn' at London was the Red Rose in St Lawrence Poultney, once the property of the Duke of Buckingham. When not at court, however, he preferred the seclusion of his Surrey mansion at West Horsley (later acquired by Sir Walter Raleigh), although even here his household numbered over a hundred gentlemen waiters, yeomen and grooms of the chamber, not to mention more menial servants.

The marquess had always tried to keep on the right side of Henry, serving on the commission for depriving Katherine of her rank as queen in 1533. For a time he had belonged to what formed the main faction at court, united by dislike of Thomas Cromwell, his main ally being Sir Nicholas Carew, Master of the Horse.[4] But when Cromwell became supreme, he spent more time in Surrey.

Links between the Courtenays and the Poles grew close, partly because of the Marchioness of Exeter's friendship with Lady Salisbury. Yet although they were staunch Catholics who loathed Cromwell and criticized royal policies in secret, they were less a political party than a group of friends, who included Lord Montague's brother-in-law Sir Edward Neville and, to a lesser extent, Lord de la Warr. The 'treason' they talked had only recently become treason under Henry's new laws, and they did not appreciate the danger from Cromwell's thought-police. Even so, before Reginald Pole's challenge became an obsession with the king they had seemed safe enough. Still in favour, Exeter was granted several confiscated monasteries. Far from supporting the Pilgrimage of Grace, he and his West Country levies formed part of the Duke of Norfolk's Army Royal.

An amiable, unambitious, calm-tempered man who was in his early forties, Lord Montague, Reginald Pole's elder brother, had also done his best to avoid antagonizing King Henry. He had dutifully served on the commissions that tried the

Carthusians and Sir Thomas More for treason, if only in an hon-
orary capacity, although we can guess that the whole business
revolted him. (He owned copies of More's books and enjoyed
reading them.) Less unwillingly, with Exeter he was among the
peers who condemned Anne Boleyn. He, too, brought a force
to fight the pilgrims. Punctilious in performing his ceremonial
duties as a courtier, he did so at Prince Edward's christening
in October 1537 and as a mourner at Queen Jane Seymour's
funeral in September.

After learning that King Henry had received Reginald's
insulting *De Unitate* during the summer of 1536, the Poles had
grown alarmed, however, realizing that in the new, Henrician
England they were only alive on sufferance. Montague wrote
to Reginald in September, declaring that when Cromwell read
extracts of the book to him he felt as if he had lost mother,
wife and children. He accused his brother of wicked ingratitude
towards a sovereign to whom he owed everything, as did his
whole family. If he did not come home, he would lose his king's
good will, his country and his family. Lady Salisbury wrote,
too, saying that because of his behaviour Henry had sent her
'a terrible message'. The king had always been good to her and
she expected her sons to serve him faithfully. Nothing had ever
upset her as much as his anger, even the deaths of her husband
or children. (She had recently lost her second son, Sir Arthur
Pole.) 'Do your duty or you will be my undoing,' she ended.[5]

Reginald confided in his friend Contarini that when these
messages from his family arrived, they upset him so much that
he very nearly gave in and went back to England.)[6] But then
he guessed that his mother and his brother had been forced to
write them in response to explicit orders from Henry which they
dared not refuse. The truth was that Lady Salisbury and Lord
Montague had even had to submit their letters to the King's
Council for approval, before they could be sent to Venice.

Despite their alarm, it is astonishing just how indiscreet the
White Rose group allowed themselves to be. When someone

rebuked the Marquess of Exeter for accepting former abbey lands, he replied, 'good enough for a time: they must have all again one day', by which he seems to have meant that in his opinion the monks were undoubtedly going to get them back. 'Knaves rule about the King,' he observed, after entertaining Cromwell at West Horsley where, in his words, he gave the Lord Privy Seal 'a summer coat and a wood knife'. Shaking his fist, the Marquess added, 'I trust to give them a buffet one day'.

He and his friends were given daily reminders of Henry's policies. Scores of religious houses, some of which contained their ancestors' tombs or were places where they had been accustomed to worship, were being demolished, often blown up with gunpowder and used as quarries. The country swarmed with beggars once fed by such houses, joined by starving monks and nuns (whose minuscule pensions went unpaid), together with their former servants and labourers.

Shrines were destroyed, pilgrims vanishing from the roads. Hallowed feastdays, celebrated since time immemorial, were arbitarily removed from the calendar. If Mass was still said in parish churches, the pope (that 'cankered and cruel serpent, the Bishop of Rome') was regularly abused from the pulpit. A new Court of Augmentations managed the plundered lands of the abbeys, while the Court of First Fruits and Tenths exploited the revenues of the Church.

Worse than all this were the new ideas about religion coming from Germany. No doubt, for some people, they induced an exhilarating certainty that faith in Christ was by itself enough to gain eternal life. But for others such a belief was a fiendish delusion that would drag men and women down to hell – the view of the White Rose group. They thought that the bishops recently appointed by the king were agents of the Devil.

Yet it was impossible to oppose Henry without an armed rising, as he was not a tyrant in the legal sense: 'Where a Borgia used poison, a Tudor used the law'.[7] During the Wars of the Roses both sides had employed Bills of Attainder against opponents

but never as a means of stifling opposition to peacetime policies. (Nor had they executed a single woman.) But in these days
people risked the scaffold if they voiced any resentment. In 1538
the Benedictine prior of Lenton in Nottinghamshire, realizing
that his house would be dissolved, was reported as saying of
King Henry, 'The Devil is in him, for he is past grace: he will
never amend in this world. I warrant him to have as shameful a
death as ever King had in England. A vengeance on him.' Within
a few weeks of the report reaching the authorities the prior was
hanged, drawn and quartered.[8]

As time went on, Lord Montague grew even blunter than the
Marquess of Exeter in expressing his disgust at the new England
being created by Henry, declaring that the 'King and his whole
issue stand accursed'. (He did not mean Mary but Henry's
short-lived sons – a reference to Warwick's curse.) Another of
Montague's comments was: 'The King gloried with the title to
be Supreme Head next to God, yet he had a sore leg that no
poor man would be glad of, and that he should not live long for
all his authority next God's.' When Sir Geoffrey received a court
post, Montague fell out with him, saying that ever since he had
been a boy he had disliked King Henry and that he was quite
sure His Grace would end up by going mad.[9]

But in October 1537 Geoffrey Pole was forbidden to come
to court. (It was on the same day as the christening of Prince
Edward, who, ironically enough, was carried by the Marchioness
of Exeter throughout the ceremony.) Perhaps someone had
reported Geoffrey shouting 'By God's blood' on hearing that
Peter Mewtas had planned to kill Reginald, and accused him of
declaring that he would have stuck his dagger into the man even
had Mewtas been standing next to the king. 'Geoffrey, God
loveth us well that will not suffer us to come amongst them,
for none rule about the court but knaves,' Montague told him
when he came home.

We know from Geoffrey that there were moments when his
brother's thoughts turned to armed rebellion, even if it was only

day dreaming. On one occasion Montague said he would rather live in the West Country than Hampshire, as the Marquess of Exeter possessed such a big following in the West, and that he regretted the death of his father-in-law Lord Bergavenny because he could easily have raised ten thousand men.[10] Lord Montague's servants echoed his opinions, in hoping that 'My Lady Mary and the Cardinal Pole would marry'. Clearly, they knew the White Rose programme. One of them promised that he would shoot anyone who killed Reginald; when he confessed this to the family chaplain, John Collins, he received a blessing instead of a reprimand.

The most outspoken member of the White Rose circle was Sir Edward Neville, once a favourite companion in the tilting yard of the king, whom he had come to loathe. Montague's brother-in-law and one of Exeter's closest friends, Neville sang songs in the gardens at West Horsley, adding words aimed at Cromwell, such as: 'knaves should be put down and lords should reign one day'. Sensing his dislike, Henry ordered Neville to keep away from Exeter, although only later did he learn that Sir Edward had several times observed, 'His Highness was a beast and worse than a beast'.[11] Neville detested Henry's courtiers as much as their master. 'God's blood, I am made a fool among them, but I laugh and make merry to pass the time,' he grumbled to Sir Geoffrey when they happened to be at court together at Westminster. 'The King keepeth a sort of knaves here that we dare neither look nor speak. And if I were able to live, I would rather live any life in the world [than] tarry in the Privy Chamber.'[12]

It is surprising that any Pole or Courtenay, let alone Neville, dared to stay a moment longer in Henrician England when they were in such obvious danger. Reginald could have given them refuge. Yet it meant leaving behind rank and position, beautiful mansions and estates. (Even Sir Geoffrey, a younger son, had married an heiress and owned a fine 'L'-shaped house at Lordington in Sussex, beneath the Downs.) The prospect of penniless exile was scarcely an alluring one. Nevertheless, Lord

Montague thought of taking refuge with the cardinal in Rome at least once, remarking, 'The King to be revenged of Reynold, I fear, will kill us all'.

Sir Geoffrey was the only member of the White Rose faction who ever seriously planned to leave the country. Although he was heavily in debt, his motives had more to do with fear of the king than moneylenders. Nervous and overstrung, he had grown terrified. Several times he asked the sea captain Hugh Holland (who brought his warning to Reginald) to take him over to Flanders, but Hugh refused, not wanting to risk being accused of aiding and betting the flight of someone who might be proclaimed a traitor. Eventually, he went to see a family friend, old Dr Croftes, the Chancellor of Chichester Cathedral, who had taken the Oath of Supremacy with the utmost reluctance and had himself thought of emigrating. He lent Geoffrey twenty gold nobles when he told him he wanted to go abroad because he feared for his life.

But next day he received a letter from Dr Croftes, saying that Our Lady had appeared to him in a dream during the night, and had warned that if Sir Geoffrey should leave England his departure would ruin the entire Pole family. So Geoffrey decided to stay, paying back the twenty nobles. Croftes then went to Lord Montague's steward, telling him that his master's brother was in severe financial trouble and Montague paid off Geoffrey's debts. Plainly on close terms with Sir Geoffrey, Dr Croftes lent him a book. It was Thomas More's *History of King Richard the Third*; perhaps Croftes had chosen it as a study in tyranny that suited the times. It may be significant that another copy was found in Lord Exeter's possession.

Among the Poles' clerical friends was John Helyar, rector of East Meon and the vicar of Warblington in Hampshire. Lady Salisbury's chaplain at Warblington Castle and an Oxford educated theologian, he violently disapproved of the king's religious policies, and in the summer of 1535 (before the cardinal's first mission) had asked Sir Geoffrey to persuade Hugh Holland to take him over to France, a trip that had duly taken place. Helyar claimed that he wanted to study at the University of Paris, but there were rumours that he had fled after 'traitorous words'. Joining the cardinal at Rome, he was given a job running the city's English Hospice. He kept in touch with the Poles, corresponding with Geoffrey. English agents in Rome quickly identified Helyar as a sworn enemy of the Henrician regime.[13]

'Pity it is that the folly of one brainsick Pole or, to say better, of one witless fool should be the ruin of so great a family,' commented Thomas Cromwell ominously in his angry letter to Michael Throckmorton of late 1537. Admittedly, on another occasion the Lord Privy Seal had reported to his master that the Poles 'had offended little save that he [Reginald] is of their kin'. Yet Cromwell realized that it was now in his power to destroy the White Rose party because the king had come to regard them as a threat. For a time, however, his spies had difficulty in obtaining any evidence. He sent his nephew to ask Exeter to be 'frank and open in certain things', tacitly offering a pardon if he would provide information to convict the Pole brothers, but the marquess contemptuously declined. Then, almost by accident, the Lord Privy Seal found a way.

Early in 1538 a failed schoolmaster from Grantham called Gervaise Tyndale arrived at Warblington, saying that he had come to recuperate at 'the surgeon house', which was the little village hospital maintained by Lady Salisbury. In reality he was one of Cromwell's spies, sent to ferret out evidence. A declared Reformer, shouting his hatred of popery from the rooftops, he found an ideal source of information in the doctor who ran the hospital, Richard Eyre, another Evangelical. Eyre told him that the countess not only dismissed servants who inclined to the New Learning, but that she forbade her tenants to read the New Testament in English. Eyre also confided that besides taking messages to Helyar, his neighbour Hugh Holland 'conveyeth letters to Master Pole the Cardinal, and all the secrets of the realm of England is known to the Bishop of Rome'. When

Tyndale quarrelled with every priest for miles around, so much angry gossip ensued that Sir Geoffrey went to see Cromwell. He admitted that he had corresponded with Helyar, but only to give him news of the village, and for a while this defused the situation.

The catalyst in what happened next was the king's illness in May 1538, when a floating thrombosis lodged in his lung. For nearly a fortnight it looked as if his death was imminent. Courtiers asked each other who would take his place on the throne – the baby Prince Edward or the Lady Mary. As soon as the king recovered, the Lord Privy Seal no doubt reported these discussions, making Henry more prone than ever to suspicion of plots against him. By now Cromwell's agents must have learned about the White Rose dream of Mary becoming queen with Reginald Pole as king consort.

At about the same time, in May or June, Tyndale and Eyre sent Cromwell a denunciation of the popish regime at Warblington Castle. While it told him nothing he did not know already, he was very interested in an allegation that Hugh Holland had acted as courier between the Poles and the cardinal. The sea-man was swiftly arrested, at Bockmer. As he was being taken away to London, hands bound behind him and feet tied beneath his horse's belly, he met Geoffrey Pole on the road, arriving from Sussex. Holland prophesied that Geoffrey would soon follow him.

Phlegmatic as ever, Lord Montague did not appear particularly worried, commenting that he always burned his correspondence. Panic stricken, Geoffrey, who did not, gave Montague's chaplain John Collins his signet ring, sending him to Lordington with instructions to burn his own letters.

Under interrogation that may have included torture (at the Tower the rack was used on stubborn witnesseses) Holland impli-cated Sir Geoffrey up to the hilt. He only testified that besides organizing Helyar's flight abroad Geoffrey had kept in touch with Reginald, but repeated his messages by word of mouth, such as the warnings about assassins. 'Show him the world in England waxeth all crooked, God's law is turned upside down, abbeys and churches overthrown, and he is taken for a traitor,' had been another warning. 'And I think they will cast down parish churches and all at the last.'[14]

Geoffrey Pole was arrested without any warning on 29 August 1538. He was kept in a damp and filthy cell at the Tower for two months, his examination deliberately postponed until 26 October so that he could be demoralized by loneliness and darkness, dirt, hunger and vermin. Interrogated seven times, he was asked fifty-nine questions and threatened with the rack, and then offered a pardon if he would cooperate – which of course meant betraying his brother and Exeter. The man who relentlessly asked question after question was William, Earl of Southampton, who had been ordered by the king to extract the right answers. A portrait drawing of Southampton in the Royal Collection shows a face that is noticeably brutal even by Tudor standards.

After his first interrogation, Geoffrey tried to commit suicide in his cell, stabbing himself in the chest with a knife, but failed. 'Sir Geoffrey Pole was examined in the Tower by my lord Admiral [Southampton],' wrote John Husee to Lord Lisle on 28 October. 'They say that he was so in despair that he would have murdered himself and has hurt himself sore.'[15] His wife, Dame Constance, was also questioned. Taken to the Tower for interrogation, she was allowed to see her husband, Afterwards she wrote to Montague, warning him that his brother was on the verge of a complete collapse and that he might blurt out something so dangerous that it might destroy the entire Pole family.

Probably Geoffrey knew what had been done in May that year to Friar John Forrest, a Franciscan who denied the royal supremacy. (Once Katherine of Aragon's chaplain, he was well known to the White Rose party.) According to the gloating Hall, Forrest 'was hanged in chains by the middle and armholes all quick [alive] and under the gallows was made a fire'.

A wooden statue of a saint was put on top of the faggots. 'This friar when he saw the fire come and that present death was at hand, caught hold upon the ladder, which he would not let go.' Adding the statue to the fire was a nice example of Henry's sense of humour.[16]

Perhaps Geoffrey, who may have been among the crowd watching the execution, feared that he might die in the same way. He broke. No jury ever dared to acquit anybody accused of treason and he realized that his only hope was to secure a royal pardon by slavishly cooperating with his questioners and telling them everything he knew, even inventing evidence if necessary. First, he wrote to the king, begging for forgiveness, and then he repeated critical remarks made by every male member of the White Rose party, including all Montague's comments about Henry. The authorities had got what they needed – not very much, but enough for their purpose.

On 4 November Exeter and Montague were arrested and sent to the Tower, soon followed by their wives and children. So were Sir Edward Neville, Dr Croftes and John Collins, the chaplain from Bockmer. On 28 November Cromwell wrote to Sir Thomas Wyatt that the Marquess of Exeter and Lord Montague had been committed to the Tower for 'sundry great crimes'; not because of mere suspicion, but because of evidence and confessions.[17] Cromwell was lying, however. Nothing serious could be proved against them, however much they may have detested King Henry. The usual show trials of the two noblemen by their peers came first, with the Lord Chancellor, Lord Audley, presiding. Montague's took place on 2 December and that of Exeter the next day. Both pleaded not guilty to the indictments, although they knew very well that it would make not the slightest difference to the outcome.

Apart from speaking contemptuously of the king, and dreaming hopefully that he was dead, the only 'evidence' against Lord Montague was of having said to Geoffrey, 'I like well the doings of Cardinal Pole, and I would we were both over the sea for this world will one day come to stripes.' A similar allegation of having spoken such words was to be made against all the accused. It was damning enough, however, in the context of Reginald's efforts to launch an invasion and stir up rebellion against Henry VIII. Inevitably, Montague was found guilty of high treason and condemned to death. In a way the sentence came as a relief to him. 'I have lived in prison these last six years,' he had declared while being questioned – a revealing comment on the terrifying claustrophobia of life in Henrician England.

The Marquess's trial was more dramatic, according to Richard Moryson in a pamphlet written shortly afterwards. In court Exeter accused Sir Geoffrey 'with frenzy, with folly and madness'. Geoffrey retorted that he had certainly been frenzied when he planned to act as a traitor in company with the accused, 'disobedient to my God, false to my Prince and enemy to my native land'. He added, 'I was also out of my wit and stricken with a sore kind of madness when I chose rather to kill myself than to charge them with such treasons as I knew would cost them their lives.' But God had saved him from killing himself. 'His work [is] that I have declared myself, my brother, the Marquess, with the rest, to be traitors.'

If Moryson can be believed, 'The Marquess was stiff at the Bar and stood fast in denial of most things laid to his charge, yet in some he failed and staggered, in such sort that all men might see his countenance to avouch that [which] his tongue could not without much faltering deny.' But although a distinguished scholar Moryson was also a government agent.[18] Despite allegations that he approved of Cardinal Pole's activities, the only charges that could be brought against Exeter were of having said, 'I trust once to have a fair day upon these knaves which rule about the King, and I trust to see a merry world one day', and of making a similar remark on another occasion. Unlike Montague there was no record of any derogatory words about King Henry. He had done nothing that was a crime under the Treason Act. But, inevitably, the Marquess too was found guilty.

Tried on 4 December, Sir Edward Neville remained defiant until the end, refusing to admit that he had committed any treason. Also tried on that day were poor old Dr Croftes from Chichester Cathedral and Collins the Bockmer chaplain, together with Hugh Holland, the sea captain. In court the two priests bravely declared their loyalty to the pope, well aware it would bring them a death sentence, Collins admitting in addition that he had prophesied, 'The King will hang in hell one day for the plucking down of abbeys'. The pair were found guilty of the treasonable offence of denying the royal supremacy, while Hugh Holland was condemned for communicating with a traitor beyond the seas.

On 9 December, a day of strong wind and pelting rain, the Marquess of Exeter and Lord Montague were beheaded on a sodden scaffold on Tower Hill. 'They had been so linked by God in sincere affection during their lives that He would not at the last hour let them be separated, both dying together in the cause of God,' Reginald wrote years later to Exeter's son.[19] Sir Edward Neville was beheaded with them. 'And the two priests and Holland were drawn to Tyburn and there hanged and quartered' is Hall's laconic record of their own, more agonizing, deaths on the same day.[20]

Attempts to incriminate the marchioness failed, although she was one of the few members of the White Rose party who had wanted a full-scale rebellion. Her correspondence with Chapuys was treason in every sense, but luckily for her the authorities knew nothing about it. When they claimed that treasonable motives must have lain behind her visits to the Nun of Kent, Elizabeth Barton, she said that she had gone to see the nun because she was worried about her children's health – almost certainly a lie but a convincing one. Even so, she remained a prisoner in the Tower until 1540.

For some weeks Sir Geoffrey Pole, who had also been found guilty of treason, remained in his cell at the Tower. By now he was dangerously unbalanced. On 28 December he made another unsuccessful effort to commit suicide, on this occasion trying to suffocate himself with a cushion, and when his wife petitioned for his release she wrote that he was 'as good as dead'. Early in 1539 Geoffrey at last received the pardon for which he had worked so hard. He was set free and allowed to go home, but could not settle down. He was a haunted man in a permanent frenzy, and the following year he attacked and badly wounded a Sussex gentleman who had borne witness against him, after which he fled to Flanders. Eventually, he made his way to Rome, throwing himself on the mercy of his brother the cardinal who forgave him. He then settled at Liège, where he received a pension from the kindly Erard de la Marck and where his family joined him.

There was another victim of the 'Exeter Conspiracy'. Sir Nicholas Carew, the Master of the Horse, had been Henry's closest friend since they were small boys, so expert in the tournament that the king had given him a tilting yard of his own at Greenwich in which to practise. After a rakish youth – Wolsey thought him a bad influence – he had settled down, frequently leading embassies to France where he was a great favourite of Francis I. As Master of the Horse he was a member of the King's Council and therefore someone of real political importance.

But on 31 December Henry's old jousting and hunting companion was accused of involvement and arrested. Shortly before his arrest the king had finally turned against him in a fit of childish pique after an angry argument over the result of a game of bowls. According to Chapuys, he was caught when a letter found among the marchioness's papers supposedly proved that he, too, belonged to the White Rose party and the 'conspiracy'. In reality, he was guilty only of having stayed unshakeably loyal to Katherine of Aragon and her daughter, despite the fact that he owed his glittering career entirely to King Henry. This heinous fault had been compounded by a witness claiming during the recent trials that Carew had often been at West Horsley and had regularly corresponded with Lord Montague.

At his trial in February 1539 Carew was charged with abetting Exeter – although how was not specified – and with discussing with him 'the change of the world'. There were also rumours that he had regularly smuggled letters of support to Queen Katherine and the Lady Mary: Chapuys suspected that Carew's destruction was part of the campaign to isolate Mary as he had always shown a chivalrous loyalty to her.

Desperately trying to save his life, Sir Nicholas recalled how the late marquess had seemed cast down on hearing of Prince Edward's birth, which ended his tenuous hopes of succeeding to the throne. His White Rose friends had all been conservatives in religion, so Carew converted to the new Henrician form of Christianity, ostentatiously reading the Bible in English – 'in the prison of the Tower, where he first savoured the likeness and sweeetness of God's most holy word,' as Hall unctuously puts it.[21] However, he was disappointed if he hoped for a pardon.

For Henry had made up his mind that his old friend was one of the principal members of 'that faction', and Sir Nicholas was duly beheaded on Tower Hill in March. As Lord Montague had shrewdly observed to Geoffrey Pole, 'the King never made man but he destroyed him again, either with displeasure or the sword'.[22] Although Lady Carew was reduced to penury by the attainder, characteristically Henry sent agents to Carew's widow to take back the diamonds and pearls, once Queen Katherine's property, that he had given her when her husband was in favour.

As a plan of action, the 'Exeter Conspiracy' existed only in the head of Henry VIII. What had worried the coldly calculating Lord Privy Seal, however, was the mere fact that a White Rose faction should exist at all. 'Henry's reaction was predictably savage, and Cromwell's predictably thorough, but they had a reality to react against.'[23] The reality was a potential and not a plot, however. Had the emperor sent an invasion force to England, it would easily have found an unguarded landing place along the South Coast, while there was reason to suspect that the West was dangerously disaffected. 'This is a perilous country,' the Dean of Exeter, Dr Simon Heynes, had reported to Henry in 1537. 'For God's love, let the King look to it in time.'[24]

While it is certainly possible that in their wilder moments Exeter and Montague might sometimes have dreamed of a rising, if only to save themselves, both men were much too negative and incompetent to have organized one. In any case, they had missed their only chance during the Pilgrimage of Grace. The fact of the matter was that Cromwell saw a chance to fuel his master's paranoia and rid himself of two powerful opponents, poisoning Henry's mind with a minimum of 'proof'. This consisted of no more than Sir Geoffrey's crazed babbling, together with reports of one or two scattered incidents that had been sent in by agents.

One such report was of how, late during the previous year, just after Prince Edward's birth, some Courtenay tenants had told West Country neighbours at Bere Regis in Dorset, 'the King hath but a little season to come and then my Lord Marquess shall be King, and then all shall be cured'.[25] This report was not referred to in the indictment, but it is more that likely that Cromwell brought it to Henry's attention. To an over-excited mind, the tenants' opinions must have seemed to confirm Dr Heynes's warning about serious disaffection in the West Country. According to Chapuys, Cromwell claimed that Exeter had intended to marry his son to the Lady Mary. No doubt he had also told the king of the marquess's intention and emphasized that if such a marriage had taken place there would not have been much future for Prince Edward.

Henry convinced himself he had escaped death by a very narrow margin indeed. In February 1539 he sent detailed instructions to Sir Thomas Wyatt in Spain to tell Charles V 'how by the Cardinal's counsel' Exeter and Montague had been planning to murder him, with his son and daughters, and that the marquess had intended to take his place 'these last ten years' – Sir Geoffrey Pole's evidence had proved this beyond any reasonable doubt.[26] Embarrassed, nevertheless, by the total lack of documentary evidence for his unhinged version of events, Henry told the French ambassador, Castillon, of a newly discovered correspondence between Exeter, Montague and the cardinal, which confirmed their guilt. (If it ever existed, the letters have never been produced.) Castillon commented sardonically that the king and Cromwell wanted to put the dead men on trial after their execution.[27]

Just how alarming Henry VIII had become may be seen from a letter of January 1539 in which a terrified Castillon begs to be recalled, because the king realizes the French are going to refuse his requests – presumably for assurances that King Francis should abandon his new alliance with the emperor. Although Henry had often chatted with Castillon in a friendly way, laughing at his jokes, the Frenchman says he is dealing with 'the most dangerous and cruel man in the world', who despite his being an ambassador will punish him for the refusal. The king 'is in a fury and has neither reason not understanding'.[28]

# 29

# Winter 1538–Summer 1539: Cardinal Pole's Last Throw

'to declare that he would be a King.'

Sir Thomas Wriothesley on Reginald Pole,
to Lord Cromwell, March 1539[1]

The end of December 1538 found Reginald Pole struggling across the Apennines through deep snow. Disguised as a layman, he was riding a horse astride – instead of on a mule side-saddle as a cardinal would normally have done – and escorted by only a small party of horsemen, since he did not want to attract the attention of English assassins who were known to be lurking in Italy and might try to ambush him. Never strong, he found the cold and the bad road exhausting, particularly the descent to Bologna, commenting that any additional snow or rain might have prevented his journey altogether. He had further mountain roads to travel before he reached Spain, through the Alps and the Pyrenees. Storms made a Mediterranean voyage impossible during the winter, however, and his mission was so pressing that he had to take this arduous route.

In the summer of 1538 King Henry's foreign policy had suffered a severe setback when Francis I and Charles realized that he had been playing them off against each other and began to negotiate an agreement by which both promised not to make any alliance with England. Henry also learned that in the near future Pope Paul intended to publish a bull excommunicating him. Always a fervent supporter of the king, Edward Hall complained that 'the cankered and cruel serpent the Bishop of Rome' (egged on by Pole) was asking foreign powers to attack England and 'utterly to destroy the whole nation'.[2] The invasion scare lasted until the spring of 1539, alarming the king to such an extent that he spent huge sums on building a dozen new castles along the coast. He also took steps against the White Rose.

In December 1539 Paul III created a new Scottish cardinal, David Beaton, ordering him to publish in Scotland the bull that excommunicated Henry VIII. Reginald, who had already written to congratulate Beaton on his promotion, was so encouraged that he asked the pope to let him have another try at toppling the king. His eloquent arguments were strengthened by sensational reports of Henry's latest outrages: not only had he desecrated Thomas à Becket's shrine at Canterbury and burnt the saint's bones, but he was said to have put the bones on trial and ensured they were found guilty of treason. (The king had the shrine's most famous jewel, an enormous ruby, made into a thumb ring.)

This was why Pole, with the pope's approval, was on his way to the Spanish court at Toledo to ask for Charles V's help. He had not wasted any time, leaving Rome just after Christmas, regardless of the weather. He must have known that his chances were even more slender than they had been in 1537. Since then it had become clear that Northern England had been cowed, while not only had men like Darcy gone to the scaffold but the White Rose families had been eliminated. The birth of a Prince of Wales meant that the Lady Mary was no longer heir to the throne. Yet he did not give up hope of overthrowing Henry and may have envisaged some sort of regency under Mary. Despite the odds, the legal murder of his brother and of his friend Exeter strengthened his determination.

As in 1537, King Henry and Cromwell took Reginald's new mission very seriously indeed. In January the king's envoy at Brussels, Sir Thomas Wriothesley, reported that he had heard the cardinal was losing favour with the pope and was 'not in such esteem at Rome as he was', implying there was nothing to worry about.[3] But by February Wriothesley – an unbalanced creature who would one day take his own life – was panicking, convinced that war between the empire and England was imminent, already imagining himself in a dungeon. 'Mr Wriothesley, your last letters of the 25th ult, show that to fair weather is succeeded, beyond all men's expectations, very cloudy weather,' Cromwell wrote to him.[4] Two months later Wriothesley reported wildly that Pole was coming to Flanders 'to declare that he would be a King'. He also hinted that when the cardinal arrived he would poison him.[5] In his fear, Wriothesley had mentioned the unmentionable – that Reginald Pole was a rival for Henry VIII's throne. Such a thought must have been in the minds of other well-informed Englishmen. (Two other sixteenth-century cardinals were to become kings – Henry I of Portugal and 'Charles X' of France.)

In February 1539 Cardinal Pole arrived at Toledo. Despite the attempts of Sir Thomas Wyatt, the English envoy in Spain, to persuade Charles V not to see him, he was given an audience that lasted for an hour. He begged the emperor to help with the deposition of Henry VIII, arguing that he was a far worse threat to Christendom than the Turks.

Pole then set out his case in an *Apologia* that listed the King of England's iniquities and his own reactions. He described in detail the martyrdom of Fisher, More and the Carthusians, the destruction of monasteries and shrines, the persecution of dead saints. The king was now turning on the English lords, having first killed the finest of them all, his kinsmen, 'who had no peers in nobility of blood' – a reference to their royal ancestry. Henry had even jeopardized the succession by rejecting those nearest to him, by which Pole meant the Lady Mary. He compared Cromwell to the demoniac in the Gospel, whose devils had entered into a herd of swine.[6]

In further letters, Reginald denounced Henry to other rulers besides the emperor. The King of England's attacks on the Church were not only damaging his afflicted island but might easily be copied all over the entire Christian world, he warned. After killing so many priests, he was turning on the no less defenceless nobility, whom he intended to annihilate. The cardinal also complained, with reason, that Henry was plotting his own death and had assassins waiting for him in France.

On 18 March Henry VIII's envoy in Spain, Sir Thomas Wyatt, sent him a disturbing message. Reginald had asked Charles to send 8,000 landsknechts and 4,000 Italian mercenaries to Flanders, for an invasion, expecting 'the wounded minds in England [the Pilgrims]' to join them.[7] Wyatt did not yet know that, unmoved by the cardinal's denunciation of Henry, the emperor had declined to take any action: after promising an embargo in Flanders on imports from England, he changed his mind. Nor would he allow publication in his domains of the bull excommunicating Henry. The English king's wily diplomacy had succeeded in turning Charles against Pole, by portraying him as a man who was trying to set a people against their ruler, someone who undermined the royal authority. It was a bitter blow for Pole, as Francis I had promised to move against Henry if Charles would do so. Avoiding Wyatt's hitmen, he left Spain and waited in vain at Carpentras for another six months before returning to Rome.

In April Reginald wrote an impassioned letter that was addressed to the Imperial Chancelllor Granvelle but was meant for Charles. 'God is my witness that once I loved and revered

Henry,' he said. 'But no good can be expected from him or his island while he stays King.' Knowing how deeply Pole loved his family, Henry had cunningly tried to use them as tools to bring him round to his way of thinking, making them write letters that accused him of betraying his king. His brother Montague's death was a call from God to fight for His cause more effectively; by killing Montague, Henry had taken away the person he loved best in the world apart from his mother.

> If they did not choose me, then every decent man in England would choose some one else from my family to ask the Emperor for help because no family has endured more for his kindred . . . his aunt [Queen Katherine] used to say that all the trouble dated from the time when she heard that my mother was no longer the Princess's governess. She had been so anxious for my mother to become the child's governess that she had gone to visit her with the King, in order to persuade her to take the post. The Queen's physician, who is now at the Imperial court, can testify to this. My family suffered a very great deal for her . . . and the Queen often declared how deeply she was obliged to us. I am saying all this to demonstrate just how much our island deserves [the Emperor's] help when it is asked for by the English family best qualified to do so. [8]

But it was in vain. Charles had made up his mind not to intervene in English affairs.

Just how frightened of an invasion Henry had been was revealed by the great 'muster' in the city of London on 8 May, which took place after the scare was over but it was too late to cancel. Most able-bodied male Londoners between sixteen and sixty took part, 15,000 marching to Westminster where the king reviewed them from his new gatehouse at Whitehall and the more skilled demonstrated their aptitude as archers or arquebusiers. Similar musters took place all over the country.

Making 'very laborious and painful journeys towards the sea coasts',[9] Henry had also visited all the major ports to inspect defence works.

His relief was evident in his noticeably relaxed behaviour a week after the muster. 'This present Holy Thursday eve the King took his barge at Whitehall and rowed up to Lambeth,' wrote John Worth to Lord Lisle at Calais. 'He had his drums and fifes playing, and rowed up and down the Thames for an hour after evensong.' The same writer notes Henry's edifying care for his subjects' morals and spiritual life, now that he was free from worry:

> The recorder of London's servant Ball showed me that last week there was one hanged for eating flesh on a Friday against the King's command . . . It is said there is another Act passed that if any priest or married man be taken with another man's wife he shall suffer death. God save the King. His Grace receives holy bread and holy water every Sunday, and daily uses all other laudable ceremonies. In all London no man dare speak against them on pain of death.[10]

The cardinal's defeat was neatly underlined by the inclusion of 'Reynold Pole, late dean of the cathedral church of Exeter' in the Bill of Attander that was enacted in May, which conveniently lumped together the leaders of the Pilgrimage with those of the so-called 'Exeter Conspiracy'. His own official crime was to 'have taken and pursued worldly promotions in the gift of the . . . Bishop of Rome'.[11] In July Pole was still hoping for the Earl of Kildare to start a rising in Ireland, but nothing came of it. His second mission had ended in utter failure.

Henry's obsessive hatred of Reginald as one of those pretenders to his throne whom he had feared ever since childhood had been particularly evident during the first half of 1539. In a letter of 13 February, clearly written in a towering rage, Henry had ordered Sir Thomas Wyatt to tell Charles V that the cardinal was 'so lewd and ingrate that no prince should esteem him worthy to be spoken with . . . his words (such traitors being commonly hypocrites) may be fair and pleasant; but howsoever the head be coloured the tail thereof is always black and full of poison'. Revealingly, Wyatt was also ordered to say that the king had raised Pole's entire family 'from nothing'.[12] Their Plantagenet mother's origins could scarcely be described as 'nothing', and it was the kind of abuse to be expected from an insecure parvenu rather than a great monarch.

Sir Thomas told everyone at Toledo who would listen to him that if Henry gave him 10,000 gold crowns and publicly proclaimed Pole a traitor, then he would wager his entire estate at home in England that he could easily arrange for the man to be killed within six months. He suggested that Rome was the best place to do the job. But this was just a piece of calculated sycophancy on the part of Wyatt, who was merely trying to please the king. He must have known all too well that plenty of other Englishmen had tried and failed to assassinate the cardinal.

Henry VIII was justified in fearing Reginald Pole. In the eyes of many Englishmen, he stood not only for the old religion and for the old nobility, but also for the old royal family. When the *Book of Common Prayer* was introduced in 1549 the West Country rose in their own Pilgrimage of Grace, carrying the banner of the Five Wounds and calling for the return of the Mass, as the new service 'is but like a Christmas game'. Among demands made by the rebels was that 'because the lord Cardinal Pole is of the King's blood [he] should not only have his free pardon, but also sent for to Rome and promoted to be first or second of the King's Council'.[13]

# 30

# May 1541:
# The Death of the
# Last Plantagenet

'The old lady being brought to the scaffold set up in the Tower, was commanded to lay her head upon the block, but . . . refused, saying "So should traitors do, and I am none." Neither did it serve that the executioner told her it was the fashion; so turning her greay head in every way, shee bid him, "If he would have her head, to get it as he could." So that he was constrained to fetch it off slovenly.'

Lord Herbert of Cherbury, *The Life and Reigne of King Henry VIII*[1]

Margaret, Countess of Salisbury, the Earl of Warwick's sister, had lived through all the conspiracies against the Tudors, from Lord Lovell's rising in the year after Bosworth to the Pilgrimage of Grace and her son's 'missions'. Her life binds together the whole tragic story of the White Rose in decline, until its final extermination. Although Henry VIII had at first admired this stately lady, in the end he decided to kill her. He did so not merely because he wanted to revenge himself on Reginald Pole, but because she was the last Plantagenet – a living reproach to the Tudor dynasty.

She had been born in 1473. Her mother, a daughter of Warwick the Kingmaker, died when she was four, while her father George, Duke of Clarence, was murdered in 1478 for plotting against his brother Edward IV. (According to rumour, he was drowned in a butt of Malmsey and for the rest of her life his daughter wore a tiny wine keg on her bracelet.) Brought up with King Edward's family, she and her brother the Earl of Warwick spent most of Richard III's brief reign at Sheriff Hutton Castle in Yorkshire.

Judging, as far as one can, from a clumsy portrait of her painted in later life (now in the National Portrait Gallery), Margaret Plantagenet inherited the good looks of the House of York, but after her world turned upside down at Bosworth, she was lucky not to disappear into the Tower or a nunnery. What made the little girl's very existence peculiarly dangerous for the new dynasty was her claim to the throne. Unlike Elizabeth of York, she had never been bastardized by Parliament. However, Henry VII's mother found a safe husband for her. This was a cousin of the Tudor king called Richard Pole, one of his most reliable henchmen, a country gentleman who, although he came from Buckinghamshire, was of Welsh origin. He had been knighted for his services at Stoke Field.[2]

At the time of her wedding in either 1486 or 1487, she was about fourteen and her husband in his late twenties. Admittedly, the match was inferior to one with the great magnate to whom her hand would have been given had her uncle Richard stayed on the throne, justifying Warbeck's charge that Henry Tudor married ladies of the blood royal to 'certain of his kinsmen and friends of simple and low degree'. Yet it was better than disappearing into a convent, and the pair seem to have been happy enough: we know from one of her letters that she mourned Richard Pole when he died. They had five children who survived infancy, four sons and a daughter.

The years of their marriage were overcast in turn by the supposed return of the 'Duke of York' from the dead, her brother Warwick's alleged plot and unjust execution, and the threat by her cousin Edmund de la Pole. None of these endangered Margaret, however, because of her husband's commitment to the new dynasty. During the middle years of Henry VII's reign she often visited court, since not only did Richard Pole hold important offices (such as Prince Arthur's Lord Chamberlain, President of the Prince's Council in Wales and Controller of the Port of Bristol), but also he became Chief Gentleman of the Bedchamber. In 1499 he was made a Knight of the Garter. Margaret herself became one of Katherine of Aragon's ladies-in-waiting as soon as she arrived from Spain.

After Sir Richard died in 1504 she spent the next few years away from Bockmer, their pleasant home amid the Buckinghamshire woodlands, and lived with the nuns of Syon Abbey, although without taking vows. (In the harsh fashion of the day her children were attached to the households of various noble families.) However, she emerged when Henry VIII came to the throne. After he handed back her Neville mother's lands in 1513 she became one of the five biggest landowners in England, with large estates in seventeen counties, notably in Hampshire and Essex as well as throughout the West Country. A dozen stewards were required to administer them. How high a place she occupied in the royal favour is shown by her investiture as Countess of Salisbury, and at the time the only English peeress in her own right.

She also acquired several fine country houses, notably Clavering Castle in Essex and Bisham Manor by the Thames in Berkshire, next to the priory, together with a London 'inn', Le Herber, which was a palatial mansion that stood on the site of today's Cannon Street Station. Her favourite, all but regal, residence, however, was the great castellated house of red brick, surrounded by a deep moat, that she built at Warblington in east Hampshire, on the Sussex border near Havant and not far from the sea. Destroyed in the Civil War, only one side of a gatehouse turret and a few other fragments survive, next to a farm, but she would still recognize Warblington church nearby (from where Dr Helyar fled abroad).

Save for Queen Katherine, no woman in the kingdom lived with more splendour than the Countess of Salisbury. Her Planatagenet arms (with the lions of England and lilies of France) were carved on the stonework and over the gateways, painted on the glass of the larger rooms' windows, embroidered on the hangings in the dining chamber and on the testers over the beds. Numerous tall 'standing cupboards' were laden with plate of gold, silver gilt and silver, together with vessels of Venetian glass. Her household included seventy-three indoor servants, among whom were a steward, a comptroller, a clerk of the kitchen, a marshal of the hall, an usher of the hall, six gentlemen waiters and even a fool.

One of her lesser houses was a castle in south-west Hampshire (now in Dorset), opposite the Isle of Wight and near the Augustinian priory of Christchurch. In the great church here she built a resting place for herself and her husband that they were never to occupy. Implausibly ascribed to Pietro Torrigiano (who designed Henry VII's tomb at Westminster Abbey) and completed in 1529, the Salisbury chantry with its fan tracery ceiling still stands in the north aisle. The last of the Plantagenets could have left no more regal a monument than this lovely little chapel.

For a long time Margaret, whom Henry VIII, in his own words, 'loved and honoured as [he did] his own grandame', was deeply respected at court. She became Queen Katherine's valued friend and a much-loved governess to the Lady Mary, almost a second mother. She ran the princess's household with amiable efficiency, her commands to the child invariably beginning with the gentle words, 'Madam, your mother would wish'. These years from 1516 to 1521 were probably among the happiest of her life. Yet the king's comparison with his grandmother was unfortunate, as he may have realized later. His father's claim to the throne came from Margaret Beaufort's remote kinship with the House of Lancaster, but there was nothing remote in any way about Lady Salisbury's descent from the House of York.

The Poles prospered. Henry VIII not only created her eldest son a peer but made her second son Arthur an Esquire of the Body and then, still more flattering, a Gentleman of the Privy Chamber, which implies that the king enjoyed his company and regarded him as a close friend. Talented, witty, a natural courtier and a hero in the tournament, Arthur was knighted, together with her youngest, least gifted, son Geoffrey. Neither had ever performed any outstanding services so the accolades were an expression of the king's respect for their mother. As we know, Reginald had equal reason to be grateful to royal favour. Her children's rise in the world seemed complete when her daughter Ursula married Lord Stafford, who was the Duke of Buckingham's heir and the greatest catch in England.

But at the duke's fall in 1521 Lady Salisbury lost favour with Henry, because after Ursula's marriage the Staffords and the Poles had grown too friendly for his liking. As has been seen, even Arthur was banished from court, suspected of involvement in the Duke of Buckingham's mythical plot, and when the king and queen left Windsor that summer, Margaret was forbidden to accompany Mary, losing her post as governess and told to keep away from court. In 1525 she was reinstated, however, while the following year Henry visited her house at Warblington. Nothing further disturbed her good relations with him until he divorced Queen Katherine.

Sometimes Margaret could be ruthless in family matters. Sir Arthur had married a rich heiress, Jane Lewkenor from Bodiam Castle in Sussex, and when he died around 1527–8, probably from the sweating sickness, without leaving sons, Margaret made his widow take a vow of chastity so that her fortune would be inherited by his daughters. (But she did not force her to enter a convent, as sometimes stated.) Twelve years later, when her mother-in-law was in no position to object, Jane asked Bishop Barlow of St Asaph for help. A keen enthusiast for the New Learning, who had no sympathy for vows of chastity, Barlow freed her from any commitment and she quickly found a new husband.

Henry's attitude towards Margaret did not alter noticeably when he decided to divorce the queen, and she was allowed to remain as the Lady Mary's governess. But everything changed as soon as he married Anne Boleyn in 1533. When he sent a lady to demand the surrender of Mary's jewels and plate, Margaret indignantly refused. She was dismissed from her post, despite offering to pay for the upkeep of the princess's household, and never saw Mary again. Before Margaret's dismissal, Queen Katherine wrote to Mary, 'I pray you, recommend me unto my very good lady of Salisbury and pray her to have a good heart, for we never come to the kingdom of Heaven but by troubles.'[3]

Although Margaret returned to court after Queen Anne's downfall (and even received a royal grant of land in Yorkshire), the king grew increasingly hostile towards the Poles after Reginald's *De Unitate*, despite her spirited pretence at being horrified by her son's behaviour. Already irritated by her loyalty to Queen Katherine and to the Lady Mary, and by her conservatism in religion, during the Cardinal's mission in 1537 Henry began to see her as a dangerous enemy.

She showed a shrewd sense of self-preservation when Sir Geoffrey was arrested. 'I pray God, madame, he do you no hurt,' said her alarmed steward. 'I trow he is not so unhappy that he will hurt his mother, and yet I care neither for him nor for any other, for I am true to my Prince,' she answered, knowing very well that her words might be reported to the authorities. A letter to her eldest son, written after Geoffrey's arrest, reveals the same wariness:

Son Montague, I send you heartily God's blessing and mine . . . This is the greatest gift that I can send you, for to desire God of his help, which I perceive [there] is great need to pray for. And as to the case as I am informed that you stand in, mine advice is to refer you to God principally and upon that ground so to order you both in word and deed to serve your prince [while] not disobeying God's commandments.[4]

On 12 November, accompanied by Bishop Goodrich of Ely, the Earl of Southampton (who had interrogated Geoffrey) arrived at Warblington to question the countess. During this initial interrogation she strongly denied having corresponded with Reginald in recent years or having burned compromising letters. On 14 November Southampton and the bishop reported to Cromwell that they had cross-examined the lady for two days, from morning till night, sometimes gently and sometimes roughly, but could get nothing out of her. She was 'manlike' in her behaviour – either her sons 'have not made her privy nor participants of the bottom and pit of their stomachs, or else she is the most arrant traitress that ever lived'.[5]

She seemed 'somewhat appalled', however, on being told that she must leave Warblington, which made them hope she was going to confess what they wanted. Taken to Southampton's house in Sussex, Cowdray, she was kept there until the following May, treated with every indignity by the earl and his wife, who refused to speak to her. (Yet Lady Southampton became so frightened of Margaret that she refused to be left alone in the house with her, while Southampton said he found her presence disturbing.) Despite relentless bullying, she gave nothing away. Her interrogators reported to the Lord Privy Seal that they had never come across anybody like her before: 'we may call her a strong and constant man rather than a woman'.

On 12 May 1539 the Countess of Salisbury was included in the Act of Attainder passed against the leaders of the Pilgrimage and those implicated in the 'Exeter Conspiracy'. She and the steward of one of her Welsh estates, Hugh Vaughan, were accused of allying themselves with the 'false and abominable traitors Henry Pole, late Lord Montague and Reginald Pole, sons unto the said Countess, knowing them to be false traitors and common enemies unto your Majesty and this your realm'. Margaret and Vaughan were further charged with 'sundry other detestable and abominable treasons to the most fearful peril and danger of the destruction of your most royal person'.[6] No details were given, but during the proceedings Cromwell rose in the House of Lords and displayed an embroidered tabard.

The tabard was accepted as damning evidence. The Deputy at Calais, Lord Lisle, received a description in a letter from one of his officials:

> There was a coat-armour found in the Duchess [*sic*] of Salisbury's coffer, and by the one side of the coat there was the King's Grace his arms of England, that is the lions without the flowers de lys, and about the whole arms was made pansies for Poles and marigolds for my Lady Mary . . . And betwixt the marigold and the pansy was made a tree to rise in the midst, and on the tree a coat of purple hanging on a bough in token of the coat of Christ, and on the other side of the coat all the Passion of Christ. Pole intended to have married my Lady Mary and betwixt them both should again arise the old doctrine of Christ.[7]

Whether the tabard had been embroidered at Margaret's command during the Pilgrimage or whether it was a cunning forgery run up by Cromwell's agents, everyone who saw it realized that its symbols spelled out the White Rose programme – Mary as queen and Reginald Pole as king consort, together with the restoration of Catholicism – which could only happen if Henry VIII were deposed. Nothing could have summed up better why Henry and Cromwell had been so frightened of the Pole family.

In autumn 1539 the countess was brought from Cowdray to spend what was left of her life in the Tower. Neither she nor her two gentlewomen, whom she was unable to pay, had any change of clothing. What they had soon wore out and was in any case inadequate for the winter, from which she suffered miserably, confined in a cold, damp and unheated cell. Only in 1541, towards the end of her imprisonment, did the latest queen, Katherine Howard, intervene and see that she was given new clothes, including a furred petticoat.

Still more distressing for the old lady was the fact that her two grandsons were also in the Tower, although neither had been attainted. In King Henry's eyes, however, they shared their parents' guilt. Gertrude Courtenay, formerly Marchioness of Exeter, was released in 1540, but her son Edward had to remain in the Tower. Some people expected that Lady Salisbury would also be released. However, she was the mother of the cardinal whom the king hated more than anyone else in the world. In consequence, she and Henry Pole were specifically excluded from the general pardon of that year.

It appears that the king ordered young Henry Pole to be treated particularly harshly, to ensure that he rotted to death. Described by the cardinal as 'the remaining hope of our race',[8] he had inherited Warwick's claim to the throne. In July 1540 the French ambassador reported that Edward Courtenay, who was then about twelve, had grown taller and been given a tutor. But 'the little nephew of Cardinal Pole . . . is poorly and strictly kept and not desired to know anything'.[9] Margaret must have feared for the boy's life, remembering how when she was a little girl certain other royal children had disappeared in the Tower.

Early in 1540 the 'Botolph Conspiracy' at Calais (which by then was not quite as prosperous as formerly but still a cherished possession of the crown) ensured that Cardinal Reginald Pole stayed very much in the king's mind. The aged Deputy, Lord Lisle – a bastard of Edward IV, born in 1461 and another survivor from the Yorkist court – had acquired a new chaplain,

Gregory Botolph, once a monk at Canterbury. Later alleged to have fled with the plate when his monastery was dissolved, he was known by friends as 'Sweetlips', but whether on account of musical, social or sexual talent is unclear. His plan was to hire 500 men and seize the town for the pope and the cardinal, whom he claimed to have seen at Rome on a recent, secret visit, and he recruited over a dozen accomplices. Yet while he may have visited Rome, it is improbable that he had met either Paul III or Pole, while his 'plot' sounds more like a confidence trick.

Even so, when Sweetlips's letters were intercepted, the authorities took the plot very seriously and he was attainted by Parliament. What happened to him afterwards is unknown, but two of his accomplices were hanged, drawn and quartered in August 1540. Ridiculously, the king even suspected poor old Lord Lisle, bumbling and hopelessly inefficient, and he was sent to the Tower. Where Pole was concerned, Henry's imagination always ran riot. His obsession may also explain why Lord Leonard Grey was executed the following year, despite having served well as Deputy in Ireland – his real offence was to have let the young Earl of Kildare escape and join the cardinal.

Undoubtedly, there was some sort of plot to rescue Margaret from the Tower. In an undated letter to a French bishop, written some time during 1540, Reginald refers to what had been planned 'for my mother's release' and to a friend of his who was the brains behind the scheme, but who had been put in prison as a result of pressure by the English authorities, although he had since been set free.[10] It has been suggested the 'friend' was Sweetlips Botolph of the Calais Plot, but the identification is far from certain.[11] If it was Botolph, then the plan can never have had much chance of success.

In 1540 the sores – the infection had spread – on Henry VIII's leg were causing him even more acute pain, unbalancing his mind still further. His monstrous obesity (we know from his armour that by now he measured a good four and a half feet around the waist and nearly five round the chest) cannot have helped either his mental equilibrium or his temper. He became more suspicious than ever, arresting the servile Bishop Sampson of Chichester for supposedly writing in secret to the pope. Early in 1541 Sir Thomas Wyatt, who was liked by everybody, and Sir John Wallop went to the Tower of London on baseless charges of corresponding with 'the King's traitor Pole', regardless of the former having done his best to arrange for Pole's murder in 1539. (Both were pardoned at the intercession of Queen Katherine Howard, Wyatt on condition that he returned to his unfaithful wife.) The king also ordered the arrest of the Gentleman Porter at Calais, Sir John Palmer, another loyal servant who was innocent of any wrong doing.

When interrogated by Cromwell, Lord Darcy had told him that he hoped 'shall there one head remain that shall strike off thy head', and in June 1540 the Lord Privy Seal, only recently created Earl of Essex, was arrested at the council table by an exultant Duke of Norfolk. Despite his frantic pleas – 'Most gracious Prince, I cry for Mercy! Mercy! Mercy!' – he was beheaded on Tower Hill on 28 July. After his death, the French ambassador Marillac heard that the king was calling him 'the most faithful servant he had ever known', which seemed to imply that he had been a victim of slander, executed in error. There were rumours that he was punished for the fiasco of his master's marriage to Anne of Cleves, the 'Flanders Mare'. Yet it was undoubtedly Henry who brought him down, deciding that in secret Cromwell was 'a miserable heretic sacramentary', to use his minister's own phrase.[12] Cranmer had tried to save him, writing to the king of the Lord Privy Seal's loyalty, diligence, wisdom and experience. But Henry believed the man had outlived his usefulness.

In April 1541 a conspiracy came to light in the West Riding of Yorkshire, an attempt by a dozen wealthy gentlemen in the Wakefield area, headed by a Mr Leigh, together with several parsons, to revive the Pilgrimage of Grace. They planned to seize and kill the evangelical Archbishop of York, Robert Holgate, who was President of the Council of the North, and then call in the King of Scots: until he arrived, they hoped to use Pontefract Castle as a base for raising supporters in a revolt against Henry's 'bad government and tyranny'.[13] However, the rising was nipped in the bud. Chapuys, who says the plot was provoked by the reprisals of 1537, believed that had it got off the ground it would have been even more dangerous than the Pilgrimage – this time the Northerners had no illusions about Henry. About 50 people were involved, of whom 25 were captured. Fifteen were put to death, and Sir John Neville of Chevet (often mistakenly described as the brains behind the plot) was executed on a charge of 'misprision', that is, failing to report the plot soon enough.

It seemed that the Northerners' spirit had finally been broken. In 1541, planning to meet James V and ensure Scotland's neutrality in the event of an invasion from Flanders or France, King Henry at last summoned up the courage to visit the North Country, and before setting out he made a clean sweep of the state prisoners in the Tower. Those involved in the recent rising were going to die in any case.

A sudden impulse made him decide to include Margaret, Countess of Salisbury. Early, either on 27 or 28 May, she was woken and told without explanation that she was to die that morning. The execution took place at 7 a.m. 'When informed of her sentence, she found it very strange, not knowing her crime, but she walked to a place in front of the Tower where there was no scaffold but only a small block,' reports Chapuys. 'She there commended her soul to God and desired those present to pray for the King, Queen, Prince and Princess.' In particular, she sent her blessing to the Lady Mary, before being told to stop talking and lay her head on the block. The ordinary executioner being absent on professional business in the North, according to Chapuys, 'a blundering youth [*garçonneau*] was chosen, who hacked her head and shoulders almost to pieces'.[14]

But the ambassador was not present. A seventeenth-century source says the old lady refused to kneel and tottered round, screaming, 'So shall all traitors die and I am none!', before being caught and held down on the block.[15] The countess was buried beneath the floor of the chancel of the chapel at the Tower of London, St Peter ad Vincula, where her skeleton – and skull – were discovered during a nineteenth-century restoration. With characteristic pettiness, the king sent commissioners down to Christchurch Priory to deface the heraldic devices on the painted roof bosses of her chantry chapel's ceiling, which presumably included her royal arms. One wonders whether there were white roses among them.

In his despatch, Chapuys gives the Countess of Salisbury a fitting epitaph. 'God in his high grace pardon her soul, for certainly she was a most virtuous and honourable lady.'[16] He adds that she and her son were killed because of their Yorkist blood, the 'last of the White Rose faction', while even Hall goes so far as to say, 'and she was the last of the right line and name of Plantagenet'.[17] The ultimate descendant of the longest reigning, most illustrious dynasty in English history, she was worthy of her royal forebears. Yet she died not only for her ancestry but also for her loyalty to the old religion, which the Catholic Church recognized in 1876 by beatifying her as a martyr.

The king's behaviour towards Margaret Plantagenet revealed his abiding fear of the White Rose. In contrast, although it was clear that she really had plotted against him, Lady Exeter was released and given a pension; spared because she did not have Yorkist blood in her veins. Henry was even frightened of Margaret's little grandson. Chapuys reported that after Margaret's death young Henry Pole, who until then 'had occasionally permission to go about within the precincts of the Tower was placed in close confinement, and it is to be supposed that he will soon follow his father and grandmother'. The ambassador adds, 'God help him!'[18] No payments for the boy's meagre diet are recorded after late 1542. How he died remains a mystery.

Marillac was convinced that the countess had been executed without warning and with such little publicity, 'in a corner of the Tower', because of fears that her killing might cause widespread outrage. Older people must surely have recalled the Earl of Warwick's murder and his curse. But Henry VIII was wrong if he thought he had exorcised the curse by killing Warwick's sister. His son would die at fifteen and his two daughters would both be childless.

# 31

# Winter 1546–7:
# Henry VIII's Final Phobia

'I saw a royal throne whereas that Justice should have sit;
Instead of whom I saw, with fierce and cruel mode,
Where Wrong was set, that bloody beast, that drank the
guiltless blood.'

*Henry Howard, Earl of Surrey: Poems*[1]

Even before the White Rose families' extermination, any threat
they might have been to Henry VIII had ended for good when
Emperor Charles V declined to give military support to Reginald
Pole's 'missions'. No doubt the cardinal might still be alive in
Italy, but he had ceased to be a danger. Even so, not content
with having rooted out the very last remnants of the White Rose
in England, the king tried to root it out abroad as well.

Two suspicious-looking Englishmen, who were arrested
when Reginald was staying at Capranica in 1541, confessed that
they had been sent to kill him. Luckily for them, he was the
legate for Bologna (papal governor) and they came before

him for trial, escaping with only a short spell on the galleys. There were other attempts on Reginald's life, all of which were unsuccessful. Yet King Henry's assassins did not always fail. In 1546 Cardinal Beaton was brutally murdered in his castle at St Andrews by a pair of Scotsmen in English pay, each rewarded with £50. Pole led a charmed life.

During the last years of Henry's reign, two factions competed for his favour. One consisted of those who had followed the late Thomas Cromwell, including evangelicals such as Archbishop Cranmer and Edward Seymour, Earl of Hertford. Opposing them were the Catholics led by the Duke of Norfolk, although by now he was suffering from chronic ill health and very much feeling his age. For a time, however, the old duke appeared to be in the ascendant after the king married his niece.

She was the tiny, auburn-haired Katherine Howard, more than thirty years younger than Henry, who became besotted with her. But in November 1541 Archbishop Cranmer broke the news to him that she was 'a whore'. Kind-hearted, empty-headed, oversexed and completely out of her depth, the poor girl was one of the most pitiful figures in Tudor history. She had taken at least one lover before her marriage and was now having a full-blooded romance with a gentleman of the Privy Chamber, Thomas Culpeper. At first the king refused to believe Cranmer, but then, shedding tears of self-pity, he told the embarrassed council he had been betrayed. The charges were soon proved, the queen's lovers being executed within a month. (In their indictment she was described as 'a common harlot'.) Only seventeen, Katherine was beheaded in February 1542 after a Bill of Attainder avoided a trial that would have made the squalid details public. She was lucky to die beneath the axe instead of being burned alive for treason.

Abroad, despite vast expenditure, Henry's foreign policy was ineffective on every front. Although English troops routed the Scots at Solway Moss in 1542, they were defeated at Ancrum Moor, and the following year the betrothal of Prince Edward to the little Queen Mary, on which Henry had set his heart – in what contemporaries called the 'Rough Wooing' – was broken off by the Scots. Three years of ruinously expensive war with France ended in 1546, having gained nothing.

As for religion, Henry continued to regard even the slightest disagreement with the 'true doctine' he had decreed as a blasphemous denial of his role as head of the Church. For, as he saw it, the law of God was in his personal care. This extraordinary assumption was evident in the Askew case.

In 1544 Mrs Anne Askew, a wealthy young Lincolnshire lady who had quarrelled with her husband over her 'sacramentarian' views, came to live in London, seeking a divorce. The year after, having joined a group of evengelicals in the city, she was arrested and frightened into recanting. As she was a friend of the latest queen, Catherine Parr, of whose own religious opinions Henry was suspicious, he took a personal interest in the case. Rearrested in 1546, Anne was questioned by the council and, despite being a gentlewoman, so cruelly racked during her interrogations that she lost the use of her limbs and even of her eyesight. In July, unable to walk, she was taken to Smithfield in a litter to be burned at the stake with other evangelicals.

The perpetually suppurating ulcer on the king's leg had turned into one among many, all giving him excruciating pain whenever the bandages were changed, which presumably happened several times a day. Sometimes he was in such agony that he could not speak. Because of his monstrous obesity (it was said that three men could have fitted inside his doublet) he needed a ramp if he wanted to mount a horse. He found walking difficult, having to lean on a stick, and in his palaces had to be carried about in a special chair. He suffered regularly from exhausting 'fevers' caused by the ulcers.

Yet although he had been hated by large sections of the population only a few years earlier – and even now the North could never forgive him – this rotting, moribund hulk of a man had become idolized as a benevolent colossus by many of his subjects, who turned a blind eye to his selfishness, cruelty and tyranny. Part of their veneration came from his having reigned over them for so long, yet most of it was due to the overwhelming impact of his extraordinary personality, shallow as it may have been. Clearly, he knew how to assume a grave and kindly air when necessary. Describing the king's last speech to Parliament, Richard Grafton (continuing Hall's chronicle) said his address gave 'his subjects there present such comfort that the like joy could not be unto them in this world'. There is no reason to doubt Grafton.[2]

Because of his ailments, Henry's temper had grown more dangerous than ever. Aware that he might have only a very short time left to live, he worried even more about what was going to happen when his young son – still only nine in 1546 – succeeded him as a minor. Although he had ensured that no more Yorkist pretenders were left in England, he was afraid that some other magnate might try and seize the throne. Richard of Gloucester's example can never have been very far from his mind.

In particular, he did not trust the aged Duke of Norfolk. A pleasant-spoken and sly little man, always blandly reassuring while lying through his teeth, Norfolk could never forget what Bosworth, fought when he was a boy of twelve, had meant for his family: his grandfather was killed and his father taken prisoner, while the Howards forfeited their duchy.[3] It had taken them years to recover their position. In consequence, no one possessed a keener sense for survival or for the main chance than Thomas Howard, who was completely without principles. 'It was merry in England afore the New Learning came up,' he famously declared in 1540. 'Yea, I would all things were as hath been in times past.' Yet despite his Catholic instincts, he was the man who had put down the Pilgrimage of Grace so mercilessly. Loathing Cromwell as he did, he had treated him with oily subservience, and then played a major part in destroying him.

Having employed Norfolk so often, Henry had no illusions about his lack of scruples, while he blamed him for the disastrous marrage to his niece Katherine Howard. Nor could the king fail to have been aware that Norfolk filled the place once occupied by Buckingham as the last remaining duke and the richest man in England, with an income verging on £4,000. He lacked Plantagenet blood, but through marrying Buckingham's daughter had acquired it for the Howards. Worse still, he possessed an alarmingly dangerously unstable son.[4]

What made the situation explosive was that the Howards stood in the way of a man who was secretly determined to rule England during the looming minority. Brother of the late Queen Jane and uncle to the Prince of Wales, Edward Seymour, Earl of Hertford knew how to make the most of his relationship to the king's favourite wife. The duke tried to defuse the situation by offering Seymour's brother the hand of his daughter Mary, the late Duke of Richmond's widow. She declined, however, while her brother Lord Surrey proclaimed his contempt for so low a marriage. What made matters worse was that Surrey had made advances to Seymour's wife. He began whispering into Henry's ear that the Howards had designs on the throne; he understood exactly how to drop hints of disaffection that the king would interpret as clear proof of treason.

In his late twenties, Henry Howard, Earl of Surrey, was a tall, horse-faced young man with a forked beard, very different from his father. A dazzling if troubled figure, he had spent a year at the French court with his friend the Duke of Richmond (the king's short-lived son), where he learned not only French but Italian, and became a genuinely great poet – one of the first Englishmen to use the sonnet. Yet despite his brilliance and although basically honourable – unlike his father – there was something shallow about him. He could be childishly frivolous, as in January 1543 when he had led a group of gilded young companions on a riot through London (shooting stone-firing crossbows at passers-by, smashing windows) that ended in the Fleet prison. Obsessed with display, he liked to ride through the city streets with an escort of fifty horsemen.

Arrogant, hot-tempered and quarrelsome, never hiding his contempt for fellow courtiers who were not nobly born, Henry Howard's attitude is encapsulated by his comment on Cromwell's fall: 'Now is that foul churl dead, so ambitious of other blood, now is he stricken with his own staff.' People like that would leave no noblemen alive, he added.[5] There is also a persistent tradition that, when very young, he had been in trouble for striking in the face Queen Jane's brother, the recently ennobled Edward Seymour, partly from disdain for his comparatively ignoble origins. Understandably, he had a talent for making enemies. At first, however, his youthful high spirits amused the king, who would have agreed with the verdict of a contemporary cleric, 'the most foolish proud boy that is in England'.[6]

Henry would not have been so fond of Surrey, however, had he read Surrey's sonnet *Sardanapalus*, which almost certainly had the king in mind, although it was probably written after the earl had lost favour.

> The Assyrian king – in peace, with foul desire
> And filthy lusts that stained his regal heart –
> In war, that should set princely hearts on fire,
> Did yield for want of martial art . . .
> Who scarce the name of manhood did retain,
> Drenchèd in sloth and womanish delight,
> Feeble of sprite, unpatient of pain.[7]

One of those men for whom war offers the best hope of staying out of mischief, Surrey served in France from 1543 to 1546, at one stage as Lieutenant General of the King on Sea and Land – commander-in-chief in the field. He turned out to be a born soldier who quickly established his authority over both starving, ill-paid English troops and tough, mutinous mercenaries, besides displaying a flair for organization. He led from the front, so much so that Henry wrote to chide him for risking his life. To the king's joy, Boulogne was taken, doubling English territory

around Calais. Although the earl had to abandon the siege of
Montreuil, he beat off a determined attempt by the French to
recapture Boulogne. However, after his humiliating rout by the
French during a skirmish near St Étienne in January 1546, when
he lost a fifth of his army and several of his standards, the earl was
demoted by Henry to Captain of Boulogne, and then recalled to
England. He had forfeited royal favour for good.

Surrey went back to the Tudor court, which was more dangerous than any battlefield. After winning the king's approval and
having wealth and honours heaped upon him, a man could all
too easily end up on the scaffold. Shortly after his return, the
earl had a disastrous argument with an officer who had served
under him at Boulogne. Losing his temper, Surrey insisted that
a council could not possibly rule England for the future Edward
VI, as Henry wanted; only one man was fit to do so and that
was his father Norfolk. The outburst was reported to Seymour,
giving him the ammunition he needed to confirm the king's
suspicions. Because the earl was descended from Edward III
through his mother, Henry decided that he saw himself as the
future King of England.

Surrey was arrested on 2 December 1546. He had just
arrived at Whitehall when the Captain of the Yeomen of the
Guard, Sir Anthony Wingfield, asked him to come outside,
saying he needed his help in persuading his father the duke
to intercede in a lawsuit. When he left the room, Surrey was
immediately grabbed by 'halbardiers' (Yeomen) who manhan-
dled him on board a waiting boat that took him to the city.
Here he was held at Ely Place and questioned by the Lord
Chancellor, Thomas Wriothesly. On 12 December, St Lucy's
Eve, he was marched from Ely Place through the city streets to
the Tower.

Norfolk was sent to the Tower on the same day, stripped of
his staff of office and his Garter badge. That evening, he wrote
beseeching the king to remember all the good service he had
done and not allow him to be destroyed by false accusations,

insisting that he was at one with Henry in matters of religion and offering to surrender his estates. He also wrote to the council requesting permission to send for three books which he needed to help him sleep: St Augustine's *City of God*, Josephus' *Jewish Antiquities* and a work attacking papal pretensions. Learning of his arrest, the delighted folk of East Anglia rose and looted all the Howard houses in the area.

Summoned before the council Surrey's sister, Mary Howard, told them he had urged her to 'endear herself' to the king and 'rule him', which was more or less what her family had tried to do through the late Queen Katherine Howard. The admission must have infuriated Henry, opening up a very sore wound. Yet there was no evidence of plots against the king's life. The prosecution fell back on heraldry, arguing that Surrey had deliberately quartered royal arms as a discreet means of asserting his claim to the throne. Mary Howard helped to substantiate the accusation by her testimony that on the cap of maintenance bearing his crest her brother had set a coronet that looked like a closed (royal) crown, with the letters 'HR' which she thought must be the king's cipher.

The prosecution's case therefore rested entirely on showing that the Earl of Surrey's intention of making himself King of England was proved by a coat of arms he had recently adopted. His father, to whom it must have seemed that Bosworth had come again, did not fail King Henry. On 12 January, the day before his son's trial, he cravenly signed a totally untrue confession:

> I have concealed high treason in keeping secret the false and traitorous act, most presumptuously committed by my son Henry Howard, Earl of Surrey, against the King's Majesty and his Laws in the putting and using of the arms of St Edward the Confessor, King of the realm of England before the Conquest, in his scutcheon or arms, which said arms of St Edward appertain only to the King of this realm

and to none other person or persons, whereunto the said Earl by no means or way could make any claim or title, by me or any of mine or his ancestors.[8]

Meanwhile, the earl attempted to break out of the Tower. Having first arranged for a dagger to be smuggled into his cell, he tried to squeeze through the garderobe (privy), a short tunnel over the moat, which was not far below. A servant was waiting for him in a boat on the Thames nearby. He had already begun climbing down the noisesome shaft when, unexpectedly, guards came into the room on a random inspection. Seeing that he was not in his bed, they ran to the privy and managed to catch him by his arm, after which he was dragged out and shackled. It was generally thought that had Surrey still been above ground, with his arms free, he would certainly have tried to knife them.

In a bizarre indictment (the draft of which had been corrected and annotated by Henry personally), Surrey was accused of displaying at one of his houses a shield that bore the Howard arms quartered with those of King Edward the Confessor. On 13 January 1547 the earl was tried at the Guildhall before a jury of knights and squires from East Anglia as he was not a peer of Parliament, after being brought from the Tower by an escort of 300 yeomen. He defended himself magnificently, speaking from nine in the morning till five in the afternoon.

Unbowed, and as haughty as ever, he told a senior member of the council, Sir Richard Rich, that he was capable of condemning his own father in return for a piece of gold. He reminded another member, Lord Paget, that his father had been a 'catchpole' (a man whose job was arresting debtors), telling him England had never prospered 'since the King put mean creatures like thee into government'. When rebuked for his attempt to escape, he replied that, however innocent a man might be, he was always condemned. Some of the jury were very unwilling to convict him, but in the end they yielded and he was found guilty of treason, the shield with Edward the Confessor's arms being taken as conclusive proof of his designs on the throne. Six days later, wearing a black satin suit trimmed with black rabbit fur, Surrey was beheaded on Tower Hill.

An Act of Attainder introduced against Norfolk, condemning the duke to death and confiscating his estates, was passed by Parliament on 27 January, signed for the dying king with a 'dry stamp' or facsimile signature. He was saved at the last moment by Henry going to his own eternal reward shortly before dawn the next day, just a few hours before Norfolk was due to climb up the scaffold on Tower Hill. The execution was postponed, indefinitely. But he had to spend the next six years in prison, released only when Mary came to the throne and dying in his bed in 1554, aged eighty-one.

Shortly after the duke's arrest, the imperial ambassador of the day, Francis van der Delft, reported a conversation with Lord Chancellor Wriothesley, who had told him smoothly 'how pitiable it was that persons of such high and noble lineage should have undertaken so shameful a business as to plan the seizure of the government by sinister means'.[9] Rumours circulated that Norfolk and Surrey had intended to murder both the king and the Prince of Wales. There was of course not a word of truth in the charge which, once again, existed only in the strange mind of Henry VIII.

The two Howards had been victims of an imagination that, as so many times before, had induced a mental condition verging on clinical paranoia; in the king's diseased mind, father and son reincarnated Suffolks, Poles and Courtenays – and King Richard.

# EPILOGUE

Henry VIII's lifelong fear that there would be an attempt to oust his dynasty came true when King Edward VI died from tuberculosis on 6 July 1553. At the time, England's real ruler was John Dudley, Duke of Northumberland (the son of Henry VII's extortioner), who persuaded Edward on his deathbed to name as his successor Lady Jane Grey, a great-grandaughter of the first Tudor king and a convinced Protestant. Dudley's real motive was that she had married his son only six weeks before, but the country did not want the Tudors to be replaced by a dynasty of Dudleys. Ignoring the proclamation of 'Queen Jane', 20,000 men rallied to the Lady Mary, who quickly established her right to the throne and was crowned at Westminster Abbey on 1 October.

To some extent the new queen's accession was a belated triumph for the survivors of the White Rose party. Despite her ferocity towards anyone unwise enough to profess the Protestant faith, she was the warmest hearted of the Tudors and never forgot the White Rose's support for her mother Queen Katherine and for herself. Exeter's son, the Earl of Devon, was released from the Tower, and when Mary's first Parliament met, his attainder was reversed so that he regained the Courtenay estates. His mother became a lady-in-waiting. The attainder of Lord Montague's two daughters was also reversed and they recovered some of Lady Salisbury's lands, specifically in recognition of the services she had rendered the queen during her 'tender age'. Margaret's daughter Ursula and her husband Lord Stafford were given back the Duke of Buckingham's great house at Thornbury.

The thirty-seven-year-old virgin queen was in need of a king consort. She did not choose a Yorkist husband, however. Although she enquired whether Reginald Pole could be dispensed from his orders, she decided that at fifty-three he was too old. Edward Courtenay, whom she created Earl of Devon and who was privileged to bear the sword of state at her coronation, was so seriously considered, despite being twelve years younger than the queen, that he established a semi-royal household. His candidature was strongly supported by the Lord Chancellor, Bishop Steven Gardiner, and Mary herself took an affectionate interest in him. But after his long imprisonment he plunged into debauchery and lost his chance. Finally, she chose Philip of Spain, although he was just as young as Courtenay.

The Spaniard was a disastrous choice and her marriage, rather than the burning of heretics, made many Englishmen turn against Queen Mary, despite the popularity with which she had begun her reign. They disliked intensely the prospect of becoming part of the Habsburg Empire. Hoping to replace Mary with her sister Elizabeth, and with Edward Courtenay as king consort, Sir Thomas Wyatt the Younger led a rebellion early in 1554 that was only defeated by the queen's courage. At first Courtenay supported the plot, but then he lost his nerve and blurted it out to Lord Chancellor Gardiner.[1]

After another spell in the Tower, Courtenay was banished from England, to wander through Italy 'frequenting courtesans'. The last of his line, Edward died at Padua in September 1556, worn out by overindulgence in women and wine, although some thought he had been poisoned by Spanish agents. (He might have survived had he accepted Michael Throckmorton's invitation to stay with him at Mantua.) Two months before his death a crackbrained schoolmaster named Cleobury impersonated the earl at Yaxley, a village in Suffolk, proclaiming 'the Lady Elizabeth Queen and her beloved bedfellow, Lord Courtenay, King'. Cleobury had even found a few followers, but they did not turn up on the day and he was quickly arrested and executed

– a story recalling Ralph Wilford's impersonation of the Earl of Warwick in 1499.[2]

Another ludicrous incident occurred in April 1557 when Thomas Stafford, who was one of the Duke of Buckingham's grandsons, landed in Yorkshire with several hundred men, seized Scarborough and proclaimed himself Lord Protector. Although he was not even the duke's heir, Thomas had already had a seal made bearing the royal arms, declaring to anybody who would listen to him that he was heir to the throne. However, local levies under the Earl of Westmorland recaptured the castle almost immediately and he was executed at Tyburn the following month.[3]

Cardinal Pole came home as papal legate in November 1554, warmly welcomed by Mary and her Habsburg husband, 'King Philip'. Later in the month, he formally reconciled England to the papacy. After Philip's departure in 1555, never to return, Reginald became the queen's most trusted confidant, presiding over a restoration of English Catholicism in the light of the Council of Trent, envisaging a new, Catholic translation of the Bible, with seminaries in every diocese to ensure that priests were properly trained. On 20 March 1556 he was finally ordained as a priest himself, and consecrated as Archbishop of Canterbury two days later. He even saved a few Protestants from the fire – he wanted to spare Cranmer but was overruled by Mary – and in his *Book of Martyrs* Foxe admits that Pole was 'none of the bloody and cruel sort of Papists'.

But time and the future Queen Elizabeth were against his attempts to introduce the Counter-Reformation, and his health was failing. As a bitter irony he was ordered by Paul IV to return to Rome and face charges of heresy, although Mary refused to let him leave the country. He died in 1558 on the same day as the queen. The last Catholic Archbishop of Canterbury, Reginald Pole was the only man to occupy the see of St Augustine who might conceivably have been King of England.

A final, ghostly whisper came from the White Rose in 1562 when Elizabeth I fell ill with smallpox and it looked as if she might die. Her heir presumptive, Mary, Queen of Scots, was a Catholic so the Calvinist Henry Hastings, Earl of Huntingdon, whose mother had been Lord Montague's daughter, was proposed as a successor by the Protestant leaders in England. The news so angered Hastings's papist cousin Arthur Pole, Sir Geoffrey's eldest son, that Pole offered his support to Queen Mary, graciously offering to forego his own claim to the throne on condition she created him Duke of Clarence: there was even talk of him marrying her. Caught plotting against Elizabeth, Arthur Pole was found guilty of treason, but the queen spared his life because of his royal blood, and he died in the Tower at some unknown date during 1570 – the ultimate Yorkist prisoner.[4]

In their staunch fidelity to a dispossessed royal family, and in their adherence to Common Law and disgust at the setting aside of the obvious heir to the throne, the last Yorkists foreshadowed the Jacobites. Supporters of the exiled House of Stuart may have been aware of this when they adopted the White Rose as their own emblem – James II had been Duke of York before he became king. However, there was no Sir Walter Scott to immortalize their sixteenth-century predecessors.

Although Mary and Elizabeth were in turn threatened by rivals (the former by her sister, the latter by her Scottish cousin), neither of them appears to have been particularly frightened by the situation. By their time, their dynasty's right to the throne was established beyond question, so that they had no sense of being parvenus. Indeed, Elizabeth's triumphant reign made it seem that the Tudors had been predestined to rule England. In consequence, the cult of the Tudor age has largely obscured the Yorkist pretenders (except, perhaps, for Perkin Warbeck) and concealed the dread in which the White Rose was held by Henry VII and Henry VII.

# CHRONOLOGY

1483   Disappearance of Edward V and the Duke of York – the 'Princes in the Tower'

1484   Edward, Prince of Wales dies – the Earl of Warwick is briefly heir to the throne

1484   Richard III recognizes his nephew the Earl of Lincoln as his heir

1485   Battle of Bosworth and accession of Henry VII

1486   Rising for Warwick against Henry by Lord Lovell and the Stafford brothers

1487   Lincoln and Lambert Simnel ('Edward VI') defeated at Stoke – death of Lincoln

1490   The Abbot of Abingdon's plot to rescue the Earl of Warwick from the Tower

1491   Perkin Warbeck comes to Ireland and is identified as 'Richard, Duke of York'

1492   Margaret of Burgundy recognizes Warbeck as her nephew

1495   James IV of Scotland recognizes Warbeck as King of England

1496   Warbeck invades northern England, unsuccessfully

1497   Warbeck lands in Cornwall but is captured

1499   Execution of Warbeck and the Earl of Warwick

1501   Flight of Edmund de la Pole, Earl of Suffolk, nephew of Richard III

1502   Attainder of Edmund, who proclaims himself 'The White Rose'

1506   Edmund is captured and imprisoned in the Tower

1509    Edmund excluded from Henry VIII's 'accession pardon'

1513    Edmund is executed – his brother Richard de la Pole becomes 'The White Rose'

1514    Recognized as 'Richard IV' by France, the White Rose prepares to invade

1515    English spies try to murder Richard, 'the king's most dreaded enemy'

1521    Execution of the Duke of Buckingham, for 'dreaming of the throne'

1522    Francis I of France asks 'Richard IV' to invade England

1525    Richard de la Pole, 'The White Rose', is killed at Pavia

1531    Lord Exeter, male heir presumptive, is sent to the Tower on suspicion of treason

1533    Bishop Fisher asks Emperor Charles V's ambassador to depose Henry VIII

1534    Charles V considers replacing Henry VIII by Mary Tudor and Reginald Pole – but rejects the idea

1536    The Pilgrimage of Grace, the gravest threat to Henry VIII during his entire reign

1537    Reginald Pole prepares to land in England but the Pilgrimage is crushed

1538    Execution of Exeter and Lord Montague, key members of the White Rose party

1539    Reginald Pole tries and fails to organize an invasion of England

1539    Attainder of the Countess of Salisbury, the only surviving Plantagenet

1541    Abortive plot to revive the Pilgrimage of Grace

1541    Execution of the Countess of Salisbury – 'last of the White Rose faction'

1547    Execution of the Earl of Surrey on suspicion of planning to claim the throne

# ABBREVIATIONS

| | |
|---|---|
| *Bacon* | Bacon, Sir F., *The History of the Reign of King Henry VII and Selected Works*, ed. B. Vickers, Cambridge University Press, Cambridge, 1998 |
| *CPR* | *Calendar of Patent Rolls (1235–1509)*, 52 vols, London, 1891–1916 |
| *CSP Milan* | *Calendar of State Papers and Manuscripts... at Milan (1385–1618)*, ed. A. B. Hinds, London, H.M.S.O. 1912 |
| *CSP Sp* | *Calendar of State Papers*, (Spain), 20 vols, ed. C. Bergenroth, P. de Gayangos and M. A. S. Hume, London, Longman, Green, Longman, Roberts,1862–1954 |
| *CSP Ven* | *Calendar of State Papers*, (Venice), *1202–1603*, 11 vols, ed. R. Brown, G. C. Bentinck and H. F. Brown, London, Longman, Green, Longman, Roberts & Green, 1864–97 |
| *Gairdner RIII* | Gairdner, J., *The History of the Life and Reign of King Richard the Third to which is added the Story of Perkin Warbeck*, rev. edn, Cambridge, Cambridge University Press, 1898 |
| *GEC* | Cockayne, G. E. (ed.), *Complete Peerage of England, Scotland, Ireland, etc. Extant, Extinct or Dormant*, 13 vols, rev. edn, ed. V. Gibbs and H. Doubleday, London, 1910–49 |
| *Great Chronicle* | *The Great Chronicle of London*, ed. A. H Thomas and I. D. Thornley, London, G. W. Jones, 1938 |

| | |
|---|---|
| *Hall* | Hall, E., *The Union of the Two Noble and Illustre Famelies of Lancastre and York*, London, [1548]1809 |
| *Leland* | Leland, J., *The Itinerary of John Leland in or about the Years 1535–1543*, 5 vols, ed. L. Toulmin-Smith, London, 1907–10 |
| *LP Hen VII* | *Letters and Papers Illustrative of the Reigns of Richard III and Henry VII*, 2 vols, ed. J. Gairdner, J., Rolls Series, 1861–3 |
| *LP HVIII* | *Letters and Papers, Foreign and Domestic, of the Reign of Henry VIII, 1509–47*, 21 vols and addenda, ed. J. S. Brewer, J. Gairdner, J. and R. H. Brodie, London, 1862–1932 |
| *Materials* | *Materials for a History of the Reign of Henry VII*, 2 vols, ed. W. Campbell, Rolls Series, 1873–7 |
| *Memorials* | *Memorials of King Henry the Seventh*, ed. J. Gairdner, Rolls Series, London, 1858 |
| *Oxford DNB* | *Oxford Dictionary of National Biography*, 60 vols, Oxford, Oxford University Press, 2004 |
| *Paston Letters* | *The Paston Letters*, ed. J. Gairdner, Gloucester, Alan Sutton, 1986 |
| *Plumpton Corr* | *The Plumpton Correspondence*, ed. T. Stapleton, CS old series (21), London, 1839 |
| *Rot. Parl.* | *Rotuli Parliamentorum (1278–1504)*, 6 vols, ed. J. Strachey and others, London, 1767–77 |
| *Vergil* | *The Anglica Historia of Polydore Vergil AD 1485–1537*, ed. and trans. D. Hay, Camden Society, Third Series 74, 1950 |

# BIBLIOGRAPHY

## Printed Primary Sources

André, B., *De vita atque gestis Henrici Septimi*, in J. Gairdner (ed.), *Memorials of King Henry the Seventh*, Rolls Series, 1873–7.

Arnold, Richard, *Customs of London*, Antwerp, 1504.

*Ballads from Manuscripts*, ed. F.J. Furnivall, London, Ballad Society, 1868.

*The Book of Howth*, in *Calendar of the Carew Manuscripts*, 6 vols, ed. J.S. Brewer, Public Record Office, London, Longman, Green, Reader & Dyer, 1867–73.

*Calendar of the Close Rolls, Henry VII (1485–1500)*, vol. 1, Public Record Office, London, Her Majesty's Stationery Office, 1955.

*Calendar of the Fine Rolls (1272–1509)*, 22 vols, Public Record Office, London, His Majesty's Stationery Office, 1911–62.

*Calendar of the Patent Rolls (1235–1509)*, 52 vols, London, His Majesty's Stationery Office, 1891–1916.

*Calendar of State Papers and Manuscripts … at Milan (1385–1618)*, ed. A.B. Hinds, London, H.M.S.O, 1912.

*Calendar of State Papers between England and Spain, (Spain)*, 20 vols, ed. C. Bergenroth, P. de Gayangos and M.A.S. Hume, London, Longman, Green, Longman & Roberts, 1862–1954.

*Calendar of State Papers, (Venice), 1202–1603*, 11 vols, ed. R. Brown, G.C. Bentinck and H.F. Brown, London, Longman, Green, Longman, Roberts & Green 1864–97.

Cavendish, G., *Thomas Wolsey, late Cardinal, his Life and Death*

*Written by George Cavendish, his Gentleman Usher*, London, The Folio Society, 1999.

*The Chronicle of Calais in the Reigns of Henry VII and Henry VIII to the year 1540*, ed. J.G. Nichols, Old Series 35, London, Camden Society, 1846.

*Chronicle of the Grey Friars of London*, ed. J.G. Nichols, Old Series 53, London, Camden Society, 1852.

*Chronicles of London*, ed. C.L. Kingsford, Oxford, Clarendon Press, 1905.

Doutrepont, G. and Jodogne, O. (eds), *Chroniques de Jean Molinet (1474–1507)*, 3 vols, Brussels, Académie royale de Belgique, 1935–7.

*The Great Chronicle of London*, ed. A.H. Thomas and I.D. Thornley, London, G.W. Jones, 1938.

Ellis, Sir Henry, *Original Letters Illustrative of English History*, 1st Series, London, Harding, Triphook & Lepard, 1824.

Hall, E., *The Union of the Two Noble and Illustre Famelies of Lancastre and Yorke* [1548], London, Printed for J. Johnson, 1809.

*Henry Howard, Earl of Surrey: Poems*, ed. E. Jones, Oxford, Oxford University Press, 1964.

Herbert of Cherbury, Lord, *The Life and Reigne of King Henry VIII*, London, 1649.

*Ingulph's Chronicle of the Abbey of Croyland*, trans. H.T. Riley, Bohn, 1854.

*Letters and Papers Illustrative of the Reigns of Richard III and Henry VII*, 2 vols, ed. J. Gairdner, Rolls Series, London, Longman, Green, Longman & Roberts, 1861–3.

*Letters and Papers, Foreign and Domestic, of the Reign of Henry VIII, 1509–47*, 21 vols, ed. J.S. Brewer, J. Gairdner and R.H. Brodie, London, Longman, Green, Longman & Roberts, 1862–1932.

Leland, J., *The Itinerary of John Leland in or about the years 1535–1543*, 5 vols, ed. L. Toulmin-Smith, London, Bell, 1907–10.

————, *De Rebus Britannicis Collectanea*, 6 vols, London, G. & J. Richardson, 1770.

*The Letters of King Henry VIII: A Selection and a Few Other Documents*, ed. M. St Clare Byrne, New York, Funk & Wagnalls, 1968.

*The Lisle Letters*, 6 vols, ed. M. St Clare Byrne, Chicago and London, University of Chicago Press, 1981.

*Materials for a History of the Reign of Henry VII*, 2 vols, ed. W. Campbell, Rolls Series, London, 1873–7.

*Medieval English Lyrics: A Critical Anthology*, ed. R.T. Davies, London, Faber & Faber, 1963.

*Memorials of King Henry the Seventh*, ed. J. Gairdner, Rolls Series, London, 1858.

More, Sir Thomas, 'A Rueful Lamentation on the Death of Queen Elizabeth', in R.S. Sylvester (ed.), *Complete Works of Sir Thomas More*, 21 vols, New Haven, Yale University Press, 1963–c.1997.

Morison, Sir R., *An Invective ayenste [against] … Treason*, London, T. Bertheleti, 1539.

*Municipal Records of the City of York during the Reigns of Edward IV, Edward V and Richard III*, ed. R. Davies, London, J.B. Nichols & Son, 1843.

*The Paston Letters* (ed. J. Gairdner), Gloucester, Alan Sutton, 1986.

*Plumpton Correspondence* (ed. T. Stapleton), Old Series 21, London, Camden Society, 1839.

Pole, R., *The Correspondence of Reginald Pole*, 4 vols, ed. T.F. Meyer, Aldershot, Ashgate, 2002.

*Registrum Magni Sigilli Regum Scotorum: Register of the Great Seal of Scotland*, ed. Thompson, J.M., Paul, J.B. et al, Edinburgh, H.M.S.O., 1882–1914.

*The Reign of Henry VII from Contemporary Sources*, 3 vols, ed. A.F. Pollard, Longmans, Green and Co., 1913.

Roper, W., *The Life of Sir Thomas More*, London, J.M. Dent, 1906.

*Rotuli Parliamentorum (1278–1504)*, 6 vols, ed. J. Strachey and others, London, 1767–77.

*Select Cases in the Exchequer Chamber before all Justices of England, 1461–1509*, ed. M. Hemmant, Selden Society 64, vol. II, 1943.

*Six Town Chronicles of England*, ed. R. Flenley, Oxford, Clarendon Press, 1911.

Skelton, J., *The Complete Poems of John Skelton, Laureate*, ed. P. Henderson, London, J.M. Dent, 1948.

*Tudor Royal Proclamations*, 3 vols, ed. P.L. Hughes and J.F. Larkin, New Haven and London, Yale University Press, 1964–9.

Vergil, P., *The Anglica Historia of Polydore Vergil, A.D. 1485–1537*, ed. and trans. D. Hay, 3rd Series 74, London, Camden Society, 1950.

———, *Three Books of Polydore Vergil's English History*, ed. H. Ellis, Old Series 29, London, Camden Society, 1844.

Wriothesley, C., *A Chronicle of England during the Reigns of the Tudors, 1485–1559*, ed. W.D. Hamilton, New Series 11, London, Camden Society, 1875.

*York House Books*, ed. L. Attreed, Stroud, Alan Sutton, 1991.

**Secondary Sources**

Angelo, S. (ed.), *Chivalry in the Renaissance*, Woodbridge, Boydell Press, 1990.

Archbold, W.A.J., 'Sir William Stanley and Perkin Warbeck', *The English Historical Review*, 14 (1899).

Arthurson, I., 'Espionage and Intelligence from the Wars of the Roses to the Reformation', *Nottingham Medieval Studies*, 31 (1991).

———, *The Perkin Warbeck Conspiracy, 1491–1499*, Stroud, Alan Sutton, 1994.

Bacon, Sir F., *The History of the Reign of King Henry VII and*

*Selected Works*, ed. B. Vickers, Cambridge, Cambridge University Press, 1998.

Baldwin, D., 'What happened to Lord Lovell', *The Ricardian*, 89 (June 1985).

Bennett, M.J., *Lambert Simnell and the Battle of Stoke*, Gloucester, Alan Sutton, 1987.

Bernard, G.W. (ed.), *The Tudor Nobility*, Manchester, Manchester University Press, 1992.

———, *The King's Reformation: Henry VIII and the Remaking of the English Church*, New Haven and London, Yale University Press, 2005.

Bindoff, T.E., *Tudor England*, Oxford, Oxford University Press, 1950.

Brewer, J.S., *The Reign of Henry VIII from his Accession to the Death of Wolsey*, 2 vols, ed. J. Gairdner, London, Murray, 1884.

Brooke, R., *Visits to Fields of Battle in England of the Fifteenth Century*, London, John Russell Smith, 1857.

Bryan, D., *Gerald Fitzgerald, the Great Earl of Kildare, 1456–1513*, Dublin, Talbot Press, 1993.

Burne, A.H., *The Battlefields of England*, London, Penguin, 1996.

Busch, M.L., 'The Tudors and the Royal Race', *History* 55 (1971).

Busch, W., *England unter den Tudors*, Stuttgart, 1892, trans. A.M. Todd as *England under the Tudors*, vol. I: *Henry VII*, London, 1895.

Childs, J., *Henry VIII's Last Victim*, London, Jonathan Cape, 2006.

Chrimes, S.B., *Lancastrians, Yorkists and Henry VII*, London, Macmillan, 1964.

———, *Henry VII*, London, Eyre Methuen, 1972.

———, Ross, C.D. and Griffiths, R.S. (eds), *Fifteenth Century England 1309–1509*, Stroud, Sutton, 1995.

Cockayne, G.E. (ed.), *Complete Peerage of England, Scotland,*

*Ireland, etc., Extant, Extinct or Dormant*, rev. edn, 13 vols, London, V. Gibbs and H. Doubleday, 1910–49.

Condon, M.M., 'Ruling Elites in the Reign of Henry VII', in C.D. Ross (ed.), *Patronage, Pedigree and Power in Later Medieval England*, Gloucester, Alan Sutton, 1979.

Conway, A., *Henry VII's Relations with Scotland and Ireland 1485–98*, Cambridge, Cambridge University Press, 1932.

Cunningham, S., *Henry VII*, London and New York, Routledge, 2007.

Delbruck, H., *Die Neuzeit*, vol. IV of *Geschichte de Kriegskunst*, Berlin, 1920.

Dickens, A.G., *Reformation Studies*, London, Hambledon Press, 1982.

Dockray, K. and Fleming, P. (eds), *People, Places and Perspectives: Essays on Later Medieval and Tudor England in Honour of Ralph A. Griffiths*, Stroud, Nonsuch Publishing, 2005.

Dodds, M.H. and Dodds, R., *The Pilgrimage of Grace 1536–1537 and the Exeter Conspiracy*, 2 vols, Cambridge, Cambridge University Press, 1916.

Ellis, S.G., *Ireland in the Age of the Tudors, 1447–1603*, London, Longman, 1998.

Elton, G.R., *The Tudor Constitution: Documents and Commentary*, Cambridge, Cambridge University Press, 1960.

———, *Policy and Police*, Cambridge, Cambridge University Press, 1972.

———, *England under the Tudors*, London, Methuen, 1974.

———, *Reform and Revolution: England 1509–1558*, London, Edward Arnold, 1977.

———, *Studies in Tudor and Stuart Politics and Government*, 4 vols, Cambridge, Cambridge University Press, 1974–92.

Fletcher, A. and MacCulloch, D., *Tudor Rebellions*, 4th edn, London and New York, Longmans, 1997.

Fonblanque, E.B. de, *The Annals of the House of Percy*, London, 1887.

Gairdner, J., *Henry VII*, London, 1892.

————, *The History of the Life and Reign of King Richard the Third to which is added the Story of Perkin Warbeck*, Cambridge, Cambridge University Press, 1898.

Gunn, S.J., *Early Tudor Government, 1485–1588*, London, Macmillan, 1995.

Guy, J.A., *Tudor England*, Oxford, Oxford University Press, 1988.

Gwyn, P., *The King's Cardinal: The Rise and Fall of Thomas Wolsey*, London, Pimlico, 2002.

Hampton, W.E., 'The Later Career of Robert Stillington', in J. Petre (ed.), *Richard III: Crown and People*, Gloucester, Alan Sutton, 1985.

Hanham, A., *Richard III and his Early Historians, 1483–1535*, Oxford, Oxford University Press, 1975.

————, 'Edmund de la Pole and the Spies 1449–1506', in S.M. Jack (ed.), *Rulers, Religion and Rhetoric in Early Modern England: A Festschrift for Geoffrey Elton from his Australasian Friends*, Sydney, Parergon, 1988.

————, 'Edmund de la Pole, defector', *Journal of the Society for Renaissance Studies*, 2 (1988).

Harris, B.J., *Edward Stafford, Third Duke of Buckingham, 1478–1521*, Stanford, Stanford University Press, 1986.

Harrison, C.J., 'The Petition of Edmund Dudley', *English Historical Review*, 87 (1972).

Hicks, M.A., 'Dynastic Change and Northern Society: The Career of the Fourth Earl of Northumberland', *Northern Society*, 14 (1978).

Howell, T.B., *State Trials*, London, 1816.

Hoyle, R., *The Pilgrimage of Grace*, Oxford, Oxford University Press, 2001.

Hutchinson, R., *Thomas Cromwell*, London, Weidenfold, 2007.

Ives, E.W., *The Life and Death of Anne Boleyn*, Oxford, Blackwell, 2004.

————, 'Faction at the Court of Henry VIII: The Fall of Anne Boleyn', *History*, 57 (1972).

Jones, M.K., 'Sir William Stanley of Holt: Politics and Family

Allegiance in the Late Fifteenth Century', *Welsh History Review*, 14 (1988).

Kaufman, P.I., 'Henry VII and Sanctuary', *Church History*, 53 (1984).

Knecht, R.J., *Francis I*, Cambridge, Cambridge University Press, 1982.

———, *Renaissance Warrior and Patron : The Reign of Francis I*, Cambridge, Cambridge University Press, 1994.

Konstam, A., *Pavia 1525: The Climax of the Italian Wars*, Oxford, Osprey, 1996.

La Rivoire de La Batie, L.E.G. de La, *Armorial de Dauphiné*, Lyons, 1867.

Levine, M., *Tudor Dynastic Problems 1460–1571*, London, Allen and Unwin, 1973.

Lipscomb, S., *1536: The Year that Changed Henry VIII*, Oxford, Lion Hudson, 2009.

Loades, D.M., *Two Tudor Conspiracies*, Cambridge, Cambridge University Press, 1965.

Luckett, D., 'The Thames Valley Conspiracies Against Henry VII', *Bulletin of the Institute of Historical Research*, 68 (1995).

MacDougall, N., *James IV*, Edinburgh, John Donald, 1989.

Mackie, J.D., *The Earlier Tudors*, Oxford, Oxford University Press, 1952.

MacLean, Sir J. (ed.), *The Berkeley Manuscripts: Lives of the Berkeleys*, 3 vols, Gloucester, Bristol and Gloucestershire Archaeological Society, 1883.

Macquereau, R., *Histoire générale de l'Europe*, Louvain, 1765.

Mayer, T.E., 'A Diet for Henry VIII: the Failure of Reginald Pole's 1537 Legation', *Journal of British Studies*, 26 (1987), pp. 305–31.

———, *Reginald Pole, Prince and Prophet*, Cambridge, Cambridge University Press, 2000.

McCormack, A.M., *The Earldom of Desmond 1463–1583*, Dublin, Four Courts Press, 2005.

Merriman, R.B., *Life and Letters of Thomas Cromwell*, 2 vols, Oxford, Oxford University Press, 1902.

Miller, H., *Henry VIII and the English Nobility*, Oxford, Oxford University Press, 1989.

Moorhen, W.E.A., 'The Career of John de la Pole, Earl of Lincoln', *The Ricardian, Journal of the Richard III Society*, 13 (2003).

Morel Fatio, A., 'Marguerite d'York et Perkin Warbeck', in *Mélanges d'Histoire offerts à M. Charles Bémont*, Paris, Félix Alcan, 1913.

Neame, A., *The Holy Maid of Kent: The Life of Elizabeth Barton, 1506–1534*, London, Hodder and Stoughton, 1971.

O'Flanagan, J.R.O., *The Blackwater in Munster*, London, 1844.

O'Malley, G., *The Knights Hospitaller of the English Langue 1460–1565*, Oxford, Oxford University Press, 2005.

Overell, A., 'Cardinal Pole's Special Agent: Michael Throckmorton, c.1503–1558', *History*, 94 (July 2009), p.315.

Pierce, H., *Margaret Pole, Countess of Salisbury 1473–1541*, Cardiff, University of Wales Press, 2003.

Pollard, A.F., *Henry VIII*, London and New York, Longmans, Green, and Co., 1905.

Porter, L., *Mary Tudor: The First Queen*, London, Piatkus, 2009.

Price, L., 'Armed Forces of the Irish Chiefs in the Early Sixteenth Century', *Journal of the Royal Society of Antiquarians of Ireland*, 62 (1932).

Rawcliffe, C., *The Staffords, Earls of Stafford and Dukes of Buckingham, 1394–1521*, Cambridge, Cambridge University Press, 1978.

Ross, C., *Richard III*, London, Eyre Methuen, 1981.

Roth, C., 'Perkin Warbeck and his Jewish Master', *Transactions of the Jewish Historical Society of England*, 9 (1922).

Rowse, A.L., *Tudor Cornwall*, London, Macmillan, 1969.

Scarisbrick, J.J., *Henry VIII*, London, Eyre Methuen, 1968.

———, 'Fisher, Henry VIII and the Reformation Crisis', in B. Bradshaw and E. Duffy (eds), *Humanism, Reform and the*

*Reformation: The Career of Bishop John Fisher*, Cambridge, Cambridge University Press, 1989.

Sessions, W.A., *Henry Howard, the Poet Earl of Surrey*, Oxford, Oxford University Press, 1999.

Skeel, C.A.J., *The Council in the Marches of Wales*, London, Hugh Rees Ltd., 1904.

Starkey, D., *The Reign of Henry VIII: Personalities and Politics*, London, George Philip, c.1985.

———, *Six Wives: The Queens of Henry VIII*, , London, 2003.

Taylor, James D., *The Shadow of the White Rose: Edward Courtenay, Earl of Devon 1526–1556*, New York, Algora, 2006.

Thompson, E.M., *History of the Somerset Carthusians*, London, John Hodges, 1895.

Wedgwood, J.C. (ed.), *History of Parliament: Biographies of Members of the Commons House, 1439–1509*, London, H.M.S.O., 1936.

Williams, C.H., 'The Rebellion of Sir Humphrey Stafford in 1486', *The English Historical Review*, 43 (1928).

Wooding, L., *Henry VIII*, London and New York, Routledge, 2009.

Wroe, A., *Perkin: A Story of Deception*, London, Jonathan Cape, 2003.

Youings, J.A., 'The Council of the West', *Transactions of the Royal Historical Society*, Fifth Series, 10 (1960).

# Notes

## Overview:
## The White Rose, 1485–1547

1. R.T. Davies (ed.), *Medieval English Lyrics: A Critical Anthology*, London, Faber & Faber, 1963, no. 156.
2. P. Vergil, *The Anglica Historia of Polydore Vergil AD 1485–1537*, Camden Society, 1950, p. 9.
3. 'The spectre of possible rivals, true or false, haunted Henry VII all the days, and maybe the nights, of his life, and inflamed the heated imagination of his son after him; many guilty and innocent heads were to roll so that the Tudors might sleep more easily.' S.B. Chrimes, *Lancastrians, Yorkists and Henry VII*, London, Macmillan, 1964, p. 158
4. A. Fletcher and D. MacCulloch, *Tudor Rebellions*, London and New York, Longmans, 1997, p. 116.
5. L. Wooding, *Henry VIII*, London, Routledge, 2009, p. 18.

## 1. Autumn 1485:
## 'this woeful season'

1. Sir F. Bacon, *The History of the Reign of King Henry VII and Selected Works*, Cambridge, 1998, p. 23. Bacon may not have known of material that has since come to light, but he had read Vergil, Fabyan and Robert André, besides several manuscript sources, and is often a remarkably shrewd interpreter.
2. R. Davies, *Municipal Records of the City of York during the Reigns of Edward IV, Edward V and Richard III*, London, 1843, p. 218.
3. *The Paston Letters*, Gloucester, Alan Sutton, 1986, 1001.

4. *Memorials of King Henry the Seventh*, Rolls Series, London, 1858, 1, 4–5.
5. Vergil, *op. cit.*, p. 8.
6. *Rotoli Parliamentorum (1278–1504)*, London,1767–77, vol. VI, 268–70.
7. Vergil, *op. cit.*, p. 144.
8. S. Cunningham, *Henry VII*, London, Routledge, 2007, p. 98.
9. Bacon, *op. cit.*, p. 19.

## 2. Easter 1486:
## Lord Lovell and the Stafford Brothers

1. Bacon, p. 65.
2. *The Plumpton Correspondence*, OS Old Series (21), London, 1839, p. 48.
3. *Ibid.*, p. 48.
4. *Material for a History of the Reign of Henry VII*, 2 vols, Rolls Series, 1873–7, vol. I, p. 143.
5. C.H. Williams, 'The Rebellion of Sir Humphrey Stafford in 1486', *The English Historical Review*, 43 (1928).
6. *LP Hen VII*, vol. I, p. 234.
7. Vergil, *op. cit.*, p. 10.
8. E.H. Fonblanque, *The Annals of the House of Percy*, 2 vols, London, [Private Circulation], 1887, vol. I, p. 300.
9. H.T. Riley (ed.), *Ingulph's Chronicle of the Abbey of Croyland*, London, 1854, pp. 513–14.
10. Bacon, *op. cit.*, p. 20.
11. *Coram Rege Rolls*, Trin. 1, Hen VII Rex. Rot. 10, quoted in Williams, 'The Rebellion', p. 188.
12. *Material, op. cit.*, vol. I, p. 434.
13. *Paston Letters, op. cit.*, p. 890.
14. J. Leland, *The Itinerary of John Leland . . . 1535–1543*, 5 vols, ed. L. Toulmin Smith, London, 1907–10, vol. 5, pp. 75–6.
15. M. Hemmant (ed.), *Select Cases in the Exchequer Chamber before all Justices of England, 1461–1509*, Selden Society 64, London 1943, vol. II, pp. 115–24
16. *Materials, op. cit.*, vol. I, pp. 513–14

17. *Calendar of the Fine Rolls,* S.M.O., 22 vols, London, 1911–62: Henry VII, 1485–1509, vol. 22, 842.

18. *Plumpton Corr, op. cit.,* p. 54

# 3. Early 1487:
## Margaret of York

1. E. Hall, *The Union of the Two Noble and Illustre Families . . .,* London, 1809, p. 430.

2. Vergil *op. cit.,* pp. 14–16.

3. Margaret de la Pole, daughter of Sir John de la Pole, a younger bother of William, first Duke of Suffolk – married Jean de Foix, Earl of Kendal ('Cumbria'), whose duather Anne became the Queen of Ladislas II of Hungary. *GEC,* vol. VIII, p. 150.

4. W.E.A. Moorhen, 'The Career of John de la Pole, Earl of Lincoln', *The Ricardian, Journal of the Richard III Society,* 13 (2003).

5. H.T. Riley (trans.), *Ingulph's Chronicle of the Abbey of Croyland,* 1854, pp. 513–14.

6. L. Attreed, *York House Books,* Stroud, Alan Sutton, 1991, vol. 2, p. 54.

7. Riley, *Ingulph's Chronicle, op. cit.,* p. 514.

8. M. Bennett, *Lambert Simnel and the Battle of Stoke,* Gloucester, Alan Sutton, 1987.

9. J.S. Brewer (ed.), *The Book of Howth,* in *Calendar of the Carew Manuscripts,* 6 vols, London, Public Record Office, 1867, vol. 5, pp.188–9.

10. *Materials, op. cit.,* vol. 2, p. 273.

11. W.E. Hampton, 'The Later Career of Robert Stillington', in J. Petre (ed.), *Richard III: Crown and People,* London, Richard III Society, 1975–81, pp. 162–8.

12. *York House Books, op. cit.,* vol. 2, pp. 540–2.

13. H. Delbruck, *Die Nenzeit,* vol. IV of *Geshicte der Kriegskunst,* Berlin, 1920.

14. J. Nichols (ed.), *The Chronicle of Calais in the Reigns of Henry VII and Henry VIII,* Camden Society, Old Series, 35, London, 1846, p. 1.

15. Vergil, *op. cit.,* p. 23.

## 4. Summer 1487:
## 'Stoke Field'

1. *Rot. Parl.*, vol. VI, 397.
2. P.L. Hughes and J.F. Larkin (eds), *Tudor Royal Proclamations*, 3 vols, New Haven and London, Yale University Press, 1964–9, vol. 1, pp. 12–13.
3. *York House Books*, *op. cit.*, vol. 2, p. 570.
4. Bacon, *op. cit.*, p. 34.
5. *The Great Chronicle of London*, ed. A.H. Thomas and I.D. Thornley, London, G.W. Jones, 1938, p. 241.
6. Vergil, *op. cit.*, p. 22.
7. *Great Chronicle*, *op. cit.*, p. 242.
8. J. Molinet, see G. Doutrepont and O. Jodogne (eds), *Chroniques de Jean Molinet (1474–1507)*, 3 vols, Brussels, Académie royale de Belgique, 1935–7, vol. 1, pp. 362–5.
9. Hall, *op. cit.*, p. 434.
10. J. Leland, *De Rebus Britannicis Collectanea*, 6 vols, London, 1770, vol. IV, p. 210.
11. A.H. Burne, *The Battlefields of England*, London, Penguin, 1996, p. 314
12. Bacon, *op. cit.*, p. 35.
13. J.M. Thompson, J.B. Paul and others (eds), *Registrum Magni Sigilli Regnum Scotorum: Register of the Great Seal of Scotland*, Edinburgh, Scottish Record Society, 1882–1914, vol. 2 (1424–1513), p. 370.
14. D. Baldwin, 'What Happened to Lord Lovell?', *The Ricardian*, 89 (June 1985).
15. Vergil, *op. cit.*, p. 24.
16. *Rot. Parl.*, *op. cit.*, vol. VI, 397.
17. B. André, *De Vita atque gestis Henrici Septimi Historia*, in *Memorials*, pp. 49–52.
18. Bacon, *op. cit.*, p. 20.

## 5. Winter 1489–90:
## The Conscience of Abbot Sant

1. Vergil, *op. cit.*, p. 32.

2. Bacon, *op. cit.*, p. 201.
3. *Paston Letters*, *op. cit.*, p. 1032.
4. *Paston Letters*, *op. cit.*, p. 1037.
5. M.A. Hicks, 'Dynastic Change and Northern Society: The Career of the Fourth Earl of Northumberland', *Northern Society* 14 (1978), pp. 78–107.
6. Hall, *op. cit.*, p. 443.
7. *Materials, op. cit.*, vol. II, pp. 337 and 339.
8. Vergil, *op. cit.*, p. 32.
9. D. Luckett, 'The Thames Valley Conspiracies against Henry VII', *Bulletin of the Institute of Historical Research*, 68 (1995), pp. 164–72.
10. *Rot. Parl.*, *op. cit.*, vol. VI, p. 436.
11. I. Arthurson, 'Espionage and Intelligence from the Wars of the Roses to the Reformation', *Nottingham Medieval Studies*, 35 (1991), pp. 145–6.
12. *Plumpton Corr*, *op. cit.*, letter lxxi; Leland, *Collectanea*, vol. IV, p. 257.
13. *Calendar of the Close Rolls, Henry VII (1485–1500)*, 2 vols, London, H.M.S.O., 1955–63, vol. 1, 672, pp. 196–7.

## 6. Winter 1491–Autumn 1492:
### One of the Princes in the Tower?

1. Bacon, *op. cit.*, p. 95.
2. Hall, *op. cit.*, p. 462.
3. *LP Hen VII*, *op. cit.*, vol. I, p. 99.
4. *Rot. Parl.*, *op. cit.*, vol. VI, p. 455.
5. *Rot. Parl.*, *op. cit.*, vol. VI, p. 454.
6. Hall, *op. cit.*, pp. 488–9.
7. J.R.O. O'Flanagan, *The Blackwater in Munster*, London, 1844, p. 37.
8. Bacon, *op. cit.*, p. 105.
9. *LP Hen VII*, Rolls Series, 1861–3, vol. II, pp. 326–7.
10. A. Conway, *Henry VII's Relations with Scotland and Ireland 1485–98*, Cambridge, Cambridge University Press, 1932, p. 49.
11. B. André, *De vita atque gestis Henrici Septimi Historia*, in *Memorials*, p. 66.

12. Hall, *op. cit.*, p. 464.

13. Vergil, *op. cit.*, p. 64.

14. *Ibid.*, p. 66.

15. Richard Arnold, *Customs of London*, Antwerp, 1504.

16. Vergil, *op. cit.*, p. 64.

17. A. Morel Fatio, 'Marguerite d'York et Perkin Warbeck', in *Mélanges d'Histoire offerts à M. Charles Belmont*, Paris, Félix Alcan, 1913, pp. 411–16.

18. Bacon, *op. cit.*, p. 102.

19. Vergil, *op. cit.*, p. 68.

20. A. Wroe, *Perkin: A Story of Deception*, London, Jonathan Cape, 2003.

21. C. Roth, 'Perkin Warbeck and his Jewish Master', *Transactions of the Jewish Historical Society of England*, 9 (1922), pp. 143–62.

22. *Archeologica*, xxvi.

23. A.F. Pollard, *The Reign of Henry VII from Contemporary Sources*, 3 vols, London, Longmann, Green, & Co., 1913, vol. 1, pp. 93–5.

24. *LP Hen VII*, vol. II, p. 321.

25. *Ibid.*, pp. 292–7.

26. *Ibid.*, pp. 388–404.

## 7. January 1495:
## The Lord Chamberlain is a Traitor

1. Bacon, *op. cit.*, p. 202.

2. G.L. Kingsford (ed.), *Chronicles of London*, Oxford, 1905, p. 203.

3. Hall, *op. cit.*, p. 463.

4. *Chronicles of London*, *op. cit.*, p. 203.

5. Bacon, *op. cit.*, p. 122.

6. Hall, *op. cit.*, p. 470.

7. Vergil, *op. cit.*, p. 74; T.B. Howell, *State Trials*, London, 1816, p. 282.

8. W.A.J. Archbold, 'Sir William Stanley and Perkin Warbeck', *English Historical Review*, 14 (1899).

9. R. Flenley, *Six Town Chronicles*, Oxford, Oxford University Press, 1911, p. 166.

## 8. Summer 1495:
## The Yorkist Invasion

1. Hall, *op. cit.*, pp. 471–2.
2. *Ibid.*, p. 462.
3. J. Gairdner, *The History of the Life and Reign of King Richard the Third*, Cambridge, 1898, pp. 291–2.
4. *Ibid.*, p. 292.
5. *Memorials, op. cit.*, pp. 393–9.
6. *CSP Ven*, vol. I, 648.
7. *Chronicles of London, op. cit.*, p. 205.
8. Hall, *op. cit.*, p. 472; Vergil B, p. 80.
9. *CSP Sp*, vol. I, 98.
10. Vergil, *op. cit.*, p. 84.
11. *Chroniques de Jean Molinet, op. cit.*, vol 1, pp. 421–2.
12. *Chronicles of London, op. cit.*, p. 205.
13. *Paston Letters, op. cit.*, p. 936.
14. *Ibid.*, p. 937.
15. *CSP Ven, op. cit.*, vol. I, 649.
16. *Ibid.*, vol. I, 651.
17. *Chronicles of London, op. cit.*, p. 205.
18. Bacon, *op. cit.*, p. 119.
19. *Ibid.*, p. 124.
20. A.M. McCormack, *The Earldom of Desmond 1463–1583*, Dublin, Four Courts Press, 2005, p. 62.
21. L. Price, 'Armed Forces of the Irish Chiefs in the Early Sixteenth Century', *Journal of the Royal Society of Antiquarians of Ireland*, 62 (1932).

## 9. Autumn 1495–Summer 1497:
## The Scots and the Cornish

1. Vergil, *op. cit.*, p. 92.
2. *CSP Sp, op. cit.*, vol. I, 169.
3. Gairdner, *History of the Life and Reign of Richard the Third*, p. 300.
4. Vergil, *op. cit.*, p. 84; Hall, *op. cit.*, p. 474; Bacon, *op. cit.*, p. 127–8.
5. *LP Hen VII, op. cit.*, vol. II, pp. 325–6.

6. W. Busch, *England Unter Den Tudors*, vol. 1, ed. J.G. Cotta, Stuttgart, 1892, trans. A.M. Todd as *England under the Tudors*, vol. 1, *Henry VII*, London, 1895, p. 105.
7. H. Ellis, *Original Letters Illustrative of British History*, 1st series, London, 1824, vol. 1, p. 23.
8. *Ibid.*, vol. 1, p. 25.
9. *Calender of State Papers and Manuscripts . . . at Milan (1385–1618)*, London, 1912, vol. I, p. 490.
10. Vergil, *op. cit.*, p. 88.
11. *Chronicles of London*, *op. cit.*, p. 210.
12. Hall, *op. cit.*, p. 475.
13. Bacon, *op. cit.*, p. 135.
14. Bacon, *op. cit.*, p. 137.
15. *Chronicles of London*, *op. cit.*, p. 215.
16. I. Arthurson, *The Perkin Warbeck Conspiracy 1491–1499*, Stroud, Sutton, 1994, p. 165, quoting TNA, PRO KB9/441/6.
17. Bacon, *op. cit.*, p. 142.
18. Gairdner, *Richard the Third . . .*, *op. cit.*, p. 317.

## 10. March 1496:
### The Grand Prior Plans to Poison the King

1. *LP Hen VII*, *op. cit.*, II, pp. 318–23. Our only source for this episode is Bernart's *Depositum*.
2. G. O'Malley, *The Knights Hospitaller of the English Langue 1460–1565*, Oxford, Oxford University Press, 2005, p. 144.
3. *Oxford DNB*.
4. I. Arthurson, *The Perkin Warbeck Conspiracy 1491–99*, Stroud, Alan Sutton, 1994, pp. 76 and 232 n. 54.
5. *The Knights Hospitaller*, pp. 146–50.
6. A. Wroe, *Perkin, a Story of Deception*, London, Jonathan Cape, 2003, pp. 166–9 and 203–4.

## 11. September 1497:
### Cornwall Rises for Richard IV

1. *CSP Milan*, *op. cit.*, vol. I, 327.
2. *CSP Ven*, *op. cit.*, vol. I, 754.

3. A.F. Pollard (ed.), *The Reign of Henry VII from Contemporary Sources*, 3 vols, London, Longmans, Green and Co., 1913, vol. 1, pp. 162–3.
4. *LP Hen VII*, *op. cit.*, vol. II, p. xli–xlii.
5. Pollard, *Reign of Henry VII*, *op. cit.*, vol. 1, p. 163.
6. *Ibid.*, p. 168.
7. *Rot. Parl.*, *op. cit.*, vol. VI, p. 545.
8. Vergil, *op. cit.*, p. 106.
9. *CSP Milan*, *op. cit.*, vol. I, 325.
10. Pollard, *Reign of Henry VII*, *op. cit.*, vol. 1, p. 150.
11. *Chronicles of London*, *op. cit.*, p. 217.
12. A.L. Rowse, *Tudor Cornwall*, London, Macmillan, 1969, p. 131
13. *CSP Milan*, *op. cit.*, vol. I, 327.
14. *Ibid.*, 329.
15. Pollard, *Reign of Henry VII*, *op. cit.*, vol. 1, p. 173.
16. B. André, in *Memorials*, pp. 73–5.
17. Hall, *op. cit.*, p. 485.
18. Vergil, *op. cit.*, p.108.
19. Vergil, *op. cit.*, p. 109.
20. *LP Hen VII*, *op. cit.*, vol. II, pp. 335–7.
21. Bacon, *op. cit.*, p. 151.

## 12. Autumn 1499:
## Bringing Down a Curse

1. Vergil, *op. cit.*, p. 118.
2. *Chronicles of London*, *op. cit.*, p. 219.
3. *CSP Milan*, *op. cit.*, vol. I, 550.
4. *Chronicles of London*, *op. cit.*, p. 219.
5. Gairdner, *Richard III*, *op. cit.*, pp. 229–30.
6. *CSP Ven*, *op. cit.*, vol. I, 760.
7. *Chronicles of London*, *op. cit.*, p. 223.
8. *CSP Sp*, *op. cit.*, vol. I, 198.
9. *Ibid.*, 221.
10. Vergil, *op. cit.*, p. 116.
11. *Chronicles of London*, *op. cit.*, p. 225.
12. Hall, *op. cit.*, p. 491.
13. *CSP Sp*, *op. cit.*, vol. I, 221.

14. *CSP Milan,*. vol I, 799.
15. *CSP Ven, op. cit.*, vol. V, 575.
16. Bacon, *op. cit.*, p. 160.
17. Arthurson, 'Espionage and Intelligence', *Nottingham Medieval Studies*, 1991, pp. 202–18.
18. *Plumpton Corr, op. cit.*, p. 141.
19. *Chroniques de Jean Molinet, op. cit.*, vol. 2, p. 467.
20. *LP Hen VII, op. cit.*, p. 1.
21. Bacon, *op. cit.*, p. 160.
22. *Chronicles of London, op. cit.*, pp. 227–8.
23. Vergil, *op. cit.*, p. 118.

## 13. Autumn 1499:
### Edmund de la Pole, Earl of Suffolk

1. Hall, *op. cit.*, p. 495.
2. Sir Thomas More, 'A Rueful Lamentation on the Death of Queen Elizabeth', in R. S. Sylvester (ed.), *The Complete Works of St Thomas More*, Yale, Yale University Press, vol. 1, p. 9.
3. *CSP Sp, op. cit.*, vol. I, 249.
4. *LP Hen VII, op. cit.*, vol. I, pp. 397, 400–1.
5. Vergil, *op. cit.*, p. 127.
6. Cunningham, *Henry VII*, pp. 187–8.
7. *LP Hen VII, op. cit.*, vol. I, pp. 131–4.
8. Vergil, *op. cit.*, p. 123.

## 14. Summer 1501:
### White Rose and White King

1. Hall, *op. cit.*, p. 495.
2. *LP Hen VII, op. cit.*, vol, I, p. 134.
3. Vergil, *op. cit.*, p. 123.
4. *LP Hen VII*, vol. I, *op. cit.*, p. 266.
5. *Ibid.*, pp. 137–8.
6. J.G. Nichols (ed.), *Chronicle of the Grey Friars of London*, Camden Society, Old Series 53, London, 1852, p. 127.
7. *Chronicles of London, op. cit.*, p. 55.

8. Vergil, *op. cit.*, p. 125.
9. *Chronicles of London, op. cit.*, p. 256.
10. Vergil, *op. cit.*, p. 126.
11. *LP Hen VII, op. cit.*, vol. I, p. 180.
12. *Ibid.*, p. 184.
13. A. Hanham, 'Edmund de la Pole, defector', in *Journal of the Society for Renaissance Studies*, 2 (1988), p. 244.
14. *LP Hen VII, op. cit.*, vol. I, pp. 134–51.
15. *Ibid.*, pp. 205–6.
16. W. Busch, *England under the Tudors*, vol. I, p. 179.
17. Hall, *op. cit.*, p. 496.
18. Vergil, *op. cit.*, p. 122.
19. Bacon, *op. cit.*, p. 180.
20. *LP Hen VII, op. cit.*, vol. I, p. 228.
21. *Ibid.*, p. 188.
22. *Ibid.*, p. 220–5.
23. *CSP Ven, op. cit.*, vol. I, 849 and 851.
24. *LP Hen VII, op. cit.*, vol. I, p. 254.
25. *Ibid.*, p. 276.
26. *CSP Ven, op. cit.*, vol. I, 861.

## 15. September 1504:
## A Conversation about the Future

1. *LP Hen VII, op. cit.*, vol. I, pp. 231–40.
2. G. Cavendish, *Thomas Wolsey, late Cardinal, his Life and Death written by George Cavendish, his Gentleman Usher*, London, Folio Society, 1999, p. 33.

## 16. Winter 1505–6: An Ill Wind

1. *Chronicle of the Grey Friars, op. cit.*, p. 28.
2. *LP Hen VII, op. cit.*, vol. I, pp. 278–85.
3. *Chronicles of London, op. cit.*, p. 261.
4. Vergil, *op. cit.*, p. 136.
5. *CSP Sp, op. cit.*, vol. I, 456.
6. Vergil, *op. cit.*, p. 136.

7. *Ibid.*, pp. 138–40.
8. *The Chronicle of Calais*, p. 126.
9. Vergil, *op. cit.*, p. 126.
10. Bacon, *op. cit.*, pp. 182–3.
11. C.J. Harrison, 'The Petition of Edmund Dudley', *English Historical Review*, 87 (1972).
12. *LP Hen VII, op. cit.*, vol. I, p. 319.
13. *CSP Ven, op. cit.*, vol. 5, 575.

### 17. Spring 1509: A Yorkist Tudor?

1. P. Henderson (ed.), *The Complete Poems of John Skelton, Laureate*, London and Toronto, J.M. Dent, 1948, p. 13.
2. Hall, *op. cit.*, p. 1.
3  *Ibid.*, p. 519.
4. Erasmus, *Opus Epistolarum Desiderii Erasmi Roterdami* (ed. P.S. and M.H. Allen and W.W. Garrod) vol. III, ep. 657, Oxford, Clarendon Press, 1906–58, 12 vols.
5. M. Bennet, 'Table Tittle Tattle and the Tudor View of History', in K. Dockray and P. Fleming (eds), *People, Places and Perspectives: Essays on Later Medieval and Tudor England in Honour of Ralph A. Griffiths*, Stroud, Nonsuch Publishing, 2005.
6. *LP Hen VIII, op. cit.*, vol. I (i), p. 11.
7. Hall, *op. cit.*, p. 512.
8. S. Angelo (ed.), *Chivalry in the Renaissance*, Woodbridge, Boydell Press, 1990, p. 110.
9. *LP Hen VIII, op. cit.*, vol. I (i), 596.
10. *Ibid.*, vol. I (ii), 2072.

### 18. 1513–21: A King over the Water

1. Hall, *op. cit.*, p. 495.
2. *LP Hen VII, op. cit.*, vol. I, p. 258.
3. *Ibid.*, pp. 273–5.
4. *Ibid.*, p. 276.
5. *Ibid.*, p. 53.
6. *CPR Hen VII, 1494–1509, op. cit.*, p. 468.
7. *LP Hen VII*, vol. I, p. 307.

8. *Ibid.*, pp. 315–20.
9. *Ibid.*, p. 321.
10. *CSP Ven, op. cit.*, vol. II, 172.
11. It looks as though the date of Richard's birth was earlier than has generally been assumed and that William, not Richard, was the youngest of the de la Pole brothers. Humphrey and Geoffrey, both clerics, died before 1513.
12. *LP Hen VIII, op. cit.*, vol. I (i), 2072.
13. *Ibid.*, 1315.
14. *Ibid.*, 1575.
15. *Ibid.*, 4691.
16. Hall, p. 569.
17. *LP Hen VIII, op. cit.*, vol. II (i), 147, 325.
18. *LP Hen VIII, op. cit.*, vol. III (i), appendix to preface (ccccxl).
19. *LP Hen VIII*, vol. II (i), 1163.
20. *Ibid.*, 742, 809, 1239.
21. *Ibid.*, 1894.
22. *Ibid.*, 2113.
23. *Ibid.*, 1973, 2081.
24. *Ibid.*, 2419.
25. *Ibid.*, 2673.
26. *Ibid.*, 2926, 3043.
27. *LP Hen VIII, op. cit.*, vol. II (ii), appendix 39.

## 19. 1519–Autumn 1520: The Duke of Buckingham

1. Vergil, *op. cit.*, p. 239
2. *CSP Ven, op. cit.*, vol. II, 1287.
3. Some sources suggest the lady was another of Buckingham's sisters, Lady Hastings.
4. *CSP Sp, op. cit.*, supplement to vols I and II, 8, 39–40.
5. E.M. Thompson, *History of the Somerset Carthusians*, London, 1895, p. 281.
6. C. Rawcliffe, *The Staffords, Earls of Stafford and Dukes of Buckingham, 1394–1521*, Cambridge, Cambridge University Press, 1978, pp. 244–51.
7. Sir J. MacLean (ed.), *The Berkeley Manuscripts: Lives of the Berkeleys*, Gloucester, 1883, vol. II, pp. 206, 215.

8. B.J. Harris, *Edward Stafford, Third Duke of Buckingham 1478–1521*, Stanford University Press, Stanford, 1988, London, 1948 pp. 147–8.
9. *CSP Ven, op. cit.*, vol. II, 1287.
10. *Complete Poems of John Skelton*, pp. 313–4.
11. Vergil, *op. cit.*, p. 263.
12. *CSP Ven, op. cit.*, vol. III, 209.
13. C.A.J. Skeel, *Council in the Marches of Wales*, London, Hugh Rees Ltd, 1904, pp. 35–6.
14. *CSP Ven, op. cit.*, vol. II, 564.
15. *LP Hen VIII, op. cit.*, vol. III (i), 1284.

## 20. Winter 1520–Spring 1521: 'A Giant Traitor'

1. W. Roper, *The Life of Sir Thomas More*, London, J.M. Dent, 1906, p. 14
2. Vergil, *op. cit.*, p. 278
3. *LP Hen VIII, op. cit.*, vol. III (i), 1070.
4. William Shakespeare, *Henry VIII*, Act 2, Sc 1.
5. *LP Hen VIII, op. cit.*, vol. III (i), 1283.
6. *Ibid.*, 1284.
7. In J.S. Brewer, *The Reign of Henry VIII from his Accession to the Death of Wolsey*, ed. J. Gairdner, London, 1884, vol. 1, pp. 391–2.
8. *LP Hen VIII, op. cit.*, vol. III (i), 1284.
9. Hall, *op. cit.*, p. 623.
10. *Ibid.*, p. 624.
11. Harris, *Edward Stafford, op. cit.*, pp. 192–3.
12. Hall, *op. cit.*, p. 624.
13. *LP Hen VIII, op. cit.*, vol. VI, 1164; Thompson, *History of the Somerset Carthusians*, p. 284.

## 21. Winter 1524–5: A White Rose Dies

1. R. Macquereau, *Histoire générale de l'Europe*, Louvain, 1765, p. 231
2. *LP Hen VIII, op. cit.*, vol. III (ii), 2340.

3. *Ibid.*, vol. III (i), 1313.

4. *Ibid.*, 1221.

5. For Philippe de Vignolles, see *LP Hen VIII*, vol. III (i), appendix to preface, ccccxliii.

6. *LP Hen VIII*, *op. cit.*, vol. III (ii), 2768.

7. *Ibid.*, 2769.

8. *CSP Sp*, *op. cit.*, 219.

9. *LP Hen VIII*, *op. cit.*, vol. IV (i), 317.

10. *Ibid.*, 324.

11. *Ibid.*, 335.

12. *LP Hen VIII*, vol. III (ii), 3118; A.M. McCormack, *The Earldom of Desmond*, Dublin, Four Courts Press, 2005, p. 64.

13. *CSP Ven op. cit.*, 1520–26, vol. III, (1120–26), 742.

14. For Marguerite de la Pole, see G. de La Rivoire de La Batie, *Armorial de Dauphiné*, Lyons, 1867, pp. 106–7.

15. Macquereau, *Histoire générale de l'Europe*, p. 231.

## 22. 1525–35: The White Rose Party

1. Shakespeare, *Henry VI*, Part 1, Act 2, Scene 4.

2. Hall, *op. cit.*, p. 703.

3. *LP Hen VIII*, *op. cit.*, vol. III (i), 386.

4. Leviticus 20: 21.

5. Hall, *op. cit.*, p. 782.

6. G.W. Bernard, *The King's Reformation: Henry VIII and the Remaking of the English Church*, New Haven and London, Yale University Press, pp. 87–101.

7. M.H. and R. Dodds, *The Pilgrimage of Grace 1536–1537 and the Exeter Conspiracy*, 2 vols, Cambridge, Cambridge University Press, 1916, vol. II, p. 181.

8. *LP Hen VIII*, vol. XIII (ii), 961.

9. Hall, *op. cit.*, pp. 780–1.

10. *Ibid.*, pp. 808–14.

11. *Ibid.*, p. 813.

## 23. 1533–4: Rebellion?

1. *LP Hen VIII*, *op. cit.*, vol. VI, 1164.

2. *CSP Ven, op. cit.*, vol. V, 575.

3. *LP Hen VIII, op. cit.*, vol. VI , 508.

4. G.R. Elton, *Reform and Reformation: England 1509–1558*, London, Edward Arnold, 1977, p. 122.

5. *LP Hen VIII, op. cit.*, vol. VI, 1164.

6. *Ibid.*, 1164.

7. *LP Hen VIII, op. cit.*, vol. VII, 136.

8. *LP Hen VIII, op. cit.*, vol. VI, 1540.

9. J.J. Scarisbrick, 'Fisher, Henry VIII and the Reformation Crisis', in B. Bradshaw and E. Duffy (eds), *Humanism, Reform and the Reformation: The Career of Bishop John Fisher*, Cambridge, Cambridge University Press, 1989, p. 163.

10. *CSP Spain*, V (i), 86..

11. *LP Hen VIII, op. cit.*, vol. VII, 1095.

12. *Oxford DNB*.

13. *Oxford DNB*.

14. *LP Hen VIII, op. cit.*, vol. XII (i), 576.

15. *LP Hen VIII, op. cit.*, vol. VIII, 35.

## 24. 1535–6: The Lady Mary
## and the White Rose

1. *LP Hen VIII, op. cit.*, vol. XIV (i), 200

2. The best study of this character change is S. Lipscomb, *1536: The Year that Changed Henry VIII*, London, Lion Hudson, 2009.

3. G.R. Elton, *The Tudor Constitution: Documents and Commentary*, Cambridge, Cambridge University Press, 1960, no. 30, p. 62.

4. For the spy network run by Cromwell, see G.R. Elton, *Policy and Police*, Cambridge, Cambridge University Press, 1972.

5. R.B. Merriman, *Life and Letters of Thomas Cromwell*, 2 vols, Oxford, 1902, vol. 1, no. 113.

6. *LP Hen VIII, op. cit.*, vol. IX, 776.

## 25. Summer 1535:
## A New White Rose?

1. *LP Hen VIII, op. cit.*, vol. V (ii), 72.

2. Mayer, *Reginald Pole: Prince and Prophet*, Cambridge, Cambridge University Press, p. 98.

3. *CSP Ven*, vol. V, 806.

4. T.F. Mayer (ed.), *The Correspondence of Reginald Pole*, Aldershot, Ashgate, 2002, vol. 1, p. 86.

5. For *De Unitate*, see T. F. Mayer, *Reginald Pole, Prince and Prophet*, Cambridge, Cambridge University Presss, 2000, pp. 13–61; also see the summary in *LP Hen VIII*, vol. X, p. 975.

6. *LP Hen VIII*, *op. cit.*, vol. XIV (i), 200.

7. T.F. Mayer, 'A Diet for Henry VIII: The Failure of Cardinal Pole's 1537 Legation', in *Journal of British Studies* 26 (1987), p. 305.

## 26. Autumn 1536:
### The Pilgrimage of Grace

1. *LP Hen VIII*, *op. cit.*, vol. XI, (iii), 786.

2. The definitive study is R. W. Hoyle, *The Pilgrimage of Grace and the Politics of the 1530s*, Oxford, Oxford University Press, 2001 – which argues that the gentry only joined in order to defuse it.

3. Dodds and Dodds, *The Pilgrimage of Grace, op. cit.*, vol. 1, pp. 88–9.

4. *LP Hen VIII*, *op. cit.*, vol. XII (i), 900, 901 and 945.

5. *Ibid.*, vol. XI, 780.

6. *LP Hen VIII*, X, 1086; Dodds and Dodds, *The Pilgrimage of Grace, op. cit.*, vol. 1, pp. 300–6.

7. *LP Hen VIII*, *op. cit.*, vol. XI, 672, 722–3.

8. C. Ross, *Richard III*, London, Eyre Methuen, 1981, p. 212.

9. *LP Hen VIII*, *op. cit.*, vol. V (ii), 114.

10. *LP Hen VIII*, XI, 957.

11. *Ibid.*, XII (i), 1013.

12. R.B. Merriman, *Life and Letters of Thomas Cromwell*, 2 vols, Oxford, Clarendon Press, 1902, vol. 2, p. 169.

13. *LP Hen VIII*, *op. cit.*, vol. XI, 1246.

14. *Ibid.*, vol. XII (i), 976.

15. C. Wriothesley, *A Chronicle of England during the Reign of the Tudors from ad 1485–1559*, ed. W.D. Hamilton, vol. 1.

16. Bernard, *The King's Reformation, op. cit.*, p. 344.

17. Dodds and Dodds, *The Pilgrimage of Grace, op. cit.*, vol. 1, p. 305.

18. *LP Hen VIII, op. cit.*, vol. XII (i), 841.
19. Scarisbrick suggests that the Pilgrimage 'could have openly enlisted latent Yorkist sentiment', stressing its failure to do so. J.J. Scarisbrick, *Henry VIII*, London, Eyre & Spottiswoode, 1968, p. 341.

## 27. Spring–Summer 1537:
## 'Mr Pole's Traitorous Practises'

1. Hall, *op. cit.*, p. 828.
2. *CSP Ven, op. cit.*, vol. V, 575.
3. *LP Hen VIII, op. cit.*, vol. V (i), 131.
4. Dodds and Dodds, *The Pilgrimage of Grace, op. cit.*, vol. II, p. 280.
5. *LP Hen VIII, op. cit.*, vol. XII (i), 779.
6. Mayer, *Correspondence of Reginald Pole, op. cit.*, vol. 1, p. 174.
7. *LP Hen VIII, op. cit.*, vol. XII (i), 1032.
8. *LP Hen VIII, op. cit.*, vol. XIII (ii), 797.
9. Mayer, 'A Diet for Henry VIII', *op. cit.*, p. 323.
10. *LP Hen VIII, op. cit.*, vol. XII (ii), 128.
11. Mayer, *Correspondence of Reginald Pole, op. cit.*, vol. 1, p. 168.
12. *Ibid.*, p. 178.
13. *LP Hen VIII, op. cit.*, vol. XII (i), 809.
14. *CSP Sp, op. cit.*, vol. V (ii), 151.
15. Merriman, *Thomas Cromwell, op. cit.*, vol. II, pp. 87–90.
16. See A. Overell, 'Cardinal Pole's Special Agent: Michael Throckmorton, c. 1503–1558', in *History*, 94 (July 2009), p. 315.

## 28. Autumn 1538:
## The 'Exeter Conspiracy'

1. Merriman, *Thomas Cromwell, op. cit.*, vol. 2, no. 281
2. M.L. Busch, 'The Tudors and the Royal Race', in *History*, 55 (1971), pp. 37–48.
3. *LP Hen VIII, op. cit.*, vol. XIII (ii), 753.
4. E.W. Ives, 'Faction at the Court of Henry VIII: The Fall of Anne Boleyn', in *History*, 57 (1972), pp. 169–88.
5. Mayer, *Correspondence of Reginald Pole, op. cit.*, vol. 1, pp. 118–19.
6. *Ibid.*, p. 118.

7. T.E. Bindoff, *Tudor England*, Oxford, Oxford University Press, 1950, p. 108.

8. Elton, *Policy and Police*, *op. cit.*, pp. 350 and 359 n. 4.

9. Dodds and Dodds, *The Pilgrimage of Grace*, *op. cit.*, vol. 2, p. 293.

10. Bernard, *The King's Reformation*, *op. cit.*, p. 431.

11. *LP Hen VIII*, *op. cit.*, vol. XIII (ii), 804.

12. *Ibid.*, 804.

13. For Helyar, see *Oxford DNB*.

14. *LP Hen VIII*, *op. cit.*, vol. XIII (ii), 797.

15. M. St Clair Byrne, *The Lisle Letters*, 6 vols, Chicago, University of Chicago Press, 1981, vol. 5, no. 259.

16. Hall, *op. cit.*, p. 826.

17. *LP Hen VIII*, *op. cit.*, vol. XIII (ii), 924 .

18. R. Morison, *An Invective ayenst [against] Treason*, London, 1539.

19. *CSP Ven.*, *op. cit.*, vol. V, 806.

20. Hall, *op. cit.*, p. 827.

21. *Ibid.*, p. 827.

22. *LP Hen VIII*, *op. cit.*, vol. XIII (ii), 960.

23. Elton, *Reform and Reformation*, p. 281.

24. J. A. Youings, 'The Council of the West', in *Transactions of the Royal Historical Society*, fifth series, 10 (1960), p. 45.

25. Bernard, *The King's Reformation*, *op. cit.*, p. 419.

26. *LP Hen VIII*, *op. cit.*, vol. XIV (i), 280.

27. *Ibid.*, 280.

28. *Ibid.*, 144.

## 29. Winter 1538–Summer 1539: Cardinal Pole's Last Throw

1. *LP Hen VIII*, *op. cit.*, vol. XIV (i), 456.

2. Hall, *op. cit.*, p. 823.

3. *LP Hen VIII*, *op. cit.*, vol. XIV (i), 114.

4. *Ibid.*, 405.

5. *Ibid.*, 456.

6. *Ibid.*, 200.

7. *Ibid.*, 560.

8. Mayer, *Correspondence of Reginald Pole*, *op. cit.*, vol. 1, p. 222.

9. Hall, *op. cit.*, pp. 828–9.

10. *LP Hen VIII*, *op. cit.*, vol. XIV (i), 967.
11. Mayer, *Correspondence of Reginald Pole*, *op. cit.*, vol. 1, p. 228.
12. *LP Hen VIII*, *op. cit.*, vol. XIV (i), 280.
13. Transcript from Lambeth Palace Library, in Fletcher and MacCulloch, *Tudor Rebellions*, p. 141.

## 30. May 1541:
## The Death of the Last Plantagenet

1. Lord Herbert of Cherbury, *The Life and Reigne of King Henry VIII*, London, 1649, p. 648.
2. H. Pierce, *Margaret Pole, Countess of Salisbury 1473–1541*, Cardiff, University of Wales Press, 2003, p. 14.
3. *LP Hen VIII*, *op. cit.*, vol. VI, 1126.
4. *LP Hen VIII*, *op. cit.*, vol. XIII (ii), 855.
5. *Ibid.*, 818.
6. Pierce, *Margaret Pole*, p. 171.
7. St Clare Byrne, *Lisle Letters*, vol. 5, no. 1419.
8. *LP Hen VIII*, *op. cit.*, vol. XIV (ii), 212.
9. *LP Hen VIII*, *op. cit.*, vol. XVI, 1011.
10. *Ibid.*, 403.
11. Pierce, *Margaret Pole*, p. 176.
12. Bernard, *The King's Reformation*, *op. cit.*, p. 574.
13. *CSP Sp*, *op. cit.*, vol. VI (i), 158. For a detailed account, A.G. Dickens, 'Sedition and conspiracy in Yorkshire during the latter years of Henry VIII in *Reformation Studies*, London, Hambledon Press, 1982, p. 5–20.
14. *Ibid.*, 166.
15. *The Life and Reigne of King Henry VIII*, p.648; *CSP Sp*, vol. VI (i), p. 332.
16. Hall, *op. cit.*, p. 842.
17. *CSP Sp*, *op. cit.*, vol. VI (i), 166.

## 31. Winter 1546–7:
## Henry VIII's Final Phobia

1. E. Jones (ed.), *Henry Howard, Earl of Surrey: Poems*, Oxford, Oxford University Press, 1973, no. 45.

2. Hall, p. 866.

3. 'devious, vengeful, foul-mouthed and essentially second rate' is G.R. Elton's verdict on the Duke of Norfolk, in *Reform and Reformation*, p. 117.

4. The latest studies of Surrey are: W.A. Sessions, *Henry Howard, the Poet Earl of Surrey*, Oxford, Oxford University Press, 1999; and J. Childs, *Henry VIII's Last Victim*, Jonathan Cape, London, 2006.

5. *LP Hen VIII, op. cit.*, vol. XVI (i), 12.

6. G. Constantyne, 'Transcript of an Original Manuscript Containing a Memorial from George Constantine to Thomas, Lord Cromwell', ed. T. Amyot, *Archaeologia* 22, London 1831, p. 62.

7. Jones, *Henry Howard*.

8. *LP Hen VIII, op. cit.*, vol. XXI (ii), 696.

9. *CSP Spain*, VIII, 364.

### Epilogue

1. D.M. Loades, *Two Tudor Conspiracies*, Cambridge, Cambridge University Press, 1965, pp. 21–3, 45–6.

2. *Ibid.*, p. 225.

3. A. Rowntree (ed.), *History of Scarborough*, London, Dent, 1931, p. 214.

4. *Oxford DNB*: H. Pierce, 'Arthur Pole'.

# INDEX